פנינים

על התורה

PENINIM ON THE TORAH
Third Series

An Anthology of Thought Provoking Ideas
Practical Insights
and Review Questions & Answers
on the Weekly Parsha

By
Rabbi A.L. Scheinbaum

PENINIM AL HATORAH
Third Series
Copyright © 1996
By Rabbi A.L. Scheinbaum

Published and Distributed by Peninim Publications
In Conjunction with "The Living Memorial"
A Project of the Hebrew Academy of Cleveland
1860 S. Taylor Road, Cleveland Hts., Ohio 44118
216-321-5838 / Fax 216-932-4597

ISBN:
0-9635120-2-1 Hard Cover
0-9635120-4-8 Paperback

Typography & Layout
PERFECT TYPE ASSOCIATES
Cleveland, Ohio
216-321-4635

Cover Design
KENNY FIXLER - K.F. GRAPHICS
Cleveland,Ohio
216-421-8520

Sefer Torah Photo
Courtesy of American Greetings Corp.

Printed in the United States of America
by Noble Book Press Corp.

מרדכי גיפטער
ישיבת טלז
Rabbi Mordecai Gifter
28570 Nutwood Lane
Wickliffe, Ohio 44092

בע"ה

ג' מר-חשון תשנ"ב

ראיתי דברי הרב הנעלה ר' אברהם ליב שיינבוים, נר"ו,
אשר ביאר בהרצאות דברים בפרשיות התורה.
ויש בדבריו רב תועלת למלמדים בבתי ספר חרדיים
יהיה ה' בעזרו להפיץ מעיינותיו חוצה
באהבה,
מרדכי גיפטער

בע"ה

ג' מר- חשון תשנ"ב

ראיתי דברי הרב הנעלה ר' אברהם ליב שיינבוים, נר"ו, אשר ביאר בהרצאת דברים בפרשיות התורה.
ויש בדבריו רב תועלת למלמדים בבתי ספר חרדיים.
יהיה ה' בעזרו להפיץ מעיינותיו חוצה

באהבה,
מרדכי גיפטר

"A People Survives So Long As It Transmits Its Heritage From One Generation To The Next"
Phil and Mary Edlis Elementary School

ב"ה

Beatrice J. Stone, Yavne High School • Hebrew Academy of Cleveland • Jacob Sapirstein Mesivta High School

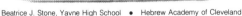

בית חנוך עברי דקליבלנד

Hebrew Academy of Cleveland

1860 SOUTH TAYLOR ROAD • CLEVELAND, OHIO 44118 • (216) 321-5838

ב"ה ר"ח חשון תשנ"ג, קליבלנד

כבוד ידידי המחנך הדגול הרה"ג ר' אברהם ליב שיינבוים
שליט"א מוציא לאור מדי שבוע בשבוע פנינים מפרשת השבוע
ממאמרי גאוני וצדיקי עולם וכבר זכה מפעל כביר זה לשבח
ולהפצה מופלגת בעירנו וגם ברחבי הארץ.

ועכשיו ברצונו וחשקו להדפיסם בספר שבשם "פנינים"
יקרא, וגם יהי' חלק ממפעלי בית החינוך לרגלי חגיגת שנת
היובל לקיומו אשר רבות בשנים הרה"ג ראל"ש הנהו מעמודי
התוך של המוסד.

הריני מברך את ידידי הרה"ג שיזכה להפיץ מעינות רבותינו
וגדולינו חוצה שהם באמת "מפז ומפנינים יקרה" וזכותם תגן
עליו עד ביאת גוא"צ בב"א.

נחום זאב דסלר

Torah Umesorah

160 BROADWAY, NEW YORK, N.Y. 10038 • 212-227-1000   Founded by Rabbi Shraga Feivel Mendlowitz ז"ל to establish day schools in every Jewish community

National Society for Hebrew Day Schools

4 Tishrei 5753
October 1, 1992

Rabbi A. Leib Scheinbaum is one of the most dynamic innovative educators I know.

It has been my privilege to work with him on several Hemshech projects for Torah Umesorah. It is always an exciting adventure and inspiration to be associated with.

A few years ago Rabbi Scheinbaum inaugurated at the Hebrew Academy of Cleveland a weekly Parashas Hashavua series called Peninim. He wisely chose commentaries on the Parsha which are particularly relevant to Day School parents, evocative thoughts and ideas which promote Torah table talks at the Shabbos table.

I was so taken with the selection of Torah thoughts and the way it was presented that I sent it out to all the Day Schools in the country as an integral part of our National PTA Sidra Series.

I understand that Rabbi Scheinbaum is publishing the Peninim in book form. The Peninim will enhance the sanctity of Shabbos in many homes for many years to come.

Sincerely yours,

Joshua Fishman

Rabbi Joshua Fishman
Executive Vice-President

JF:ls

———— תורה ומסורה ————

PREFACE

The first copy of *Peninim* was distributed in the greater Cleveland community five years ago. Since that day, this endeavor has been blessed with amazing *siyata dishmaya*; it has been disseminated weekly in dozens of synagogues and schools throughout the country. *Peninim* has been welcomed as a refreshing and enriching weekly compendium on the *parsha*. I am humbled by this *zechus* and fervently pray to Hashem *Yisborach* that I merit the ability to continue promulgating authentic *Torah* thoughts and values.

Peninim presents a broad-based anthology of thought-provoking ideas, homilies, and practical insights. These are based upon the *Parashas Hashovua*, but are applicable in varied situations. The concepts presented include *divrei Torah* which are culled from and based upon the thoughts and interpretations expounded by our revered *gedolei Yisrael* of the past and present. They reflect authentic *Torah* perspective on life. Recognizing the need for an annual anthology of these insights, we published the first anthology in what we hoped would become a series of compendiums on the *Torah*. We take great pride in presenting to the public the third volume in the series. We hope that this volume will be greeted with equal enthusiasm as its predecessors and reach out to a larger national audience.

The comments and insights compended in this volume are geared for beginner and scholar alike, as many practical messages may be gleaned from this work. The review questions and answers are likewise formulated for various levels. It is our sincere hope that the insights anthologized in this volume will give effective expression to the mind and soul of its readers, affording them the opportunity for personal development and educational enrichment through *Torah* study.

Avrohom Leib Scheinbaum
Rosh Chodesh Iyar 5756
Cleveland Heights, Ohio

ACKNOWLEDGMENTS

No successful project is accomplished by the efforts of a single individual. Whatever a man achieves is predicated upon the forces, both direct and indirect, which have influenced him throughout his life. To this end, I feel it is incumbent upon me to acknowledge those individuals who have in one way or another affected the development of this project.

One can never fulfill the requirement to acknowledge and appreciate the gratitude owed to parents and mentors. My father, *Reb Noach Scheinbaum, z.l.*, was a man of sterling character whose uncompromising integrity inspired all who knew him. Together with my mother, *Mrs. Glika Bogen*, he labored with love to ensure his children a genuine *Torah* education. May she, together with her husband, *Mr. Simcha Bogen*, enjoy health, longevity, and *nachas* from their families. My father-in-law, *Reb Shlomo Zalman Brunner, z.l.*, was a man whose entire life was a lesson in the *middah* of *chesed*. Together with my mother-in-law, *Mrs. Feige Feldman*, they imparted a legacy of *ahavas Yisrael* and *ahavas chesed* to their children. May she and her husband, *Mr. Moshe Leib Feldman*, be blessed with health, longevity and *nachas*.

My first Rebbe, *Horav Tzvi Hirsh Meisels, z.l.*, served as mentor to my entire family. His inspiration will always be with us. I owe an eternal debt of gratitude to that great citadel of *Torah*, the Telshe Yeshivah and to its *Roshei Hayeshiva, shlita*, for all the years I spent there studying *Torah*. I would especially like to single out my two *rebbeim* who are no longer with us, *Hagaon Horav Chaim Mordechai Katz, z.l.*, and *Hagaon Horav Refoel Boruch Sorotzkin, z.l.* Their lives epitomized *gadlus ba'Torah*.

The Hebrew Academy of Cleveland has been my "home" for the last sixteen years. I am indebted to *Rabbi N. Z. Dessler, shlita*, whose guidance and friendship have been essential requisites in whatever success I have achieved. My esteemed colleagues, my dear students and all those who listened, commented and offered constructive criticism, I owe you my heartfelt thanks.

I would also like to take this opportunity to thank my dear friends, *Judy* and *Morry Weiss*, for their continued support throughout my accomplishments. Their friendship and encouragement has always been very important to me.

The success of this project is due to a concerted effort on the part of a group of dedicated individuals who have given so much of themselves. My daughter, *Ahuva*, prepares and produces the weekly *Peninim*. Her suggestions to and patience with the author have been major factors in *Peninim's* success. **Mrs. Marilyn Berger** edits the weekly copy. Her careful editing of this work once again demonstrates her ability for enhancing the written word. *Rabbi Malkiel Hefter* is always there, ready to help in any way. His smile lends so much cheer to this work. He is a pleasure to work with.

A special thanks to **Boruch Berger** of New York and *Rabbi Menachem Hommel* of England and to all the others who distribute *Peninim* in their respective cities.

In order that any *sefer* be adequately appreciated, it must be prepared in a clear and esthetically appealing style. This finished volume was made possible through the devoted efforts of my dear friend, *Rabbi Doniel Neustadt*, an erudite *talmid chacham* whose vast storehouse of knowledge has greatly benefited this work. He labored strenuously to present a *sefer* that was both spiritually and esthetically appealing. The cover design was the creation of *Kenny Fixler*, a master in graphic design, whose works have enhanced many *Torah* projects.

The reinforcement and support of my family have always been the driving forces behind my work. My children have accepted an absentee father and have given me the moral support and stimulus to pursue this endeavor. My son *Zalman* reviewed the entire manuscript. His suggestions were well received.

Last, but not least, I pay tribute to my wife, מנב"ת *Neny*. She helped me to continue my studies for many years after our marriage and willingly shared in my *harbotzas Torah*, wherever it may be. She has been a tower of strength and an unfailing source of encouragement without whom this work would never have been completed. She sacrifices much, often assuming the role of mother and father, so that I may pursue my work. Her valor as a woman and her forbearance as a wife have proven to be instructive to our children and an inspiration to me. She truly personifies *Shlomo Ha'Melech's* famous dictum, "אשת חיל מי ימצא ורחוק מפנינים מכרה, "*A woman of valor who can find, far beyond pearls is her value.*" May we, together with our children, merit that the love of *Torah*, its study and its dissemination, be the hallmarks of our home.

Avrohom Leib Scheinbaum
Rosh Chodesh Iyar 5756
Cleveland Heights, Ohio

Table of Contents / התוכן

*The Living Memorial is proud to pay
tribute to those who have made
this volume a reality*

Sidney and Phyllis Reisman

*and to the patrons of Peninim who
have each dedicated one Sefer
of the five Chumashim.*

Sefer Bereishis
Mendy and Ita Klein

Sefer Shemos
Bob and Chaya Schottenstein

Sefer Vayikra
Steven DeFren and daughter Rachel

Sefer Bamidbar
Charles and Debbie Zuchowski

Sefer Devarim
Mark and Peggy Yagour

למזכרת נצח בהיכל הספר

לז"נ

אבי מורי

ר' נח ב"ר יהודה אריה שיינבוים ז"ל

נפטר כ"ב כסלו תשכ"ו

תנצב"ה.

***

לז"נ

מר חמי

ר' שלמה זלמן

ב"ר יצחק ברינער ז"ל

נפטר ב' דר"ח אייר תשכ"ח

תנצב"ה.

***

לז"נ

אחיותי שנקטפו בילדותן ע"י הנאצים הארורים ימ"ש

רחל לאה ע"ה

פריידא ע"ה

שרה אסתר ע"ה

שיינבוים

נשמתן עלתה בטהרה י"ג תשרי תש"ב

ספר בראשית

Sefer Bereishis

Dedicated by

Mendy and Ita Klein

In Honor of Our Children and Granddaughter
Amir and Edna
Yoni, Dina, Nati
and Shani

*With pride in the knowledge
that you will continue to foster our tradition of
bringing Torah and joy to others.*

"כי ידעתיו למען אשר יצוה את בניו ואת
ביתו אחריו ושמרו דרך ד' לעשות צדקה ומשפט"
*'For I have loved him, because he commands his children and
his household after him that they keep the way of Hashem,
doing charity and justice.' (Bereishis 18:19)*

פרשת בראשית
PARSHAS BEREISHIS
▶◀

בראשית ברא אלקים
In the beginning (Hashem) created. (1:1)

The *Talmud (Megillah 9a)* tells us about king Ptolemy, who gathered seventy two elders and implored them to translate the *Torah* into Greek. Rather than translating it in the correct form, in their translation.they wrote "אלקים ברא בראשית" - *"Hashem created the Beginning."* Rashi attributes the deviation from the original text to logical reasoning. One would not have expected the name of the Creator to precede the creation itself (*M'harsha*). Therefore, had the elders preserved the sequence of the original text, Ptolemy might have misconstrued the Greek word for *"in the beginning"* to be the proper name for another deity who had created Hashem.

Horav Moshe Shternbuch, Shlita, questions this hypothesis. Why should the *Torah* make a statement at the onset which could be misunderstood? He explains that the *Torah's* intent was specifically to be ambiguous in order to communicate the proper attitude toward *Torah* study. *Torah* is given to those who seek its truth. Indeed, as *Chazal* note, at the end of these three words, בראשית ברא אלקים, the Hebrew letters which comprise the word "אמת" or "truth". One whose approach to *Torah* study is not honest will inevitably find ways to distort its truth.

Often we meet people who regrettably strayed from the prescribed path of worship. They may defend their attitude by citing questions regarding the philosophy and traditional values of Judaism. One must understand, however, that the moral posture of the questioner is probably the single most important factor in any critique of Judaism. Some questions remain unanswered no matter what position one adopts. Other questions disappear immediately upon the questioner's change of orientation. Furthermore, one's level of

5

tolerance for unaddressed issues is often consistent with the perspective from which he views them. One who is nurtured in an atmosphere that is both meaningful and rewarding will not be distressed as acutely as one who does not enjoy such a positive milieu.

The religious believer exalts in his ability to serve the Divine. His motivation emanates from a pure love for Hashem and His *Torah*. Questions and ambiguities are not obstacles in his chosen course. He seeks only the opportunity for a deepened understanding of Hashem's imperative, not a rationale to fulfill it. As we once again begin the *Torah*, the greatest code of truth, we must rededicate ourselves to studying it from a committed orientation. For the believer there are no questions, and for the non-believer there are no answers.

***

ויאמר אלקים נעשה אדם בצלמנו

"And Hashem said, Let Us make man in Our image." (1:26)

Horav Avigdor Miller, Shlita, notes that The word "צלם"- *image*- is derived from the Hebrew word "צל"- shadow. Man is, therefore, to be viewed as a reflection of Hashem. In effect, the *Torah's* statement is a declaration of man's distinction. In (*Avos 3:18*) it is stated, "חביב אדם שנברא בצלם, חבה יתרה נודעת לו שנברא בצלם". *"Beloved is man that he was created in the Image; it is a special love that was revealed to him, in that he was created in the Image."* Through this *pasuk*, the *Torah* asserts that man is held in high esteem in the eyes of his Creator.

When one views a shadow, he is immediately reminded of the object which the shadow reflects. Man is constantly reminded of his Creator. The dignity and majesty of the human face is a testimonial to Hashem. The faces of people around us are reminders that Hashem is looking at us through their eyes. Indeed, Hashem "looks" at us from the heavens, but the faces of men remind us of this reality. When one is embarrassed to be perceived as a sinner in the eyes of man, he is taking a step towards an even greater shame, being sinful in the eyes of Hashem. All of the emotions we feel and express toward men are ultimately shaped by our attitude toward Hashem.

***

6

כי בו שבת מכל מלאכתו אשר ברא אלקים לעשות

"For with it He ceased from all His work which Hashem had created for it to continue to work." (3:2)

Horav Yechezkel Avramsky, z.l., explains that when Hashem created the world, He left opportunity for man to participate. He gave man the role of partner in creation by placing him in control of the revelation of nature's hidden treasures. When man explores the knowledge which is at the source of every natural power, he gains some control over the processes. His experience "tasting" creation makes him privy to the sublime pleasure produced by the mastery of the spiritual realm over the physical world.

Over the ages, man has delved into the secrets of nature. He has sought to reveal the sources of nature's hidden treasures in order to harness them for the benefit of mankind. Indeed, all of nature's superficially concealed secrets are waiting for man to uncover. Every invention is a result of man's patient and careful study of these secrets and his applying them to routine needs. As we continue to delve, we are mandated to reflect upon the wisdom of the Creator. We are obligated to pay homage to the One who ordained this world with its amazing treasures.

Indeed, man does not fulfill his obligation of "לעשות" by merely revealing the natural processes. They are but forces, without any spirit. The purpose of all the toil in developing these ideas is to enable man to recognize Divine Providence at work. If one's "work" is only directed at alleviating some of life's discomforts, so that his concept utilization extends only to his physical gratification, then he degrades all that he achieves. The ability to consecrate mundane labor by dedicating its fruits to Hashem is the essence of the "לעשות", obligation.

***

לא טוב היות האדם לבדו אעשה לו עזר כנגדו

"It is not good that man should be alone, I will make him a helpmate opposite him." (2:18)

The *Torah*'s description of Chava as a helpmate "opposite" man seems peculiar. A helpmate should work side by side in a parallel relationship, rather than opposite! The *Midrash* infers from this expression that a wife can be either a "helpmate" or an "opposition". If man is worthy, his wife will be a source of support and a helpmate. If he is unworthy, she becomes his opponent. Indeed, as the *Tiferes Tzvi* extends this idea, a helpful wife is one who encourages her husband to study *Torah* to the full extent of his ability. This applies to any endeavor. A wife's encouragement can be one's greatest source of moral and spiritual support.

As Hashem created a wife and a partner for Adam, He simultaneously created the first "relationship". It, therefore, is appropriate to study this paradigmatic relationship not only from the husband-wife perspective, but also from the perspective of true friendship. The term "עזר", or helpmate, clearly indicates that woman has been created in order to give man the physical, moral, and spiritual partnership which he requires. Man's task on this earth is too awesome for him to bear in solitude. He needs a helpmate at his side. Consquently, the term reserved for woman is invested with the highest nobility. A helpmate is an equal partner, not someone who remains in his shadow. The notion of being "opposite" suggests a specific form of support.

The husband-wife relationship should be one in which each partner is prepared to stand "opposite" the other, lending support through intellectual appreciation. Unconditional love should not cause a spouse to support an irrational act on the part of a life partner. Nor should criticism be the sole basis of one's relationship. One should stand opposite, providing primary source of review and approval. Life partners should seek each others imprimatur. This should apply to all relationships. A true friend is not one whose support transcends even the foolhardy, but one who is prepared to offer a constructive critique when appropriate.

The *Talmud* in *Eiruvin 18a* suggests that the first person was a self-sufficient androgynous being. Hashem said, "לא טוב היות האדם לבדו". It is not good that man should be alone as a self-sufficient creature, devoted only to himself. He, therefore, divided this first being into two distinct people, man and woman, each reflecting unique qualities. Either one alone is incomplete. The perfection of the human personality occurs when man and woman live for one another in total harmony, functioning together as one unit, even while each

8

performs their own individual tasks. Indeed, as the *Raavad* states, woman was created from man's body in order to establish the tone for marriage. Had she been created from dust like man, they would have gone their own separate ways, independent of one another. Hashem created one from the other in order to designate their reciprocal need to live together as one unit, in constant need of each other.

The *Raavad* states that this manner of creation also defines the approach necessary to establish a stable marriage relationship. The couple's attitude should be one in which each views the other as an inherent component of him or herself. One should be as concerned about his or her mate as he is about himself.

This paradigmatic relationship should serve as the basic model for all relationships among fellow men. We should identify with our fellow Jews' needs as being intrinsically our own. We will then have attained the apex of fulfilling the *Torah's* perspective of the *middah* of *"chessed"*, kindness.

QUESTIONS LEVEL-A

1. Which two words describe the world before creation?

2. All forms of vegetation were created on the _____ day.

3. From what material did Hashem create Adam?

4. What were Kayin's and Hevel's respective professions?

5. How old was Noach when his first child was born?

QUESTIONS LEVEL-B

1. Why did Hashem bless the fish and the fowl?

2. Were Adam and Chava permitted to eat meat?

3. How did the snake changed physically after it was cursed?

QUESTIONS LEVEL-C

1. Why does the *Torah* use the plural tense in regard to the creation of water- *Yamim* ; was it not all one body of water?

2. Why didn't Hashem bless wild beasts as He blessed the fish and the fowl?

3. With which language was the world created?

QUESTIONS LEVEL-D

1. Why does it not say "ויהי ערב ויהי בקר", regarding the creation of the seventh day?

ANSWERS LEVEL-A

1. תהו ובהו.
2. Third.
3. From the earth.
4. קין worked the soil, while הבל was a shepherd.
5. 500 years old.

ANSWERS LEVEL-B

1. Since they are always hunted, Hashem gave them a special blessing.
2. No.
3. It had feet, but they were cut off.

ANSWERS LEVEL-C

1. Since the fish in the water situated in one part of the world have a different taste than the fish in another part of the world, the *Torah* refers to the water in the plural.

2. The blessings that would be given to the wild beasts would also apply to the snake, and Hashem did not want the snake to receive a blessing.

3. לשון הקודש.

ANSWERS LEVEL-D

1. There is a *halacha* that מוסיפין מחול על הקודש. One must add to *Shabbos* from the weekday period. Therefore, it does not say ויהי ערב ויהי בקר since *Shabbos* did not begin exactly at the moment that it became "ערב" but earlier.

פרשת נח
PARASHAS NOACH
►◄

נח איש צדיק תמים היה בדורותיו

"Noach was a man, righteous and wholehearted". (6:9)

The characterization of Noach as a *tzaddik*, a devout and righteous man, is enigmatic. Indeed, *Chazal* themselves question Noach's unique personality. He was, however, the only individual who Hashem saved from the devastation that engulfed an entire world. Corruption, violence, and debauchery effected a tragic end to that world. One man stood alone with his family, in contrast to these people, unaffected by their immoral way of life. Hashem told him to build an ark in order to save himself and to go forward to rebuild the world.

"כי אותך ראיתי צדיק לפני בדור הזה" – *For you I have seen righteous before Me in this generation.* In no other place in the *Torah* does Hashem describe a man as a *tzaddik*. Nonetheless, *Chazal* state that Noach's faith was equivocal. *"He lacked faith, for had the water not reached his ankles he would not have entered the ark."* Indeed, the angels demanded that he perish with the rest of his generation.

This unique phenomenon, in which *Chazal* question one whose character Hashem has praised, prompts the obvious question, "What was wrong with Noach? Were did his weakness lie? And wherein did he fail?" *Horav Moshe Swift, z.l.,* suggests that the answer lies in the contrast between Noach and two other great leaders, Avraham and Moshe. For days, Avraham *Avinu* stood entereating Hashem on behalf of the evil inhabitants of Sodom and Gomorrah. He threw himself into war in order to save his nephew, Lot. Moshe *Rabbeinu* similarly devoted his life to *Klal Yisrael*. On the other hand, Noach spent 120 years building an ark and preparing the equipment, but he did not influence the moral development of a single person in his generation. Noach was not able to retrieve even one individual from devastation. Consistent with this concept, the *Zohar* states *"Since Noach did not*

11

pray for the people, the flood of destruction was therefore named after him." As Yeshayohu *Hanavi* says "כי מי נח זאת לי". We associate Noach with a world that was destroyed, rather than with the new world which he eventually built.

One may succeed in amassing a great fortune, but if the world does not benefit from his wealth, what good has it brought him? One can be the greatest physician, but if he does not expend his talents by treating the sick, his skill is useless to society. A *tzaddik's* presence offers great merit for his generation, but if he does not influence his peers to correct their ways, he remains as "צדיק לפני"- as the *Torah* says about Noach, a "צדיק לפני"- a *tzaddik* before Me, but not to mankind.

The lesson to be derived from Noach's tragic yet glorious life is that one cannot build a Jewish homelife only for oneself. We must endeavor to exercise our influence on our family and on the society within which we live. Noach's glorious life went from the high of איש צדיק to the low of איש אדמה, the heavenly man to the earthly man. His own child Cham, who had witnessed such devout piety as a child, was driven to such an act of indecency, as recorded in the *Talmud*. How tragic it is for the old father whose life comes to an end with the words "ארור כנען"- *"cursed be Canaan"*, cursing the child whom he saved from the flood. How many people have tragically passed on cursing the day that shame was brought upon them by their own descendants? The challenging question stands accusing us all; are we building an ark only for ourselves, or for others, too? We must exert our influence upon those around us, so that we do not remain alive just to Hashem while being dead to the world around us.

***

ותשחת הארץ לפני האלקים

"And the land was corrupt before Hashem." (6:11)

Rashi comments that the ultimate verdict for the destruction of that generation was based upon the people's stealing. The *Ozorever Rebbe, z.l.,* explains that the arrogance demonstrated by the manner of this stealing signified a decadence so sinister that repentance for this sin was highly unlikely. Their form of stealing was unique in that it was not biblically prohibited, since the people were careful to steal less

12

than the value of a *"perutah"* (which is the criterion for establishing an act of stealing). They obviously derived no benefit from such an insignificant theft. They stole for the pure sake of stealing; they sinned for the thrill of sinning. They seemed to be noble and dignified people who diligently researched the law, seeking loopholes to enable them to accomplish their immoral acts within a legal framework.

Such an attitude could never lead to repentance. What did they do wrong? They were able to find the proverbial *"heter"*, permission, for their miscreancy. He interprets the *pasuk* in the following manner: *"And the earth was corrupt before Hashem,"* but Hashem is aware of an individual's true intentions. It was the fact that they sought ways to legally steal (with permission) that sealed their destruction. One who sins "only" before Hashem will be punished before man.

***

ויחל נח איש האדמה ויטע כרם

"And Noach, master of the land, planted a vineyard." (9:20)

When Noach went ashore following his lengthy journey on the ark, his first activity was to plant a grapevine. Later, he drank its wine "and became inebriated." This act ultimately led to an embarrassing situation which culminated in his cursing his grandson, Canaan. When we view the positive and negative actions of our forebears, we must delve into their origins in order to learn from them. What was Noach's mistake and what lessons may be derived from it?

Horav A. H. Lebowitz, Shlita, cites *Sforno* who interprets Noach's violation in the following manner. *"And Noach began"-* his mistake lay in the manner he generated his activity upon arriving safely on the land. He began with an action which lacked refinement and did not reflect appropriate judgment. This impropriety led to a tragic misdeed. A slight error at the onset can create havoc and tragedy in the end. Because wine is not a nourishing substance, Noach should not have made it his first priority upon debarking from the extended trip on the ark.

This seems peculiar. Wine does have both practical and holy uses. Indeed, wine is required in the observance of many *mitzvos*. Undoubtedly, someone of Noach's noble character must have planted the grapevine with the proper intentions, for the sake of Heaven.

Wherein lay his sin? *Horav* Lebowitz explains that the sin originated in a misdirected sense of priorities. Planting a grapevine is a prerequisite for serving Hashem, but it does not take precedence over other activities necessary for rebuilding the world. The grapevine symbolizes pleasure and not necessity. This should not have been Noach's first act. This slight indiscretion led to disaster for himself and for his descendants.

With this thesis, we are confronting a transgression in the form of unbecoming behavior. We have a popular Jewish dictum of עס "פאסט נישט", it is inappropriate. Some view this merely as good advice. This should not be the case, for a sin which originates here and now can have far reaching implications. We tend to overlook certain types of inappropriate behavior, with the common defenses, "What am I doing wrong?" or "Where is it cited in *Halacha*? As *Horav* Lebowitz explains, activity unbecoming a *Torah* observant Jew need not be written explicitly in the *Torah*. A mandate issued from our *Torah* leadership deeming a certain activity or manner of dress unbecoming should be sufficient. As Hashem's chosen people, we are especially obligated to act in a dignified manner consistent with our royal status. Transgression is relative to the sinner and the One before Whom one sins.

***

הוא היה גבור ציד לפני ד'

"He (Nimrod) was a crafty hero (hunter) before Hashem." (10:9)

In Tanach the phrase *"before Hashem"*, suggests that an activity is performed in accordance with Hashem's will. *Horav S.R. Hirsch, z.l.,* suggests that here, too, *before Hashem* - means simply in the name of Hashem. Nimrod had a quiet "pious G-d pleasing" manner, which was the culmination of his wickedness. The name "Hashem" had not yet become lost. When properly understood, the same Name implies the equality of men. It takes benevolence and love normative and applicable to all. Nimrod was the first person to distort this Name, using it to suppress and subjugate his fellow man - all in the name of Hashem. He demanded recognition of his power - all in the name of Hashem. Nimrod went so far as to claim divinity for himself. He was the prototype of ensuing dynasties, who with cunning and guile crowned themselves with the halo of holiness. He was the first to destroy the lives of others - all in the name of Hashem.

QUESTIONS LEVEL-A

1. How many floors did the תיבה have?

2. What did Noach erect when he went out of the תיבה?

3. Who was the father of כנען?

4. What did the people build that incurred Hashem's anger?

5. A) How old was תרח when he died? B) Where did he die?

QUESTIONS LEVEL-B

1. For which sin was the final verdict sealed on the דור המבול?

2. What was the purpose of each floor of the תיבה?

3. Did the decree of the מבול affect the fish?

QUESTIONS LEVEL-C

1. Did נח immediately enter the תיבה upon the outbreak of the מבול?

2. How deep (in the water) was the תיבה?

QUESTIONS LEVEL-D

1. What are the שבע מצוות בני נח?

ANSWERS LEVEL-A

1. Three.

2. מזבח.

3. חם.

4. A tower that was supposed to reach the heavens.

5. A) 205 years old. B) In חרן.

15

ANSWERS LEVEL -B

1. גזל.

2. The top level served as a place for humans, the middle one was for the animals, and the bottom one served as a storage place for waste.

3. No.

ANSWERS LEVEL-C

1. No. He waited until the waters forced him to enter the תיבה.

2. 11 *Amos* .

ANSWERS LEVEL-D

1. 1) עבודה זרה- Idol worship. 2) ברכת השם -Blaspheming Hashem's Name. 3) גזל -Stealing. 4) שפיכות דמים- Murder. 5) גילוי עריות - Adultery. 6) אבר מן החי - Eating a limb from a living animal. 7) דינים- Establishment of courts of law.

פרשת לך לך
PARASHAS LECH LECHA
▶◀

לך לך מארצך
"Go away from your land." (12:1)

We may note the contrast between the *Torah's* introductory description of Noach and its initial description of Avraham. The *Torah* praises Noach, citing his righteous character and faultless behavior. The *Torah* does not present Avraham *Avinu* with a similarly positive orientation although he is acknowledged as a righteous and G-d-fearing man. The *Maharal* explains that Avraham is not described as one who possesses unique characteristics and noble qualities, so that one will not infer that these qualities are the basis for his distinction. Had this been the reality, *Am Yisroel* would be at risk to lose its special status if the people do not live up to his example. Consequently, the *Torah* presents Avraham simply as an individual, without lauding his virtue. This approach demonstrates that Avraham and his descendants were chosen by Hashem solely because it was His desire. This "arbitrary" choice will never be annulled. *Am Yisrael's* relationship with Hashem is founded upon Hashem's sacred love for them. The *Maharal's* explanation should serve as a lesson in the appropriate perspective by which one should view his fellow Jew. Just as Hashem loves all Jews, for they are *zerah kodesh,* sacred offspring, despite their mistakes, we are obligated to do the same.

***

ואת הנפש אשר עשו בחרן
"And the soul(s) that they had gotten in Haran." (12:5)

Chazal teach us that the world will exist for six thousand years. These years are divided into three, two thousand year periods. The first is the period of "תהו ובהו" - nothingness. The second period is the *Torah* era. The third is the Messianic period. The Rabbis indicate that the initial period of *"Tohu V'Vohu"* lasted from Creation until Avraham *Avinu*

17

successfully reached out to the masses to convert their idolatrous beliefs to monotheism. This is the meaning of the words, *"the souls they had gotten in Haran."* Avraham brought these itinerant souls under the protective wings of Hashem. This is a powerful condemnation of the two thousand years prior to Avraham. There were undoubtedly other righteous people who reached out to the people. Indeed, Shem and Ever maintained a *Yeshivah* to transmit the precepts of *Torah*. What was so unique about Avraham's orientation that it became the harbinger of the millennium of *Torah*?

This question is raised by many commentators. In his notes on the *Rambam* in *Hilchos Avodah Zarah*, the *Raavad* indicates the reason that Avraham is credited with wielding such a high level of influence. He explains that Avraham succeeded in smashing the idols, while his predecessors did not. Others moralized and taught positive precepts, but Avraham eradicated the evil from their midst. One has the obligation to involve himself with those who are estranged from the *Torah* way of life. He must realize, however, that complete success in reaching the unaffiliated will be achieved only when the evil is completely eradicated from their midst. Introducing the uninitiated to the positive aspects of *Torah* life, the beauty of *Shabbos*, the serenity of the observant Jewish home, and the stability of *Torah* education, is effective only when one exerts a simultaneous effort to focus upon the elimination of their prior misconceptions. The "idols" must be broken in order to effect a lasting return to *Torah* observance.

The *Raavad* continues to explain that other *tzaddikim* did, in fact, rebuke and influence the masses. They were not able to destroy the idols, however, since the idol worshippers hid them. Only Avraham was able to locate and actually break these idols. The *Kesef Mishnah* notes that the *Raavad's* answer is perplexing. Did Avraham possess a unique technique by which he detected the idols which had eluded the others before him? Idol worship was not clandestine in those days; on the contrary, it was publicly flaunted.

We suggest that the answer lies in the manner in which the idolators concealed the idols. The idols themselves were not physically hidden. Rather, the people denied their ownership. When an individual was accused of possessing an idol, he would immediately deny his relationship to it. He protested either that he was holding it for someone else, that he had just borrowed it, or that it belonged to his wife. These disclaimers provided a diversion from the superficial search for idol-worshippers. Avraham, however, maintained a relentless effort to eradicate every vestige of idol worship from the masses. His success was a reward of his total dedication to this goal.

***

ושמתי את זרעך כעפר הארץ

"And I will make your seed as the dust of the earth." (13:16)

הבט נא השמימה וספר הכוכבים... ויאמר לו כה יהיה זרעך

"Look please towards Heaven and count the stars... and He said to him, "So shall be your seed." (15:5)

והרבה ארבה את זרעך ככוכבי השמים וכחול אשר על שפת הים

"And I will unconditionally multiply your seed as the stars of the Heaven. And as the sand which is on the seashore." (22:17)

The *Torah* metaphoricully compares *Am Yisroel* to three different substances. *Horav Moshe Feinstein, z.l.,* suggests the following interpretation of this symbolism. In the first analogy, sand serves as a boundary for the sea. The boundary restrains the sea's overflow and the ensuing damage of human life and property. Likewise, when man is overwhelmed by physical or emotional troubles, he finds it difficult to serve Hashem with a relaxed attitude. Thus, Hashem offers us His blessing. This blessing enables us to restrain these difficulties from overwhelming us and interfering with our service to Hashem.

In the second analogy, the dust of the earth serves mankind in various ways. It provides the raw material for food, shelter, and clothing. Similarly, *Klal Yisrael* benefits all of mankind, since it constitutes the sole reason for the world's existence. Another lesson to be derived from this analogy is the importance of humility as a character trait. We must maintain a low profile, so that we are able to impart our *Torah* knowledge to others.

As stars rise above mankind, so, too, are we blessed with ascendancy above the nations, according to the third analogy. Although we are enjoined to be humble, we must still retain our uniqueness and self-respect. In order for an individual to be prepared to reach out to others, he must first establish within himself a symbiotic fusion of these two analogies - dust and stars. He must view himself as knowledgeable and capable of helping others. Simultaneously, he must act with humility and modesty. We must each be aware of our unique blessing and the awesome responsibility that accompanies this opportunity.

***

אני הנה בריתי אתך והיית לאב המון גוים

"As for Me, behold My Covenant is with you, and You shall be the father of a multitude of nations." (17:4)

Rashi explains that as Avraham became the father of the world, he would attain "spiritual paternity" over all nations. Avraham feared that the isolation which resulted from his circumcision would create a barrier separating him from the uncircumcised world. This obstacle might serve to confine his spirit from radiating out to the pagans, preventing him from bringing them closer to Hashem. He was threatened with the failure of his whole life's work. Converted pagans would not acquiesce to the imperative of circumcision. Thus, Hashem solemnly assured Avraham that he would become the spiritual father of a multitude of nations.

The term "אב" often refers to spiritual paternity. This notion is confirmed through the letter ה *(hay)* which Hashem added to Avram's name as He made this promise. The sound of the letter ה is just a barely audible breath, not an articulated sound. Thus, the letter ה is among the most inconsequential letters, symbolizing a material void. Integrated into the name of the Patriarch, the ה indicates that Avraham's paternity over the world is not to be a substantive one, but rather a spiritual one.

As *Rashi* notes, this paternity extends over *"a multitude of nations"*, including both Jewish and non-Jewish peoples. The unique but universal character of this nation was first proclaimed at the threshold of the formation of the Jewish people. It is apropos that this declaration was presented simultaneously with the commandment of *Bris Milah*. *Bris Milah* creates a physical barrier which segregates *Am Yisroel* from other peoples, underscoring the distinctiveness of Jews more than any other *mitzvah*. This separation also allows the Jewish people to shelter its national prowess from the external influences which threaten it. In order for the Jewish people to accomplish its personal mission, it must focus solely on the persuasive force which emanates from absolute truth. This orientation necessarily precludes missionary work and inhumane methods such as those practiced by the fanatics of other religions.

Horav Eliyahu Munk, z.l., suggests, therefore, that it is incumbent upon the Jewish leaders to limit the people's interaction with the external world. Such exposure could tarnish the unique character of the Jewish people. In order for the Jewish ideal to persevere, *Bnei Yisroel* must remain aloof and true to its heritage, principles, and values. Consequently, the Jewish nation will be better equipped to carry out its mission. The significant power of Judaism's truths is that it can enable Jewry to realize its potential without sacrificing any aspect of its existence. In this sense the separatist imperative of circumcision serves as an effective means of preservation.

QUESTIONS LEVEL - A

1. Why did Avraham eventually go to Egypt?
2. Why was Pharaoh punished by Hashem?
3. How many kings were involved in a war with each other?
4. What is the treaty which Hashem made with Avraham called?
5. In the treaty, what did Hashem promise Avraham?

QUESTIONS LEVEL - B

1. Who was given the power to bless whomever he wanted?
2. Why did Avraham stop chasing the kings at the city of Dan?

QUESTIONS LEVEL - C

1. Why did Hashem tell Avraham to go live in *Eretz Yisroel*?
2. What caused Lot to become so rich?

QUESTIONS LEVEL - D

1. Why do we complete the first *bracha* of *Shmonei Esrei* with מגן אברהם but we do not mention the other *Avos* ?

ANSWERS LEVEL - A

1. Because of the famine.

2. He took Sarah away from Avraham.

3. 4 kings against 5 kings.

4. *Bris bein ha'besarim.*

5. He will give him the land.

ANSWERS LEVEL - B

1. Avraham.

2. He knew *B'ruach Hakodesh* that his children would sin there.

ANSWERS LEVEL - C

1. A) Only in *Eretz Yisrael* will he have children. B) Only in *Eretz Yisrael* will Hashem make his character known.

2. Because he traveled with Avraham.

ANSWERS LEVEL - D

1. Since it says *you shall be a blessing,* we therefore conclude with Avraham's name.

פרשת וירא
PARSHAS VAYEIRA
▶◀

והאלקים נסה את אברהם
"And Hashem tested Avraham." (22:1)

Chazal state that this was the tenth time that Hashem tested Avraham *Avinu's* devotion. The first nine tests were only preparations for the *Akeidah*, the ultimate test of faith. *Horav Nissan Alpert, z.l.*, offers two insights regarding the *Akeidah* which shed light on this incident and its ramifications for the future of our People. Throughout Avraham's previous tests, he clearly displayed his tenacious devotion and utter loyalty to Hashem's imperative. Indeed, in Uhr Kasdim he was prepared to die for his belief. At the *Akeidah*, however, he indicated his willingness to give up all that he possessed for Hashem. All his efforts, teachings, and accomplishments would have been sacrificed with Yitzchak on the *Akeidah*. He was about to publicly contradict everything which he had been teaching about a loving G-d, whose hallmarks are benevolence and altruism. He was suddenly directed to perform the most irrational act of his life by the G-d upon whom this belief focused. Perhaps the greatest test of faith is to perform an act which is not justifiable under ordinary circumstances. The ultimate validation of one's conviction is the ability to pierce through the veil of ambiguity and remain steadfast in one's belief in Hashem. People will always raise questions regarding Hashem's Divine Providence and make demands for explanations. We should respond with expressions of belief in Hashem despite the shadow of uncertainty.

There is yet another aspect of the *Akeidah* which demands interpretation. Why was this test oriented towards Yitzchak, his son? Until this juncture every trial was of a personal nature, focusing on Avraham's own compliance. *Horav* Alpert suggests that until now it was not clear whether Avraham's devotion had been transmitted to

Yitzchak. Did this devotion begin and end with Avraham, or was this the beginning of a family, and, consequently, a nation? Would Yitzchak show the same resolute faith which his father had taught the world, or would it become extinct with Avraham? Was this belief inculcated into the next generation, or was it a sterile spirituality? Was Avraham a "father" whose lifelong goal was to transmit this heritage to his offspring? The involvement of Yitzchak in the test transformed it into the ultimate test of Avraham. This trial would assess the extent of Avraham's spiritual success and his ability to transmit his spirituality and faith to future generations.

We may suggest another aspect of Avraham's trial. We tend to view *Kiddush* Hashem (sanctification of Hashem's Name) through the perspective of one's willingness to abdicate his life for the sake of Hashem. We often overlook another form of *Kiddush* Hashem. The ability to maintain one's faith in Hashem despite serious hardships has the capacity to establish spiritual affirmation. The Jewish People's ability to withstand suffering and deprivation is testimony to the eternity and to the greatness of their spirit.

There is a famous story told about the *Bluzover Rebbe, z.l.,* which took place as he lit the *Chanukah* candles in the concentration camp. Standing amidst death and desperation, he recited the first two *brachos* (blessings) over the candles. As he was about to recite the third *bracha* of *"shehechiyanu"* - blessing Hashem for keeping us alive and preserving us- he suddenly stopped, looked around the room into the faces of the other inmates, and then recited the blessing. Later, he explained why he had hesitated. How could he say, *"Blessed are you Hashem who has kept us alive, and preserved us, and enabled us to reach this season?"* How could he utter this blessing amidst the hundreds of dead bodies which were lying literally in the shadow of the *Chanukah* candles - when thousands of Jewish skeletons were walking around the camp and millions more were being massacred? How can one praise Hashem for being kept alive to witness this travesty?

He turned around, however, and noticed the throng of Jews who, despite their obvious misery, stood resolute with tears streaming down from their glistening eyes. Their faces expressed faith and concentration as they listened to the rite of the kindling of the candles.

He, therefore, felt it was mandatory to exalt Hashem. A people who continues to serve Hashem despite all of the anguish which its members have undergone truly exemplifies the concept of *Kiddush Hashem.* Avraham's distinctiveness lay not only in his willingness to die for Hashem, but also in his inclination to serve Him despite such extremely adverse circumstances.

***

ויהי אחר הדברים האלה והאלקים נסה את אברהם

And it was after these words and Hashem tested Avraham (22:1)

Rashi cites the *Talmud* in *Sanhedrin 89b* which explains that these words apply to the "words" of the *Satan.* The Satan attempted to condemn Avraham for not offering a sacrifice to Hashem during the plentiful banquet he had arranged in honor of Yitzchak. Hashem responded to the Satan, *"Even if I had told him to sacrifice his own son, he would do it! Did he not make the whole banquet in honor of his son?"* Hashem immediately commanded Avraham to perform the *Akeidah.* The fact that Avraham did not offer any form of sacrifice seems puzzling. While he had the faith and moral stamina to withstand the trial of the *Akeidah*, he did not offer a *korban* in thanksgiving to Hashem during the banquet in honor of Yitzchak.

Be'er Yosef suggests the following explanation for Avraham's behavior. Avraham's aspiration in having progeny was to fulfill a single goal, the perpetuation of the monotheistic belief in Hashem. When Yitzchak was born, the source of Avraham's enjoyment was the hope that the continuity of his life's work would now be realized. There was no personal motive in this wonderful banquet he prepared in honor of Yitzchak's birth. Rather, it was a *seudas mitzvah* in the holiest degree. There was no need for a physical manifestation of sacrifice at this banquet. The whole banquet was in his son's honor, as he was perpetually prepared to "sacrifice" this wonderful son in the service of Hashem. There was no need for a specific ritual "sacrifice" when the the entire orientation of the banquet was sacrifice.

***

ויאמר יצחק אל אברהם אביו ויאמר אבי... ואיה השה לעולה

And Yitzchak said to Avraham, his father, father where is the lamb for the sacrifice? (22:7)

Avraham *Avinu* reached the pinnacle of *avodas* Hashem, service of Hashem, during the *Akeidas* Yitzchak. He was asked to act upon his boundless love for Hashem by demonstrating his willingness to offer his beloved son Yitzchak as a sacrifice. The enthusiasm, zeal, and love which Avraham demonstrated throughout this endeavor continue to serve as an eternal merit for his children until this day. The *Midrash* portrays Yitzchak as a partner equal to his father throughout this major trial fully aware of what was transpiring.

The *Midrash* relates that the *Satan* cleverly attempted to lure the pair into failure in their mission. After failing to dissuade Avraham, he turned to Yitzchak hoping to deter him from continuing towards the successful achievement of his goal. In an attempt to dissuade Yitzchak, he presented many convincing arguments, all in vain. The *Satan* then daringly asserted, that following Yitzchak's death all of his prized possessions would revert to Yishmael, his half-brother. Surprisingly, this argument caused Yitzchak to hesitate momentarily. Although he continued to walk with his father, he haltingly questioned him concerning the location of the sacrificial lamb.

Horav A.H. Lebowitz, Shlita, cites this *Midrash* with great emphasis. From the vast storehouse of the Satan's arsenal, the only weapon capable of piercing Yitzchak's defenses to bring about a hesitancy in his alacrity to serve Hashem was a small dose of *kinah,* jealousy. Yitzchak stood prepared to offer himself as an *"olah temimah"* - perfect sacrifice to Hashem. The thought of Yishmael usurping his inheritance, however, allowed a small vestige of jealously to awaken within him. Even the delicate, selfless Yitzchak was momentarily stirred, ever so slightly, by the evil passion of jealousy.

There is but one way to effectively resist the powerful force of jealousy. It is through total dedication to Hashem. By establishing a binding allegiance to Him, one can overcome the constraints of jealousy. When one exercises his *bitachon,* faith, in Hashem, he never feels threatened by any situation or deprived of any material possession. His faith in Hashem enables him to wholeheartedly believe that Hashem will take care of him in every respect.

True *bitachon* must be inexorable. The *Chazon Ish* states that the storekeeper who proclaims his devout trust in Hashem when things are going well, only to complain bitterly when a competitor opens a business down the block, does not have complete *bitachon*. Faith in Hashem which is sincere sustains one through the bad times as well as the good times. When inundated with life's trials and tribulations, one must reach out to his storehouse of faith, to confront and quell pangs of doubt and jealousy. One who trusts in Hashem will, in turn, triumph in His salvation.

QUESTIONS LEVEL A

1. What was Avraham's immediate reaction when he saw the strangers?
2. Were there a total of 10 *tzaddikim* in the cities Hashem wanted to destroy?
3. What did Avimelech do to Sarah?
4. What was the name of the שר צבא of Avimelech?
5. Which part of the animal was caught in the twigs?

QUESTIONS LEVEL B

1. How old was Avraham at the time the *malachim* came to visit?
2. Did the *malachim* actually eat from the food that was served?

QUESTIONS LEVEL C

1. Which *malach* was sent to heal Avraham from his *bris milah*?
2. Who was the one who cried out from Sedom to Hashem?

QUESTIONS LEVEL D

1. What was Yitzchak's birthdate?

ANSWERS LEVEL A

1. He ran to greet them.
2. No.
3. He took her from Avraham but he did nothing else to her.
4. Phicol.
5. His horns.

ANSWERS LEVEL B

1. 99 years old.
2. No. They just made believe that they ate in order not to differ from the way of the world.

ANSWERS LEVEL C

1. Rafael.
2. A girl in Sedom who was tortured for housing visitors.

ANSWERS LEVEL D

1. He was born on the 15th of *Nissan* - the first night of *Pesach*.

פרשת חיי שרה
PARASHAS CHAYEI SARAH
▶◀

ויהיו חיי שרה מאה שנה ועשרים שנה ושבע שנים שני חיי שרה

"And the life of Sarah was one hundred years and twenty years and seven years; the years of Sarah's life." (21:1)

Horav S. R. Hirsch z.l., notes that this is the only place in *Tanach* in which the *Torah* records a woman's age. There are two peculiarities in the text. After stating "ויהיו חיי שרה" - *and the life of Sarah* - rather than "שני חיי שרה" *the years of Sarah's life*, the *Torah* finds it necessary to repeat this information at the end of the *pasuk*! Indeed, the simple textual interpretation is not that Sarah lived 127 years, but that she lived one hundred years, twenty years, and seven years. *Chazal* have duly noted that Sarah's life was divided into three periods which reflect the entire span of human life: the age of childhood, the time of maturing youth, and completed old age.

   Chazal state that one who has perfectly matured maintains the ability to transmit the crowning quality of each age into the next stage of life. Hence, the term "בא בימים" literally translated as *"he walks in his days,"* means that his days are not complete. He takes all of the moral and spiritual acquisitions, of his past days and carries them into the next stage of his natural life. He does not allow any of his past attainments to whither away. Instead he transports them into the future. His future is built upon the achievements of his past. Sarah took the beauty of childhood with her into maturing womanhood and the innocence of the twenty year old girl with her into the grave. This view which *Chazal* presented contrasts sharply with that expounded by contemporary society. *Chazal* seek beauty not in the maturing woman, but in the child; innocence not in the child, but in the maturing adult. We speak of "childish innocence." It would be truly sad if childhood would be enviable because of its innocence. Innocence presupposes the possibility of guilt. Only one who has matured into adulthood, confronting the struggle of his passions and

29

matured into adulthood, confronting the struggle of his passions and managing to conquer them, is fit to be crowned with the wreath of innocence!

These years are, therefore, referred to as חיי שרה *the life of Sarah*. She "lived" in all of them. Her entire 127 years of existence was a life of cheer, importance and satisfaction. She did not regret any part of it. Nonetheless, the *Torah* concludes with the term שני חיי שרה *the years of Sarah's life*; these were but years out of the actual life of Sarah, only one part of her life. Life is not to be measured by the span of time allotted to us to live here, but by the whole physical and spiritual existence granted to us by the Almighty. As *Chazal* state, *"The righteous ones live on after death, as they go to ever progressing development in an unlimited future."*

***

וה' ברך את אברהם בכל

"And Hashem blessed Avraham with everything." (24:1)

Rashi explains that the word "בכל" alludes to the fact that Avraham was blessed with a son, since the numerical equivalent of "בכל" equals that of "בן", which means "son." It seems peculiar that the *Torah* would be so circumspect, rather than explicitly stating that Avraham was blessed with a son. *Horav Nissan Alpert, z.l.,* offers two insightful answers to this question. Although parents make every attempt to raise children in an appropriate manner, sometimes it is to no avail. Some children grow up and unfortunately do not see "eye to eye" with their parents. The type of wife envisioned by the father is not consistent with the son's perspective of a mate or vice versa. In Yitzchak's situation, a harmonious outlook existed between father and son. Avraham had fathered a son whose total outlook was compatible to his own. He was blessed with "בכל" - everything - a son who was his in every sense of the word.

He suggests another thought which is specifically applicable to those fathers who devote so much of their time and energy to communal endeavors. Their lives are totally entwined in community affairs, often at the expense of their own families. These individuals contrast to those who exemplify the "perfect" parents, whose entire lives revolve around their families. Their devotion to family knows no cognizant of the "other" children in the community. Truly blessed is he who can succeed in accomplishing his missions, both at home and in the community. This can occur when parents educate their children to the importance of *"chesed"*- kindness to others. When one shares with his children the performance of various communal endeavors, such as charity, visiting the sick, helping the downtrodden, one achieves two objectives. First, one sensitizes children to the importance of helping a fellow Jew. Second, one actually performs this *mitzvah*. Such an educational process will succeed in creating a strong, harmonious family environment, in which parents participate in a meaningful relationship with their children. This was Avraham's blessing: he succeeded "בכל", in everything. By involving his son in his life's work, he was able to fulfill his obligations to both the community and his family.

***

ויאמר אברהם אל עבדו ... ולקחת אשה לבני ליצחק

"And Avraham said to his slave... and take a wife for my son for Yitzchak." (24:2-4)

The *Torah* devotes a large amount of space to the process of Yitzchak seeking a wife and subsequent marriage. This is indicative of the importance that is attributed to this major event. Indeed, there is no event in the life of a Jewish father which is more important than the marriage of his child. No details are left to chance. Avraham elaborates for Eliezer the specific criteria required for Yitzchak's wife, who is to carry on the mantle of Jewish motherhood. The *Torah* details the fact that this first Jewish marriage was arranged through an intermediary or in the classical term, *"shadchan."* In fact, the *Torah* seems to emphasize the virtue of this method of choosing life mates.

The *Michtav M'eliyahu* explains Avraham's rationale for entrusting a third party, albeit his faithful slave, with the task of seeking the next Matriarch. The Jewish approach to marriage recommends this method as the route to marital happiness. The man who looks for a wife on his own leaves himself open to external influences or temporary feelings which may very well vanish after the marriage. Objectivity in choosing a mate is a prerequisite which cannot be compromised. The consequences of choosing based upon external pressures are tragic. A third party, who has the advantage of age, experience, and wisdom is more likely to be objective. A third party's decision can be free from internal prejudices and emotional factors. Hence, his choice represents a better guarantee of mutual understanding for the couple's future. Perhaps this first recorded "*shidduch*" should serve as a paradigm for later generations.

***

אשר לא תקח אשה לבני מבנות הכנעני

"That you will not take a wife for my son from the daughters of the Canaanites." (24:2)

The spiritual and moral abyss between a son of Avraham and a daughter of Canaan is so profound that any relationship between them remains forever illusive. The son of Avraham must never come under the influence of a Canaanite woman. We see Avraham, however, accepting marriage with an Aramean woman of his land and birthplace. In as much as both of these nations were idolators, what is the distinction between them? The *Ran* explains that the difference is in their basic character. The Arameans were of a moral and pure character, whose affinity to idolatry was a correctable intellectual deviation. The Canaanites, on the other hand, were morally corrupt, perverted to the very depth of their souls.

Avraham could not aspire to find a morally pure and chaste woman among them, who would be fitting to share the physical and spiritual engenderment of the Jewish people with his son.

QUESTIONS LEVEL - A

1. By which title did *Bnei Cheis* refer to Avraham?

2. Who was Avraham's chief servant?

3. How many camels did Eliezer take with him when he left Avraham's house?

4. How did Lavan react when he saw the gifts that were given to Rivkah?

QUESTIONS LEVEL - B

1. Why was it easy to recognize Avraham's camels?

2. Who was the first person described in the *Torah* as putting on a veil?

3. A) Who was *Keturah*? B) Why was she given this name?

QUESTIONS LEVEL - C

1. What is the meaning of "עובר לסוחר"?

2. What special miracle did Eliezer experience on his way to Rivkah?

QUESTIONS LEVEL - D

1. The bodies of seven *tzaddikim* did not decay. Who were they?

ANSWERS LEVEL - A

1. "נשיא אלקים".

2. Eliezer.

3. 10.

4. He immediately invited Eliezer to stay with him.

ANSWERS LEVEL - B

1. They were muzzled.

2. Rivkah.

3. A) Hagar.   B) "שנאים מעשה כקטורת".

ANSWERS LEVEL - C

1. Currency which is universally accepted.

2. קפיצת הדרך.

ANSWERS LEVEL - D

1. Avraham, Yitzchak, Yaakov, Binyamin, Moshe, Aharon, Miriam. According to some opinions - Dovid *Hamelech*.

פרשת תולדות
PARASHAS TOLDOS
►◄

ויתרצצו הבנים בקרבה
"And the sons struggled within her" (25:22)

The *Talmud* states that the implacable hatred which Eisav exhibited for Yaacov was foreshadowed in their mother's womb. The eternal struggle between Eisav and Yaakov began even before birth. Hence, says *Horav S. R. Hirsch, z.l.,* the paths of these two rival brothers seems to have been pre-established. This approach is consistent with the teachings of some scholars who contend that the first gestures of a human being are indicative of the tendencies and desires which become evidenced throughout his life. From the most tender age, the child conceals the man. The skilled educator is mandated to display acute sensibility to the mental makeup of the young student. In this way the educator can adroitly cultivate the student's capabilities in order to prepare him to be a useful member of society. One should not suppress an individual's attitude or impose an alien orientation upon him, for the future man is already present under the surface. One succeeds in guiding, advising, and ultimately helping the young student only through absolute understanding and infinite patience.

The story of Yaakov and Eisav is a living example of positive and negative approaches to education. The former consists of observing the child, taking heed of his abilities, structuring realistic goals for him, and educating him in accordance with his own learning style. חנוך לנער על פי דרכו ‎- *"Educate the young man according to his presumed life's path."* The latter approach lies in perceiving the child not as he is, but as he ought to be. All too frequently this method ends in total defeat for the mentor and utter disaster for the student.

***

34

ויגדלו הנערים ויהי עשו איש ידע ציד איש שדה ויעקב איש תם ישב אהלים

"And the boys grew up, and it came to pass that Eisav was a man who understood hunting, a man of the field, and Yaakov a single minded man dwelling in tents. (25:27)

Eisav was not a simple person who wantonly lusted after his heart's passions. He was an intelligent human being who had developed his own philosophy of life. Eisav's ability to "fool" Yitzchak, a feat which even the Satan could not successfully accomplish, provides evidence of this. In distinguishing Yaakov from Eisav, the *Torah* characterizes their chosen vocations as the manifestation of their divergence. The *Torah* describes Eisav as *"one who understood hunting, a man of the fields,"* while, in contrast, it characterizes Yaakov as *"a single minded man dwelling in tents."* Yaakov is not presented as the *tzaddik,* while Eisav is not viewed as the *rasha.* Nonetheless, this is what they were. Where in the *Torah's* description of them lies the foreshadowing of their future development?

Horav Dovid Bliacher, z.l., explains the contrast between one "who dwells in the tent" and one who is *"a man of the field"* in the following manner. These two descriptions suggest polarized life orientations. The ישב אהלים is one who maintains a disciplined lifestyle, living within a framework of predetermined restrictions. His theological consciousness and philosophical speculation is limited to his level of understanding. He is acutely aware of his inability to gain insight into matters which are beyond his sphere of comprehension. His faith and trust carry him through moments of ambiguity. He does not sense that his intellectual capacity is "stunted" by the limits on thought and activity. He realizes that man must live within the confines of discipline, mandated by a Superior Being. The power of belief in a higher moral authority and the concomitant fear of disobeying the untamperable religious law can overwhelm an individual. No other power could demand the complete subordination of one's will. The outcome not only serves as the best method of effecting man's good life, but it also generates a euphoric feeling of joy, serenity, and satisfaction.

In contrast to this orientation is the "איש שדה", the free thinking individual who does not live within the framework of Divine restriction and obedience. He relies completely upon his own

35

intellectual faculties. The premise of his theory is that man should be able to differentiate for himself between right and wrong. He should not be intellectually "dwarfed' by restrictions which he feels are not rational. He feels that limitations should not be placed on virtue. Hence, Eisav went to all lengths to honor his parents, unaware that there are moments when other *mitzvos* take precedence. He felt that if one must give a tithe of foods, then salt and straw should likewise be tithed. He rebelled against any externally imposed form of constraint.

The *Torah's* seemingly innocuous characterization of Yaakov and Eisav is a profound description of the chasm that exists between the *Torah* observant Jew and his free-thinking secular counterpart.

***

ויצעק צעקה גדולה ומרה עד מאד

"And he (Eisav) cried out with a great and exceedingly bitter cry.
(27:34)

The *Torah* depicts two brothers who go their separate ways. Eisav was the quintessential hunter, blood thirsty, shrewd and cunning. With his eloquent pious fraud, he was able to cultivate the love of his father. Yaakov, on the other hand, was the son who inherited his fathers characteristics. He was the simple student, the home loving son who served his parents obediently and piously.

Moreshes Moshe points out that these two sons grew up with divergent lifestyles. Yaakov requested that Eisav transfer the spiritual birthright to him because it had no meaning to Eisav. Eisav readily agreed to the arrangement, since he had no interest in preserving the spiritual heritage. Yitzchak, unaware of this eternal transaction, was deceived by Eisav's smooth speech and pretense. Thus, Yitzchak called Eisav to his bedside for the final blessing. A son like Eisav cannot be entrusted with such a noble spiritual heritage, with the Jewish values that will one day transmitted to the world. Therefore, Rivkah advised Yaakov to conceal the truth from his father and ensure the blessings which he had fairly acquired. The rest is history. Eisav entered, only to find out that "his" blessings had been taken by his younger brother. He cried out bitterly with animosity towards Yaakov.

From that day onward, we, the sole inheritors of this heritage have been scorned by the sons of Eisav. Critics from numerous sources have heaped a mountain of hatred upon Yaakov, who stole the blessings, and, in turn, upon his physical and spiritual descendants. Perhaps the statement in the *Zohar* that *Moshiach* will not arrive *"til Eisav's tears will dry up"* alludes to this. To continue to pay the penalty for those tears that Eisav shed is an awful retribution. What is the meaning of the *Zohar*? Have not our people shed enough tears at the hand of Eisav's descendants that they long ago should have overwhelmed the tears of Eisav?

Nonetheless, the birthright has been a major source of contention, the pivotal source of anti-semitism which has emanated from Eisav's descendants throughout the years. The description of the Jews as "the chosen people" has spurred the greatest conflict in every era. How can we dry Eisav's tears so that we will exist in tranquility in order to serve the Almighty in serenity? Eisav's tears will cease when the nations of the world reconcile themselves with the "lie"of Yaakov's "stealing" the birthright. This can occur only when the Jew justifies his spiritual superiority by his mode of lifestyle. He can thereby claim the right of possession to Eisav's birthright and consequently, Yitzchak's blessing. Too often the apparent distinction between Jew and non-Jew is so slight that an objective observer could hardly notice any variance. Was it truly necessary for Yaakov to deceive his father and cause Eisav's tears, so that Eisav's descendants would continue to abuse the heirs of this hard won birthright? Undoubtedly, this question is at the heart of the *Zohar's* statement. As long as Eisav's tears have not dried, as long as we have not justified our spiritual ascendency and moral dominance, we will continue to be in exile.

The Jew has a difficult goal and awesome responsibility to fulfill. By asserting his spiritual superiority and his uniquely Jewish lifestyle, the Jew must mitigate an action which Yaakov performed for his sake many years ago. When the whole world sees that " כי שם ד' נקרא עליך," the Name of Hashem is written all over the Jew in all of his endeavors, mankind will be reconciled with the historic fact that the blessing was conferred upon us. It will necessarily be fulfilled through our children.

QUESTIONS LEVEL - A

1. What did Yitzchak and Rivkah do when they saw that they had no children?
2. How did Eisav look when he was born?
3. To which land was Yitzchak forbidden to go?
4. Who overheard Yitzchak speaking to Eisav about the blessings?
5. Did Yitzchak also bless Eisav?

QUESTIONS LEVEL- B

1. What type of food is served to a mourner after the funeral?
2. In what way did Hashem bless Yitzchak in G'ror?

QUESTIONS LEVEL- C

1. Why does the *Torah* specify that Rivkah was the daughter of Besuel?
2. Who gave Eisav his name?

QUESTIONS LEVEL- D

1. A) At which age did Eisav really become a *rasha*?

B) How can this be calculated?   C) Why then does *Rashi* say he was thirteen years old?

ANSWERS LEVEL- A

1. They prayed to Hashem
2. He was red and hairy all over.
3. Egypt.
4. Rivkah.
5. Yes.

ANSWERS LEVEL- B

1. Foods that are round, such as eggs, lentils etc. to symbolize mourning which comes around to everyone.

2. He produced 100 times more than would usually have been produced.

ANSWERS LEVEL- C

1. Even though her father was a *rasha*, she still remained arighteous 2. Everyone.

ANSWERS LEVEL- D

1. A) Eisav was 15 years old when he actually went out and performed a sin. B) *Rashi* says that on the day that Avraham *Avinu* died, Eisav committed his first sin. Hashem shortened Avraham's life in order that he not see this. Avraham, who was 175 years old when he died, was 160 years old when Eisav was born. Hence, Eisav was 15 years old when Avraham died. C) One does not become a *rasha* overnight. At age 13 Eisav was beginning to show his leanings towards evil. but his first sin was at age 15.

פרשת ויצא
PARASHAS VAYEITZEI
►◄

ויקח מאבני המקום וישם מראשתיו וישכב במקום ההוא

"And he took from the stones of the place and placed them at his head, and he lay down to sleep there" (28:11)

Rashi cites the *Talmud* in *Chullin 91a* which states that the twelve stones began arguing with each other, each urging Yaakov to rest his head upon it. Hashem immediately merged them all into one large stone. The *Gerer Rebbe (R.'A.M.), z.l.,* questions this consolidation. Yaakov could rest his head upon only one area of the stone. He insightfully suggests that when the stones merged, they blended into one stone with such harmony that they were no longer distinguishable from one another. Every aspect of the consolidated stone was a fusion of all the stones together. This is the essence of *"achdus,"* unity. We should strive for a harmonious blending of personalities, such that as a community we respond as one. Through the undermining of jealousy and other manifestations of intragroup discord, we merit the appreciation of *"Who is like Your nation Yisrael, one People in the land..."*

***

וישא את קולו ויבך

"And (Yaakov) raised his voice and cried" (29:11)

After a long journey, Yaakov *Avinu* finally arrived in Padan Aram and encountered his future wife, Rachel. One would expect Yaakov to have expressed profound joy at the momentous occasion of this first meeting. Instead of rejoicing, however, Yaakov cried. *Rashi* explains that Yaakov cried because he was grieved that he came to Rachel empty-handed. In contrast, his father, Yitzchak, had been sent with jewelry to meet his future wife, Rivkah. Yaakov's sudden poverty is attributed to an unusual altercation between Yaakov and Elifaz, Eisav's son. When Yaakov ran from his parents' home, he narrowly

40

escaped the venomous wrath of Eisav. At his father's behest, Elifaz chased after Yaakov in order to kill him. When Elifaz caught up to Yaakov, he was suddenly unable to perform his mission. Having been raised in a house replete with the sanctity of *mitzvah* performance, he was incapable of committing murder. Elifaz, the consummate student, turned to Yaakov to advise him of a way to fulfill his father's imperative, even though it was contrary to *Torah* law. Yaakov advised Elifaz to take all of his money, which would render him "dead" in a small way, since Yaakov would be incapable of supporting himself and others. The *Baalei Tosfos* explain that although Elifaz was apparently exempt from fulfilling his father's wishes, he nonetheless wanted to find a way to comply while simultaneously conforming with *Torah* law.

Horav A. H. Lebowitz, Shlita, observes that Elifaz's dilemma and ensuing actions demonstrate a remarkable level of appreciation for the value of a *mitzvah.* Because his mission was in direct violation of the *Torah,* he could have rationalized walking away without even trying to execute it. He implored his uncle, however, to contrive some scheme in which he could simultaneously fulfill both obligations: his father's negative wishes and *Torah* law. Thus, Elifaz demonstrated dedication to the *mitzvah* of honoring his parents.

We should also note Yaakov *Avinu's* total devotion to *mitzvos.* He was willing to give away all of his possessions in order to enable another individual to perform a small facet of a *mitzvah,* despite the negative orientation of this *"mitzvah"* towards them. Even more amazing is the fact that this is the same Yaakov who jeopardized his life in order to protect the *"small jars"* (*Rashi 32:25*) which he owned.

Do we nurture equal love for every *mitzvah?* True, we might never attain that level of devotion reached by Yaakov *Avinu,* but our goals must be set towards that objective. Complacency in *mitzvah* performance can be devastating. We should view each obstacle we confront as a challenge to be overcome, while we perceive every *mitzvah* as an opportunity to gain eternity. With these thoughts as a guiding perspective, every *mitzvah* will take on a new meaning.

***

41

וירא והנה באר בשדה... והאבן גדולה על פי הבאר... ויגל האבן מעל פי הבאר

"And he saw a well in a field... and a great stone was on the mouth (top) of the well... and he rolled the stone from the top of the well." (29:2-10)

The *Torah* emphasizes Yaakov's superhuman physical strength by relating that he was able to roll the stone off the top of the well. *Rashi* elaborates on this theme by stating that the *Torah* notes Yaakov's physical strength. It seems peculiar that the *Torah* would find it necessary to stress such a mundane trait. Is Yaakov a secular hero that his physical strength must be exalted? Is one's personality and character to be measured by his physical prowess?

Siach Mordechai answers that obviously, characterizing someone according to his physical ability is both inaccurate and inappropriate. The importance of one's physical ability lays in the benefit derived from its use. How does one employ this unique gift which Hashem has conferred upon him? The wicked apply this G-d-given gift in order to take advantage of those who are weaker than they. Their actions contrast to those of the righteous who channel their physical capability in service of their fellow man. They are constantly dedicated to making life more pleasurable for those in need. Such an appropriate employment of one's G-d-given physical attributes should be stressed, so that others will be inspired to emulate it.

***

מלא שבע זאת ונתנה לך גם את זאת בעבדה אשר תעבד עמדי עוד שבע
שנים אחרות. ויעש יעקב כן...

Complete this week and this one also will be given to you for the work which you will do for me for another seven years. And Yaakov did so. (29:27-28)

We may be puzzled by Yaakov's passive acquiescence to Lavan's proposal. Surely, Lavan had no legal or moral claim for Yaakov to work another seven years to receive Rachel as a bride, which their original contract had stipulated. After seven years, Lavan acted reprehensibly towards Yaakov by putting Leah under the *chupah* in place of Rachel. Yaakov clearly owed Lavan nothing, since he had explicitly stated his desire to marry Rachel. Why did Yaakov accede to Lavan's manipulation without objection?

Horav Dovid Feinstein, Shlita, suggests that Yaakov's actions were motivated by his sensitivity to Leah's feelings. He knew that Leah's self-esteem would be destroyed if he were to protest working seven years for Leah in place of Rachel. Imagine Leah's despondency, her feelings of dejection, over this hypothetical reaction.

Horav Feinstein notes the great demands that the *Torah* places upon us in our relationships with our fellow man. Rather than demean Leah, Yaakov was willing to dedicate an additional seven years of his life to working for the unethical Lavan in an atmosphere entirely antithetical to *Torah.* Inherent in the arrangement, Yaakov was giving up another seven years of *Torah* study! Yaakov did not view these seven years as unnecessary *"bitul Torah",* cessation of *Torah* study, since its performance was critical to Leah's continued self-esteem. How much more so should we be ever vigilant in our speech and actions in order not to cause harm to another person's feelings.

QUESTIONS LEVEL- A

1. What percentage of his wealth did Yaakov promise to give to Hashem?

2. From which of Yaakov's actions do we note his physical strength?

3. What were the names of the sons of Bilhah?

4. Who warned Lavan not to bother Yaakov in any way?

5. A) Who met Yaakov when he was returning to *Eretz Yisroel?*

B) What name did Yaakov give to his place?

QUESTIONS LEVEL- B

1. Why was Leah afraid she would have to marry Eisav?

2. What excuse did Lavan give for tricking Yaakov into marriage with Leah?

QUESTIONS LEVEL-C

1. A) Where did Yaakov go immediately upon leaving home? B) How

43

many years was he there? C) How much sleep did Yaakov get during this time?

2. Why was Zilpah given to Leah as a maid servant?

QUESTIONS LEVEL- D

1.Which three great *tzaddikim* met their wives as a result of a well?

ANSWERS LEVEL- A

1. Ten percent.

2. He lifted the stone off the well by himself.

3. Dan and Naftali.

4. Hashem.

5) . A) Angels. B) Machanayim.

ANSWERS LEVEL- B

1. It was said "*two sons were born to Rivkah and two daughters to Lavan, the older son to the older daughter and younger son to the younger daughter.*" She (Leah) was the older daughter and Eisav was the older son.

2. *It is not our custom to give the younger daughter before the older one...*"

ANSWERS LEVEL- C

1. A) To study *Torah* in the *Yeshivah* of Shem and Eiver. B) 14 years. C) He never lay down to sleep. He was always studying *Torah*.

2. This was done in order to fool Yaakov. Usually the younger maidservant went to the younger daughter, hence Zilpah should be given to Rachel. Since Yaakov thought he was marrying Rachel he expected to get Zilpa as the maid servant.

ANSWERS LEVEL- D

1. Yitzchak, Yaakov and Moshe.

פרשת וישלח
PARASHAS VAYISHLACH
▶◀

ויקם בלילה הוא ויקח את שתי נשיו ואת שתי שפחתיו ואת אחד עשר ילדיו

"And he rose that night and took his two wives and his two maidservants and his eleven children." (32:23)

Rashi cites the *Midrash* that questions Dinah's whereabouts. He explains that Yaakov, fearing Eisav's desire for Dinah, hid her in a chest in order to prevent Eisav from seeing her. For denying Eisav this opportunity, Hashem punished Yaakov by causing Dinah to fall into the hands of Shechem. As the *Midrash* states, Hashem reprimanded Yaakov, saying: *"You prevented the possibility of a kindness to your brother; she will instead be taken by an enemy. You denied her marriage to one who is circumcised; she will instead marry an uncircumcised infidel. You refused her marriage in a permitted fashion; she will be married in a forbidden manner."*

Horav Yerucham Levovitz, z.l., comments on this *Midrash*, asking where Yaakov's sin lies? He followed the prescribed *Halacha*, which compares giving ones daughter in marriage to a man who is ignorant to one who ties her up and places her before a lion! *(Pesachim 49b)* Was it appropriate for Yaakov to have been so severely punished for not allowing his daughter to fall prey to the treacherous Eisav, the epitome of evil?

He explains that Yaakov was certainly <u>obligated</u> to lock Dinah in the chest. *Tzaddikim* however, are judged for any slight infraction of Hashem's will. Yaakov is faulted for a slight movement; he closed the chest just a little more forcefully that was necessary, a movement detected only by Hashem. This miniscule deviation from perfection precipitated Yaakov's punishment in the form of the Shechem ordeal and the consequent disgrace of his family. This is but a glimpse of the standard by which Hashem measures the righteous!

וירא כי לא יכל לו ויגע בכף ירכו ותקע כף ירך יעקב בהאבקו עמו
על כן לא יאכלו בני ישראל את גיד הנשה

"And (the stranger) saw that he could not defeat him (Yaakov), he touched the upper joint of his (Yaakov's) thigh, and Yaakov's hip joint became dislocated as he wrestled with him. Therefore Bnei Yisrael do not eat the displaced nerve. (32:26-33)

The *Talmud, Chullin 90b,* cites a difference of opinion between R' Yehudah and the *Chachamim* regarding the prohibition of *gid ha'nashe,* the thigh muscle. The *Chachamim* state that this prohibition applies to the thigh muscle of both the right and left hind legs, while R' Yehudah has the opinion that it applies only to the right hind leg. His reasoning is based upon the premise that the angel struck Yaakov on the right side. The *Chachamim*, in contrast, feel that he was struck from behind, affecting both sides. Since the prohibition is in memory of Yaakov's struggle, what happened that night is critical to the establishment of the *Halachah.*

Be'er Yosef suggests a somewhat homiletic appreciation of the *Halachah* in regard to the narrative. It has been noted that this angel was actually the Satan whose calculated attack on Yaakov caused him to deviate from his belief in Hashem. Although he failed to overpower Yaakov, he did succeed in dislocating his thigh. The hip and loins serve as metaphors for the future descendants of Yaakov, whose faith in Hashem would be weakened.

The *mitzvos* of the *Torah* are divided into two categories: those that concern man's relationship with Hashem (*Bein Adam La'Makom*) and those that address man's relationship with his fellow man (*Bein Adam La'Chaveiro*). The two *luchos* which contain the Ten Commandments and allude to all 613 of the *mitzvos* are similarly divided. The right side reflects those *mitzvos* concerning man's obligation towards Hashem, while the left side focuses on those *mitzvos* which address man's relationship with his fellow man. Man must adhere to both aspects of Hashem's imperative. One who neglects to follow *mitzvos Bein Adam La'Makom* is viewed as incomplete or "limping" on his right side, while one who fails to respond to *mitzvos "Bein Adam La'Chaveiro"* is perceived as lame on his left side.

The angel approached Yaakov with a desire to harm both

sides of him, his *mitzvos Bein Adam La'Makom* and *Bein Adam La'Chaveiro*. He did not succeed in either endeavor. This is implied by the angel's statement, "*For you battled with G-d and with man and prevailed.*" Yaakov prevailed in warding off attacks on both aspects of *mitzvah* performance. Upon noticing his defeat, the angel made one last try and struck Yaakov's hip, representing his descendants, aiming to weaken their *mitzvah* observance.

We may note that the latter generations, although they may have been weak in their relationship with Hashem, nonetheless continue to perform many acts of *chesed* toward their fellow man. These may perhaps be viewed as metaphorically limping on their right side. This is reflected in R' Yehuda's decision prohibiting only the right side of the animal. The *Chachamim* feel that if one's belief in Hashem is weakened, if his *mitzvah* performance *Bein Adam La'Makom* is remiss, then he will not be able to maintain his meritable charitable activities (*mitzvos Bein Adam La'Chaveiro*). Consequently, *Chazal* believe that the prohibition of *gid ha'nashe* extends to both hips.

***

ויאמר לא יעקב יאמר עוד שמך כי אם ישראל כי שרית עם אלקים
ועם אנשים ותוכל

"And he said: No longer shall your name be said as Yaakov but Yisrael, for you battled with angels and with men and have prevailed" (32:29)

There are many explanations regarding the episode of Yaakov's battle with the "man." Indeed, the divergence between the literal and symbolic meanings of the episode is reflected in the many interpretations applied to this passage. Many commentators view the narrative as a parable for the righteous individual's inner struggle against the forces of evil. Yaakov stands alone in the vastness, in the deep silence of the night, a mortal being in confrontation with the Divine messenger. This mysterious encounter represents the numerous struggles which surface on the eve of an approaching ordeal.

The *Sh'lah Hakadosh* views this struggle in the night as a foreshadowing of the decisive battle which is to occur on the morrow, in broad daylight. Man is judged in the silence of the preceding night.

It is in this abyss of darkness that man's moral value and inner strength must be asserted in order to prevail against the forces of evil. If man emerges triumphant, he will be personally blessed by the angel of evil, in preparation for the imminent trials which yet await him. In the crises of our lives, our destiny is decided in the dark night, in the secret recesses of the human conscience.

The *Brisker Rav* suggests a similar homily. He questions *Rashi's* statement that the "men" with whom Yaakov fought were Lavan and Eisav. Why does *Rashi* assume that Yaakov had prevailed over Eisav, when he had not yet confronted him? *The Brisker Rav* explains that the "man" with whom Yaakov struggled was Eisav's guardian angel. As the *Midrash* states, their "wrestling" raised dust all the way up to the Heavenly throne. In other words, this battle actually occurred in Heaven. If Yaakov managed to succeed in Heaven, then he would emerge victorious over Eisav himself on earth.

We must always concern ourselves with what is taking place in Heaven. Are we prevailing up there? Did we pass the test of judgement on Heaven? If we are to be victorious in Heaven, then we should have no fear on earth. Man's continued concern should be only, "What will they say up in Heaven?" Man should subdue his heart and purify his thoughts, dedicating them only to the Almighty. Hashem will thereby enable him to defeat all the powers of this world which are designed to constrain him. This resolve will enable the individual to fend off all harsh decrees. No longer will he be intimidated by earthly obstacles, for he has acquired the greatest strength, trust in Hashem!

***

כי שרית עם אלקים ועם אנשים ותוכל

"For you battled with G-d and with man and have prevailed"
(32:29)

Targum Onkelos interprets the angels' words in the following manner: *"For you fought before G-d with man and have succeeded."* Consequently, the name *"Yisrael"* refers to one who fights "before' Hashem. *Horav Eliyahu Munk, z.l.,* notes that there is no indication that this name refers specifically to the battle with men. Our strength lies not in our physical struggle with human beings. Judaism's eternal struggle is <u>within</u> society. Its goal is the establishment of the kingdom of Hashem on earth. In this struggle, however, the Jew does not gather physical weapons of violence. On the contrary, his symbolic armament is his spiritual values. He fights for the preservation of his idealistic principles, which are being constantly threatened by the environmental forces. His method reflects respect for human dignity, never inflicting physical damage upon those who do not respond positively to his agenda. Jewry's ongoing struggle is never directed against human beings.

QUESTIONS LEVEL- A

1. For what purpose did Yaakov send messengers to Eisav?

2. Which river did Yaakov cross the night before he met Eisav?

3. A) To where did Eisav travel after meeting with Yaakov? B) Where did Yaakov travel from there?

4. A) Where did Rachel die? B) Where was she buried?

5. A) How many wives did Eisav have? B) Who was a *pilegesh* to Elifaz, the son of Eisav? C) Who was their child?

QUESTIONS LEVEL- B

1. Why did Yaakov say that all he possessed was a ox and a donkey?

2. Why isn't Dinah mentioned as part of the group that met Eisav?

QUESTIONS LEVEL- C

1. For what two reasons did Yaakov send messengers to Eisav?

2. A) Do angels have permanent names? B) How do we know this?

QUESTIONS LEVEL- D

1. The *Midrash* states that "ox" refers to Yosef and "donkey" to Yissacher: A) What aspect of *Avodas* Hashem do each of these tribes represent? B) Why did Yaakov pick these tribes to showcase for Eisav?

ANSWERS LEVEL- A

1. To try to make peace with him.

2. Yabok.

3. A) Seir. B) Succos.

4. A) On the road to Bais Lechem B) In the same place.

5. A) Three B) Timnah C) Amalek

ANSWERS LEVEL- B

1. To show him that the *bracha* of "הוי גביר לאחיך" was not fulfilled.

2. He hid her in a box so that Eisav would not see her and want to marry her.

ANSWERS LEVEL- C

1. To notify him of his arrival; To seek his friendship.

2. A) No. B) When Yaakov asked the angel his name, the angel said that his name is based on whatever mission he is performing.

ANSWERS LEVEL- D

1. A) Yosef is the *tzaddik* and Yissachar represents *Torah* study. B) Yaakov showed Eisav that physical strength did not impress him. The spiritual level of a person has the greatest value.

פרשת וישב
PARASHAS VAYEISHEV
▶◀

וישראל אהב את יוסף מכל בניו כי בן זקנים הוא לו ועשה לו כתנת פסים

"And Yisrael loved Yosef most of all his sons, because he was the child of his old age, so he made him a fine (multi- striped) cloak."

(37:3)

Yosef was the recipient of Yaakov's special favor because of his unique attributes. As *Rabeinu Bachya* states, Yosef's personality combined the outstanding qualities of all the other brothers. Yaakov perceived in Yosef a continuation of himself. Their facial features strongly resembled one another's, and their life histories were strikingly similar. *Pirkei D'Rav Eliezer* states that Yaakov loved Yosef because he prophetically foresaw that Yosef was destined for eminence.

Above all, Yaakov loved Yosef for his *Torah* knowledge. *Rashi* cites *Onkelos* who defines בן זקנים as בר חכים - the wise son. This is consistent with the *Midrash* which states that Yaakov imparted to Yosef the *Torah* knowledge he had gained from the *Yeshivah* of Shem and Ever. Yaakov provided a *Torah* education for each of his sons, exerting great effort to raise them as *tzaddikim*. To Yosef, however, he revealed secrets of the *Torah* which he shared with no one else. Nonetheless, it seems peculiar that Yaakov would teach Yosef "more" *Torah* than he had imparted to the other brothers.

We may suggest the following thought. The father and son relationship can be established in many ways. The two can go on outings together or work cooperatively on various projects. Another method to concretize this relationship is through *Torah* study. When a father and son establish a *"chavrusa",* learning partner, relationship, this alliance is bonded for eternity. This partnership is not an emphemeral or vacuous experience, which continues on only as long as each member derives benefit from it. Rather, it is a holy

51

relationship in which both individuals are fused into one being. Yosef was Yaakov's *"ben zekunim."* Their association was nurtured by *Torah* study. While Yaakov supervised the *Torah* study for all of his sons, Yosef was his *"chavrusa"*!

***

ויבא יוסף את דבתם רעה אל אביהם

"And Yosef reported evil about them (his brothers) to their father." (37:7)

Upon hearing about Yosef's constant tale-bearing, the brothers convened a *Beis Din* and judged him according to *Halachah*. They judged him as a *rodef* - pursuer, one who chases another with the intention to kill him. The *Halachah* is clear in this case. The verdict was based upon the principle that the pursuer is liable for death, as long as there is no other way to save the pursued. The *Sforno* writes that the brothers were so clear in their judgement that they experienced no pangs of remorse. In fact, after they threw Yosef into the pit, they sat down to eat. They perceived their actions as neither wrong nor tragic. They did what the situation demanded of them!

Even twenty two years later, upon witnessing their father's continued anguish over his loss, they still did not question their deed. When Yosef was prepared to imprison one of the brothers, they conceded among themselves that perhaps they were being punished for not taking pity on Yosef when he pleaded with them. At no time, however, did they change their opinion regarding their original verdict. They still felt that Yosef's actions merited the death penalty. Indeed, the judgement was so unambiguous that when Yosef revealed himself to them, the brothers were prepared to kill him had not an angel intervened. *(Tanchuma)*

The *Alter of Kelm, z.l.,* suggests that this episode communicates an important insight into human nature. When one has a first impression of a given situation, it becomes rooted in his subconscious. This conception will gradually become a part of his psyche, so that his mindset is reconstructed in accordance with his initial assessment. Even if the original matter has been forgotten, he will nonetheless conform to his original decision. The verdict that Yosef deserved death was so ingrained in the brothers' nature that, even though they were prepared to ransom him and bring him home immediately upon recognizing him, they acceded to their natural instinct and desired to kill him. That first impression still clouded their ability to judge clearly. How careful must one be when passing judgement on a matter upon which he has previously developed a strong opinion. Unless one can completely absolve himself of all previous notions, he cannot offer a pure critique, since he is subconsciously hindered by his earlier prejudice.

***

ויהי איש מצליח ויהי בבית אדניו המצרי

"And he (Yosef) became a successful man, and he stayed in his Egyptian master's house." (39:3)

The epithet "Egyptian," is repeated several times in this chapter as if to draw our attention to the immense transformation taking place in Yosef's life. From the sublime heights of holy life in Yaakov's home, Yosef was dragged down to the abysmal depths of the depravation that was Egypt. The immoral character of the Egyptian lifestyle was the direct antithesis of the upbringing in Yosef's home. Potifar's wife, rejecting all moral scruples, was the prototype of the Egyptian woman.

Horav Eli Munk, z.l., suggests that the *Torah* intentionally set out to emphasize this contrast. In order to fully appreciate the profound piety of Yosef *Ha'tzaddik*, one must first reflect upon what he was confronting. Yosef must have possessed exceptional qualities in order to have reached this exalted position in Potifar's house.

Similarly, we should consider the background of those who have braved the counter-currents of an assimilationist society and have discovered the road which leads them to the *Torah*. Their resolute courage is to be lauded. The travail which they had to experience in order to reach and be accepted by the observant community should be appreciated. Perhaps the most significant aspect of their endeavor is the world from which they came. When one perceives the distorted sense of values which has caused the moral breakdown of society, one can truly admire *baalei teshuvah*. Their superhuman courage and strength of character should be a lesson for us all.

ויהי אחר הדברים האלה חטאו משקה מלך מצרים והאפה
לאניהם למלך מצרים

"And it came to pass after these things, that the <u>butler</u> of the king of Egypt, and his <u>baker</u> had sinned against their master, the king of Egypt."(40:1)

Later on in the story the *pasuk* refers to them in a slightly different way. *"And Pharoah became angry against his two officials, the <u>prince</u> <u>of</u> <u>the</u> <u>butlers,</u> and the <u>prince</u> <u>of</u> <u>the</u> <u>bakers."</u> (40:1)* While in the first *pasuk* they are simply referred to as butler and baker, they are referred to as "prince" of the butlers and "prince" of the bakers in the second *pasuk. Horav S. R. Hirsh, z.l.,* notes the apparent mockery reflected in the pathos of these "princes." They are princes to those beneath them in status, but to those above them they are merely slaves to be manipulated at the whim of their superior. When one's stature is dependent solely upon his relation to the king, his princely position is -- at best -- precarious. The king holds the life of these "princes" in his hand, as if they were his chattel. To him they are not princes; they are simply butlers and bakers.

This would seem an appropriate message for those who delude themselves with self-aggrandizement as soon as they ascend to a position of semi-importance. The opinion of underlings is of little consequence. What really matters is one's image in the eyes of those to whom he is beholden. We may extend this to a spiritual perspective. We often concern ourselves with the opinion of man, while we neglect to reflect upon the only opinion which is of primary significance - that of Hashem.

QUESTIONS LEVEL- A

1. What kind of special garment did Yaakov give to Yosef?
2. For how much was Yosef sold by his brothers?
3. What was the royal position of Potifar?
4. Who was Yehudah's father-in-law?

QUESTIONS LEVEL- B

1. Why did Yosef associate himself with the *Bnei Hashfachos*?

2. Who met Yosef as he was searching for his brothers?

QUESTIONS LEVEL - C

1. How many times was Yosef sold?

2. What special sign did Hashem give to Yaakov regarding his share in *Olam Habah*?

3. For which special *middah* did Tamar merit to be the mother of kings?

QUESTIONS LEVEL- D

1. Who was the angel that made Yehudah go to Tamar?

ANSWERS LEVEL- A

1.*Ksones pasim* - a multi-colored coat.

2. 20 silver pieces.

3. Prince of the butchers.

4. Shua.

ANSWERS LEVEL- B

1. Since they were always slighted by the other brothers, Yosef made a point to befriend them.

2. The angel Gavriel.

ANSWERS LEVEL- C

1. Three times. He was sold to the Yishma'elim who in turn sold him to the Midyanim who in turn sold him to the Egyptians.

2. Hashem told him that if none of his children would die during his lifetime, he would not go to *Gehinom*.

3. *Tznius*.

ANSWERS LEVEL- D

1. The angel Michael.

פרשת מקץ
PARASHAS MIKEITZ
►◄

ועתה ירא פרעה איש נבון וחכם וישיתיהו על ארץ מצרים. יעשה
פרעה ויפקד פקידים על הארץ וחמש את ארץ מצרים בשבע שני השבע

**"So now let Pharaoh look for a man discreet and wise. And set
him over the land of Egypt. Let Pharaoh do this, appoint officers
over the land and impose a fifth on the land of Egypt during the
seven years of plenty."** (41:33,34)

Yosef advised Pharaoh to seek a wise man who would be capable of
managing Egypt during the ensuing years of plenty and famine. Yosef
was chosen for this position because of his profound wisdom. He
proceeded to suggest that food be stored during the years of plenty in
order to provide sustenance for the Egyptian people during the
approaching years of famine. At first glance, Yosef's advice hardly
indicates great wisdom! Any person with minimal intelligence would
realize that one must prepare for the years of famine during the years
of abundance. What was the mark of Yosef's great wisdom?

Horav Y. Lubshensky, z.l., suggests that upon careful scrutiny,
Yosef's advice appears to be indicative of one who is particularly
perceptive. People who are not currently in need will rarely concern
themselves about the future. Countries that have surplus food, often
squander this excess, never giving thought to the morrow. An
individual who concerns himself with the future during moments of
abundance is a wise unique individual. Thus, Yosef illustrated his
prudence. He was able to <u>see</u> the problems that would occur
tomorrow, despite the illusionary abundance of today.

We glean this idea from the words of *Chazal* in *Pirkei Avos*:
"Who is a wise man? He who sees what will be born!" One who is
able to anticipate the future, to perceive it as if he were <u>seeing</u> it now,
is truly a wise man. It is not sufficient to <u>know</u> what is in store for the
future, one must experience this knowledge now.

56

כי נשני אלקים את כל עמלי ואת כל בית אבי

"For Hashem has made me forget all my previous misfortune and all my father's house." (41:51)

The usual translation for נשני אלקים is *"Hashem has made me forget, (all my previous misfortune and all my father's house)."* This notion engenders a distasteful feeling. It seems objectionable that Yosef would be anxious to disassociate himself with his elderly father and all of his family. *Horav S.R. Hirsch, z.l.,* notes that this would explain Yosef's deficiency in getting in touch with his family for such a long time. To state, however, that Yosef's heart was so cold is simply preposterous! The various commentaries imply justifiable reasons for Yosef's inaction.

Horav Hirsch cites another interpretation for the word נשני. The word נשני also means "to be a creditor" and can, therefore, mean: *"Hashem has made my misfortunes and my family into creditors."* Hashem had transformed what had formerly seemed to be calamity into the medium for attaining the greatest joy. The realization that one is deeply indebted to his misfortune and family is the hallmark of greatness. One's objective should be to pierce though the veil of ambiguity that clouds various life situations in order to vividly see Divine Providence directing every step. Yosef *Ha'tzaddik* was not only righteous in his own right, he was also able to see the "righteousness" of Hashem's guidance in everything.

We may suggest another thought. Sometimes it is good to forget! Imagine that Yosef went through life with bitter animosity, loathing his brothers for what they had done to him. He would calculate and add every bit of misery to his hatred, until it became insurmountable. This obsessive hatred would have eventually destroyed him. How many individuals and institutions have fallen prey to the effects of hatred? In due time a simple offense can be blown out of proportion. This occurs because we refuse to forget yesterday's offense which blatantly glares us in the eye many years later, demanding revenge. Yosef thanked Hashem for giving him the ability to open his arms to his brothers and view their actions in the proper perspective.

***

כלנו בני איש אחד... לא היו עבדיך מרגלים

"We are all sons of one man....your servants are not spies."
(42:11)

The *Ramban* offers insight into the dialogue between Yosef and his brothers. Yosef questioned the need for <u>all</u> the brothers of such a prestigious family to journey to Egypt to purchase food. Obviously, such a mission could have been accomplished by a few of the brothers, together with an entourage of servants. The brothers responded that *"we are sons of one man"* - and our father, seeking to minister to the needs of brotherhood and unity, insisted that we travel together. Such a journey of togetherness would promote brotherly love.

Horav A. H. Lebowitz, Shlita, notes that Yaakov's decision offers a profound insight onto the significance of *achdus* - unity. If Yaakov was so concerned about the dangers of the trip that he refused to permit Binyamin to accompany them, why did he allow <u>all</u> of the brothers to go? Should not the risks of such a journey preclude the whole family from going? What about the *bitul Torah,* cessation of *Torah* study, for all the brothers? Unity and brotherhood are not merely noble attributes. They are the basis of *Torah* life and the foundation of *Yidishkeit.* The essential trait of *"love your fellow man as yourself"* is the fundamental principle of the entire *Torah.* It was, therefore, necessary for Yaakov to emphasize that *mitzvah* at all costs.

We must add that *Ahavas Yisrael,* love for a fellow Jew, cannot be fulfilled simply by active involvement in communal affairs, while simultaneously neglecting the needs of the individual. Our concern for *Klal Yisrael* - the whole people - must generate from a genuine sensitivity to the individual Jew. One who works relentlessly for national Jewish causes, while neglecting the Jew at home or on the street, does not reflect the true essence of *Ahavas Yisrael.*

***

ויאמר ישראל למה הרעתם לי להגיד לאיש העוד לכם אח

"And <u>Yisrael</u> said, why have you dealt ill with me, to tell the man that you had yet a brother." (43:6)

From his loss of Yosef until this juncture, the *Torah* refers to the Patriarch as <u>Yaakov.</u> This is the first instance in which the *Torah* refers to him with the name Yisrael, signifying strength. The name Yaakov implies a depressed state of mind in which one feels despondent It describes one who is "limping behind" circumstances (as in עקב עשו - Eisav's heel), unable to master over them.

Horav S.R. Hirsch, z.l., explains his sudden change in the following manner: The believing Jew only feels despondent when he is at a loss to know what he should do. The righteous Jew becomes depressed by two things: guilt for having done wrong and doubt regarding the correct course of action to follow. He never fears the future, for he places his complete trust in Hashem. As long as Yaakov was in doubt about whether or not he should allow Binyamin to leave, his name appears as Yaakov.

From the moment that his departure seemed a pressing necessity because his life was in peril (whether he stayed home and starved or he went on the treacherous trip), Yaakov culled his resources and became Yisrael. As soon as a Jew realizes it is beyond his human powers to provide for himself, he is told, 'גול על ד' (*Tehillim 37:5) "roll over to Hashem."* This refers to that which is too difficult for one to handle alone. Therefore, with quiet resolve, the Patriarch reproached his sons only for having unnecessarily mentioned their youngest brother at all. In regard to the future, however, he placed his resolute faith in Hashem.

QUESTIONS LEVEL- A

1. What is considered the major river in Egypt?

2. What did Pharaoh see in the second dream?

3. What new name did Pharaoh give to Yosef?

4. A) Who were Yosef's two sons? B) Who was born first?

5. In what order did Yosef seat his brothers at the table?

QUESTIONS LEVEL- B

1. A) What is the meaning of the words ותפעם רוחו? B) Who else had a similar reaction to a dream?

2. Which word tells us that Yosef did not want to take personal credit for interpreting Pharaoh's dreams?

3. How much grain was Yosef able to collect in Egypt?

QUESTIONS LEVEL- C

1. What does צפנת פענח mean?

2. Why does the *Torah* mention that Yosef and his brothers drank together and became intoxicated?

QUESTIONS LEVEL- D

1. A) Where in the *Parsha* do we find a קטן who is referred to as איש?

ANSWERS LEVEL- A

1. יאור - Nile.

2. Seven healthy ears of corn grew on one stalk, and then they were swallowed completely by a second set of seven thin ears that grew after them.

3. צפנת פענח.

4. A) Ephraim, Menashe B) Menashe.

5. Oldest to youngest.

ANSWERS LEVEL- B

1. A) His heart pounded. B) Nebuchadnezar.

2. בלעדי.

3. He collected so much that they stopped counting.

ANSWERS LEVEL- C

1. Someone who is able to figure out hidden enigmas.

2. We derive from here that from the day of מכירת יוסף until that day, neither Yosef nor his brothers drank any wine.

ANSWERS LEVEL- D

1. Menashe, who was about nine years old at the time, is referred to as איש - - ויעש האיש כאשר אמר יוסף.

פרשת ויגש
PARASHAS VAYIGASH
▶◀

מהרו ועלו אל אבי ואמרתם אליו כה אמר בנך יוסף

"Hasten and go up to my father and say unto him, so said your son Yosef" (45:9)

והנה עיניכם ראות... כי פי המדבר אליכם

"And behold your eyes <u>see</u>... that it is my mouth that speaks to you" (45:12)

וירא את העגלות אשר שלח יוסף... ותחי רוח יעקב אביהם

"And when he (Yaakov) saw the wagons which Yosef had sent... then the spirit of Yaakov their father revived." (45:27)

When Yosef and his brothers met, they reconciled. Yosef quickly dispatched his brothers to bring their aged father to Egypt. He subtly communicated to his father that he still remained his son in the truest sense of the word - כה אמר בנך יוסף. "Although I am geographically distanced from you, I am nonetheless your Yosef. I never yielded to temptation or capitulated to the adverse influences of the Egyptian lifestyle." He continued this dialogue by underscoring his ability to speak *lashon ha'kodesh*, the holy language. *"Your eyes see that it is my mouth that speaks to you."*

The text seems peculiar. Does one actually <u>see</u> the spoken word? On the contrary, one <u>hears</u> the spoken word! Yosef was, however, emphasizing the fact that he was <u>speaking</u> from his mouth. One can have sounds emanating from his mouth, while he is really expressing the feelings of his heart. When the mouth and heart are inconsonant with one another, hypocrisy results. <u>What</u> a man says is not as important as <u>how</u> he says it. Yosef exemplified consistency between his outward expression and his internal orientation. He <u>spoke</u> from the mouth. "My character has not changed," he told his brothers. "My *lashon ha'kodesh* is the same. I have maintained the same sanctity of life upon which I was nurtured in our father's home." Yosef deliberately sent wagons - עגלות - to remind his father of the last *Torah* lesson in which they had been engrossed at the time when he left so suddenly. When the exciting news that his son was alive physically and spiritually reached Yaakov, he was revived - ותחי רוח יעקב. He lived again in the lives of his children. *Horav Moshe Swift, z.l.,* poignantly describes Yaakov's revival. We live in a world of opportunity in which every child has the resources to develop into just about anything. When a child leaves home and goes out into the world, he can become a blessing, provided he maintains the same *Shabbos*, the same learning, the same *Kashrus* and the same perspective of Judaism learned at home. He must continually learn and review the same *Torah* that was taught to him in his father's home.

The precious treasures of *Torah, Talmud,* and the Codes should not be relegated as literary treasures to the cultural glories of a bygone age. As Yosef said to his father, I still remember the subjects that we studied together, because I still study them. It is a noble sentiment to treasure a father's *seforim*, Jewish books, but a son who is a *Talmid Chacham* is the greatest tribute to his father. When the same *seforim* are read and studied by the children and grandchildren then: ותחי רוח יעקב אביהם - Yaakov lives all over again!

We may wonder what Yaakov's secret was. What was so unique about his *Torah* with Yosef that even after so many arduous years, Yosef still remembered exactly what they had been studying together? We may suggest that the answer lies in Yaakov's personal involvement. A father's personal study with his child is very special. A child develops a unique esteem and love for those precious moments of spiritual relationship. Children remember with rapture the spiritual moments spent with a parent, the *Torah* learning, the standing next to each other praying in *shul*, the father's blessing on Friday night. These memories are the most treasured. We should make every effort to spend quality spiritual time with our children, so that the memories of the shared past will play a role in forging the spiritual future.

***

62

ויאמר יעקב אל פרעה מעט ורעים היו ימי שני חיי

"And Yaakov said to Pharaoh... few and unhappy have been the days of the years of my life." (47:9)

The *Daas Zekeinim* cite the *Midrash* that states that Hashem shortened Yaakov's life-span as compared to Yiztchak's because of this remark. Hashem told Yaakov, *"I saved you from Eisav and Lavan and returned Dinah and Yosef to you, and yet you complain that your life has been short and unhappy. You shall not live as long as your father did!"* *Horav Benzion Bruk, z.l.*, in a thesis on the depth of judgement which Hashem applies to the righteous, cites this *Midrash* as the source of a great moral lesson for us. Imagine, if you will, one who has suffered overwhelming pain and suffering and has undergone severe tribulation. He is cut off from his beloved son, and he has even mourned him as dead. Somehow he survives these tragedies to be reunited in his homeland with his long lost son. By heavenly grace, he is able to aspire to a future of health, happiness, and tranquility. This person has experienced both aspects of life: pain and suffering, as well as joy and serenity.

When this individual begins retroactively to complain about his past suffering, he will be soothed by the current reality. True, he was at death's door and suffered great indignations, but now he is alive. He should be happy with his lot. He should not prolong the past, but rather he should focus upon the satisfaction of the present. Yaakov endured enormous suffering throughout his life. Now, however, he was at peace, surrounded by his entire family. Rather than reminisce about the pains to which he was subjected, he should have rejoiced in his survival.

How important it is for us to open our eyes and experience the goodness which Hashem grants us! Everyone has his own "baggage" of hardships. To allow ourselves to be completely overwhelmed by troubles, never thinking about the good moments which we are accorded, is wrong. A malcontent attitude to life is not only self-destructive, but it is not a Jewish orientation.

***

ואלה שמות בני ישראל הבאים מצרימה

"And these are the names of Yisrael's children who came to Egypt." (46:8)

From the ensuing list of names, we see that all of Yaakov's children maintained their names. Only these original names are used whenever the children are mentioned in the *Torah*. By recording these names, the *Torah* emphasizes the importance of keeping names of Jewish origin especially when facing dangers of assimilation, such as those which threatened *Bnei Yisrael* who entered the Egyptian exile. Maintaining their Jewish names created for the Jewish people a moral and spiritual safeguard. It also served as a self- defense mechanism against the winds of assimilation. Indeed, one of the principle merits of *Bnei Yisrael* cited when they were redeemed from Egyptian bondage was that *they did not change their names*. This was their way of affirming their Jewish identity.

Horav Eli Munk, z.l., suggests that we consider another reason for enumerating each one of the tribes. In this instance, we see that all of the members of Yaakov's family lived together in perfect harmony. They were unified in the service of a single lofty ideal, and they stood prepared to defend this belief against any incursion. Like the branches of a tree which are all nourished from one root, the seventy members of this Patriarchal family received their spiritual nourishment from one source. This family served as the nucleus of *Am Yisrael*. Therefore, it is of great consequence to record the names of these family members for posterity. Similarly, it is appropriate to accentuate this portrayal of an ancient Patriarchal family, resolute in faith, pious in action, and esteemed by Egyptian royalty. Highlighting this distinguished family illustrates that the origins of *Am Yisrael* were neither from some recluse nomadic tribe, nor from a group of disoriented revolutionaries, nor from an august brotherhood of prophets, but rather from a family whose origins were untainted by any form of defilement.

QUESTIONS LEVEL- A

1. What was Yehudah prepared to do in order that Binyamin be set free?

2. What did Hashem tell Yaakov while he was on the way to Egypt?

3. How many of his brothers did Yosef take to Pharaoh?

4. How much grain were the Egyptians to give to Pharaoh from the land they used?

5. Was the land of Goshen a good place for Yaakov's family to live?

QUESTIONS LEVEL - B

1. What was Yosef's first question when he made himself known to his brothers?

2. Why did Yaakov send Yehudah to Goshen?

QUESTIONS LEVEL - C

1. What other meaning, besides "father," does the word אב have in this *parsha*?

2. What blessing did Yaakov give to Pharaoh when they met?

QUESTIONS LEVEL- D

1. A) Did Yosef rebuke his brothers for selling him? B) Which two words did he say to them?

ANSWERS LEVEL- A

1. He was willing to become a slave in place of Binyamin.

2. Hashem told Yaakov that He would "go down" with him to Egypt, that Yaakov will become a great nation there, and that Yaakov will be buried in *Eretz Yisrael*.

3. Five. 4. One fifth. 5. Yes.

ANSWERS LEVEL- B

1. העוד אבי חי

2. A) To prepare a place for Yaakov to settle. B) To prepare a place to study for him.

ANSWERS LEVEL- C

1. A friend and a patron.

2. He blessed him that the Nile River would rise and water the land when he would approach it.

ANSWERS LEVEL- D

1. A) He did not rebuke them. B) He only said to them אני יוסף. This was more than enough to cause them to have remorse for what they had done.

65

פרשת ויחי

PARASHAS VAYECHI

שמעון ולוי אחים... כלי חמס מכרתיהם

Shimon and Levi are brothers... cursed be their anger for it is fierce and their fury for it is hard."(49:5,7)

Rashi notes that even during his reproach to Shimon and Levi, Yaakov designated only their anger as inappropriate. Their action and resulting consequences were not Yaakov's focus. Rather, he deplored their origin. Unrestrained fury ignited their fiery response to their sister's debasement. Indeed, anger is viewed by the *Arizal* as the ultimate contaminant of morality. When anger begins to direct a man's conduct, the sparks of holiness which permeate his soul depart from him, only to be replaced by the powers of spiritual impurity.

Countless times *Chazal* have described the consequences suffered by a person who becomes angry. Although this is ever true regarding the common man, it is especially significant when a *Torah* scholar falls prey to this disgraceful trait. The most pronounced result of anger is that one loses all of his dignity and spirituality. *Chazal* cite many examples to validate this point.

One can attempt to control his anger by focusing on the possible calamitous consequences of anger. *Horav Chaim Shmuelevitz, z.l.,* explains that, unlike the purveyor of many other character traits, one who is angry usually feels that his anger is an appropriate response. The effect of anger is such that one deceives himself into believing that his response is justifiable. *Horav* Shmuelevitz states that the way to overcome this problem is to understand that anger, however legitimate, has a harmful influence upon a person. His reasoning is that anger's effect should not be viewed only from within the framework of retribution for a sin, but rather as its natural consequence.

Torah differs from all forms of wisdom. In contrast to other forms of wisdom, *Torah* directly relates to the character of one who accepts its precepts. A G-d-given profundity, *Torah* takes root only in one who is morally fit to carry the mantle of *talmid chacham, Torah* scholar. One whose personality has become sullied by base character traits is unfit to serve as a vessel for the transmission of *Torah*.

***

בן פרת יוסף בן פרת עלי שור

"Yosef is a charming son, charming to the eye." (49:22)

The commentaries offer varied interpretations of Yaakov's blessing to Yosef. They all share the common concept that Yosef's blessing is imbued with the warmest terms of affection. Yaakov keeps his most commendatory blessing for Yosef, the one who is twice referred to as "son." After all his suffering, Yosef receives his due acclaim and reward.

Horav Eli Munk, z.l., defines Yosef's distinction in the following manner: Yehudah was proclaimed the undisputed leader over the brothers. He demonstrated natural authority and enjoyed uncontested popularity. Yosef, however, whose spiritual and physical attributes were greater, always provoked the jealousy and hatred of the brothers. Consequently, he could not aspire to the position of leadership, even though he was spiritually superior to Yehudah. It was Yosef, not Yehudah, who merited the title of *tzaddik,* righteous one. His father referred to him as "the crown among the brothers." He was the one who, unnoticed by his brothers, wore the diadem of moral perfection. Yaakov conferred this exceptional tribute upon Yosef as a result of the strength of character which Yosef exhibited on two decisive occasions in his life. Yaakov was able to recall these instances through the euphemisms presented in his blessing.

Yosef's first moral triumph was his ability to maintain his purity in Egypt, despite the daily temptations. Egypt was a land where moral perversion was practiced in the most ignoble form. Yosef, however, remained unaffected by this decadent environment. He was able to resist the constant flirtations of his master, Potifar's, wife. Even at the risk of death, he did not yield to these temptations.

The self-mastery and stoicism demonstrated by Yosef in his struggle against the attractions of the senses was reaffirmed in the realm of moral virtue. His brothers had harassed him, and they eventually sold him as a slave to be forgotten forever. The pain and sorrow which Yosef experienced during this time of separation from his father and family, the constant travail to which he was subjected, would have driven a lesser man to revenge. Yet, as viceroy of Egypt with unlimited powers, he was still able to forgive the perpetrations of his suffering. He proved himself capable of generosity by renouncing the opportunity to display hatred, however justifiable it might have been. Instead of turning away from his brothers, he magnanimously showed compassion by welcoming them with open arms.

On his deathbed, Yaakov venerated his son who had understood the meaning of mankind's moral mission more deeply than the others. His nobility of heart and exceptional natural gifts combined to form the character of a true *tzaddik* and heir to the crown of Yaakov. He merited the appellation of honor, *tzaddik*, because during moments of great temptation he exhibited a mastery over himself by remaining absolutely faithful to the tenets of his moral belief.

***

ויאמר יוסף אל אחיו אנכי מת ואלקים פקד יפקד אתכם והעלתם את
עצמתי מזה

"And Yosef said to his brothers, I am dying and Hashem will surely remember you...and you shall bring up my bones from here." (50:24,25)

After a distinguished career leading *Bnei Yisrael*, Yosef prepared to leave them with the words of encouragement that were to ring in their ears forever. Hashem will remember you! Yosef entreated his brothers to be sure to remove his bones from Egypt when they departed from exile. Yosef was not interred with the Patriarchs in *Me'oras Hamachpailah*. Rather, he was buried in Shechem. *Horav Avigdor Miller, Shlita,* suggests the following reasons for this. First, Yosef's burial place was to serve as a monument to Hashem's justice and His Providence. Yosef's ordeal began in Shechem and it ended there some 250 years later when his bones were returned to that same place. The story of Yosef is symbolic of *Am Yisrael's* exile and eventual return to their own land. There is another purpose for Yosef's interment in Shechem, which is located in Ephraim's portion. Ephraim was the leading tribe opposing the kingdom of the House of David. Yosef's burial in Ephraim's land would serve as a reminder of their progenitor's virtue, as well as the requirement to remain loyal to Hashem despite the envy of the tribe of Yehudah.

The entire narrative concerning Yosef is ordained as a parallel to and a foreshadowing of the history of *Am Yisrael*. Yosef was singled out by his father and given a unique multicolored garment, which stimulated much of the original envy and enmity towards him. Similarly, *Am Yisrael* was also chosen to receive the *Torah* with its multifaceted precepts. This gift engendered the envy and animosity of the nations. Like Yosef, our prophets have been granted singular visions of the great future waiting for us. Just as the brothers plotted against Yosef and eventually sold him into slavery, so, too, have we fallen prey to the machinations of our enemies and been driven from our land into exile.

Potifar's wife unsuccessfully tempted Yosef. Similarly, although we have been subjected to the blandishments of strange gods and foreign ideologies, we have refused to succumb. Yosef was later falsely accused by his master, just as we have been unjustly denigrated in every generation. As Yosef was eventually redeemed from his incarceration to shine forth in greatness, so, too, will we be restored and elevated to our former lofty position.

QUESTIONS LEVEL - A

1. Why was Yaakov unable to see?
2. Which three sons did Yaakov scold in the *Brachos*?
3. Which brother was compared to a lion?
4. Who would have many olive trees in his land?
5. What did Yosef ask of his brothers before he died?

QUESTIONS LEVEL-B

1. A) Were any of Yaakov's sons considered wicked? B) How do we derive this?

2. A) For how many years was Yosef viceroy over Egypt? B) How can this be calculated?

QUESTIONS LEVEL-C

1. Which two brothers really wanted to kill Yosef?

2. A) From whom did Yaakov purchase his portion in the *Me'oras Hamachpailah*? B) Where did he get the money for this?

QUESTIONS LEVEL-D

1. There are two types of kindness - doing what someone wants, and doing what someone needs.

A) Which one of these would you consider a *chesed shel emes?* B) Why?

ANSWERS LEVEL-A

1. He was blind due to old age.

2. Reuven, Shimon, Levi.

3. Yehudah.

4. Asher.

5. Yosef requested that they take his bones out of Egypt when they eventually left.

ANSWERS LEVEL-B

1. A) No. B) It says: וישתחו ישראל על ראש המטה – שהיתה מטתו שלמה.

2. A) 80 years. B) He became viceroy when he was 30 years old, and he died at the age of 110.

ANSWERS LEVEL-C

1. Shimon and Levi.

2. A) He purchased it from Eisav. B) He took his earnings he had accumulated from Lavan, and traded it for Eisav's portion in the *Me'oras Hamachpailah.*

ANSWERS LEVEL-D

1. A) Doing what a person needs is a higher form of *chesed.* B) A *chesed shel emes* is a true and just form of kindness. Fulfilling the needs of an individual is *chesed shel emes*, since this is a right and just thing to do. Doing what someone wants isn't always the right thing, since people do not always want what is right, only what they think is right.

ספר שמות
Sefer Shmos

Rabbi Shimon said: There are three crowns; the crown of Torah, the crown of priesthood and the crown of kingship. But the crown of a good name excels them all. (Pirke Avos)

Dedicated in loving memory of our dear fathers

Alvin E. Schottenstein
חיים אברהם יונה בן אפרים אליעזר הכהן ז"ל
נפטר ז' תמוז תשד"מ

Alvin E. Schottenstein was a much-loved and respected business leader in Columbus, Ohio. As busy as he was in the world of commerce, he was a humanitarian and philanthropist with a humble spirit and generous heart. He was always available to those seeking help. His devotion to his family, his community and to Eretz Yisrael was his precious legacy.

Irving Altman
יצחק אייזיק בן עקיבא הכהן ז"ל
נפטר ר"ח אב תשכ"ח

Irving Altman was an אוד מוצל מאש, 'a firebrand saved from the fires of the Holocaust'. He came to America with his faith in Hashem intact, and imbued with the learning he received in his parents' home in Bardejov, Slovakia. His sterling character and warm nature, his humility and piety, and his acts of kindness, were his hallmarks. His Torah values and pride in Yiddishkeit was his legacy that was transmitted to his family.

By
**Bob and Chaya Schottenstein
and sons, Isaac, Ephraim and Avi**

פרשת שמות
PARASHAS SHEMOS

ואלה שמות בני ישראל הבאים מצרימה
"And these are the names of Bnei Yisrael who came into Egypt."
(1:1)

Rashi cites the *Midrash* which states that *Bnei Yisrael* were counted twice as a result of Hashem's great love for them. They were counted when they were about to go down to Egypt. They were counted a second time after their deaths. They made their mark both in life and in death. It is not sufficient to have lived and made one's mark only during one's lifetime. How many of us bequeath a legacy after death for our children and ensuing generations to inherit? People are born and die. During their lifetimes, many lead productive lives. Each individual must examine, however, whether he has transmitted an everlasting legacy for his children and others to follow. Has his life's endeavor served as an inspiration?

Our only true possessions are those which are eternal; *Torah* and *mitzvos*. Alas, we often journey through life gathering the ephemeral while rejecting the eternal. One must strive to bequeath an inheritance worthy of remembrance to his descendants. An individual whose accomplishments live on after him has not really died. The twelve tribes left their mark in life, as well as in death. Their legacy of faith and courage inspired their descendants, enabling them to cope with the anguish of Egyptian bondage.

***

וירא ה' כי סר לראות ויקרא אליו אלקים מתוך הסנה
"And when Hashem saw that he turned aside to see, Hashem called to him from the midst of the bush." (3:4)

Horav M. D. Soloveitchik, Shlita, notes the *Torah's* emphasis on Moshe's *"turning aside to see."* Such a wondrous fire burning in the desert should have attracted attention. Moshe, however, was the one who (was) סר לראות - turned to identify this unique fire. Moshe sought every opportunity to perceive, to attain whatever wisdom he could grasp. His love of wisdom was a natural result of his search for truth. This is the essence of a true *talmid chacham*. He is the consummate student of wisdom, always searching to satisfy his incessant desire for spiritual excellence.

One who is complacent and does not "turn aside" to see, to appreciate the great wonders which Hashem has wrought, forfeits his opportunity to become closer to Hashem. Man must initiate interaction with Hashem. Only then will he merit the encounter.

***

של נעליך מעל רגליך כי המקום אשר אתה עומד עליו אדמת קדש הוא

"Take off your shoes from your feet, for the place wherein you stand is holy ground." (3:5)

This is the first reference in the *Torah* to the consecration of sacred ground. Hashem instructed Moshe to remove his shoes when treading upon this sacred soil. The custom to walk barefoot in the *Bais Hamikdash* originated from this *pasuk*. Indeed, even today the *Kohanim* remove their shoes when they approach the *Duchan* to bless the people. Although shoes have become an accepted convention to cover a part of the body, they were essentially designed for protection. *Horav Moshe Swift, z.l.,* suggests that Hashem's imperative to Moshe has a profound meaning for us. One whose feet are protected can walk blindly, not heeding where he treads. Direction is not limited for the one who is externally protected. If one takes off his "shoes," however, he must be forever cautious and alert to danger.

The call came to Moshe, *"Take off your shoes, because you stand on holy ground."* You must remove your shoes in a holy place. You cannot walk blindly in Hashem's house. You cannot act in Hashem's house as you would in your own home. Your mode of dress, your manner of speech, your whole demeanor must be dignified in Hashem's house. You must walk warily, keeping your eyes open, your tongue guarded, and your thoughts concentrated. Wipe off the mud and filth when you enter Hashem's Sanctuary. Only after this type of preparation, did Hashem address Moshe.

We may extend this idea with regard to one's relationship with Hashem's devotees, individuals whose lives are dedicated to His holy service. One who has merited the mantle of *Torah* scholarship should be perceived in a different light. Our entire approach to interaction with them must reflect the most sublime form of reverence. Our attitude must be one of "remove your shoes", reflecting dignity, affability and refinement. One who has consecrated his life's endeavor in this manner becomes an embodiment of sanctity.

***

ויאמר ה' ראה ראיתי את עני עמי אשר במצרים ואת צעקתם שמעתי
כי ידעתי את מכאביו

"And Hashem said I have surely <u>seen</u> the affliction of My people who are in Egypt and their cry I have <u>heard</u> ... because I know of their pain." (3:7)

Hashem appeared to Moshe for the very first time in a burning thorn bush. *Rashi* explains the symbolism of the bush as representing Hashem's "personal" sensitivity to *Klal Yisrael's* pain and anguish - עמו אנכי בצרה. Indeed, as *Rashi* states later in *Parashas Mishpatim* (24:10), even after the redemption Hashem kept brickwork from the time of the Egyptian bondage under His Heavenly throne. This attribute of caring for others and sharing their affliction is an essential attribute of a *Torah* leader.

Upon seeing the burning bush, Moshe pondered why it was not being consumed. As he neared the bush, he was suddenly so overcome with awe that he hid his face. This constituted Moshe's instinctive reaction to Hashem's identifying Himself to Moshe. The *Torah* relates that Moshe later entreated Hashem to allow him to see His glory. The privilege was denied to him at this time. The *Talmud* cites the following response by Hashem, "*When I wished it, you did not, now that you wish it, I do not.*"

This seems puzzling. Moshe's previous concealment of his face was a direct result of his sudden apprehension of Hashem. Was this not a natural response to the overwhelming feeling of awe which gripped Moshe? Why should Moshe be responsible for his reaction to this unique phenomenon?

Horav Meir Bergman, Shlita, clarifies this matter in the following way. We are implored to *"walk in His ways"* - והלכת בדרכיו. As Hashem is merciful and compassionate, so, too, should we be. What are the essential parameters of "walking in Hashem's ways"? Obviously, one must share in alleviating the plight of the downtrodden in any way that he can. Does this obligation also apply to instances in which one is not able to offer any hope or concrete help? What is our obligation vis a vis our brethren who are captives in foreign countries, subjected to inhuman physical and spiritual degradation? Does this injunction also pertain to instances in which we are not in a position to ease their plight?

Unfortunately, in our present society success is judged by behavioral standards. *Horav* Bergman posits that this type of measuring device is invalid. The *Torah* states that we are to <u>listen</u> to the cry of the oppressed, even when we cannot respond with action. To emulate Hashem means not only to act and to do, but also to <u>listen</u> and to feel. Hashem does not only answer the problems of the afflicted; He also <u>listens</u> to them.

Sharing the burden of the ailing and the weak has two components. Clearly. one must offer concrete assistance whenever possible. A second form of cooperation also has great significance. This is the ability to lend an empathetic ear to another's suffering. At certain times, action is not the practical response to another's affliction. Some individuals are unfortunately beyond the need for action. They, in turn, require a listening ear, a warm feeling of knowing someone is there to listen and to share in their affliction. This "listening ear" extends itself to a willingness to recognize another's suffering. It may even be suggested that one who refuses to help another is incapable of <u>seeing</u> another's misery.

Horav Bergman utilizes this concept to respond to the original question concerning Moshe's refusal to approach the bush. Hashem told Moshe that He, indeed, <u>sees</u> *Bnei Yisrael's* affliction and <u>hears</u> their cries of pain. This is due to a single reason - כי ידעתי את מכאביו. "I <u>know</u> of their pain." There is a direct correlation between <u>knowing</u> anothers' pain and <u>seeing</u> and <u>hearing</u> their affliction.

This was the message to Moshe: I am appearing to you from a burning bush, to symbolize My affinity to *Bnei Yisrael's* affliction.

Therefore, I am capable of knowing their pain. Hashem called out to Moshe, "Come near! Share in the pain of *Am Yisrael*!" Moshe refused, reacting to his feelings of awe and apprehension. Indeed, *yiraas shomayim* is all encompassing, but it should not take precedence to the welfare of *Klal Yisrael*. Moshe should have emulated Hashem, והלכת בדרכיו, and moved forward to participate with Hashem in *Klal Yisrael's* affliction. Hashem judges the righteous with a very fine measuring stick. In accordance with Moshe's lofty spiritual level, he was delinquent in his sensitivity to the plight of *Bnei Yisrael*. Consequently, when he later wanted to behold Hashem's glory, Hashem denied him this privilege.

QUESTIONS LEVEL- A

1. Why was the Egyptian king scared of the Jewish people?

2. What were the names of the Jewish mid-wives?

3. What excuse did the mid-wives give for not carrying out Pharaoh's orders?

4. Why did Moshe request that Hashem send someone with him to talk to Pharaoh?

5. In what way did Pharaoh punish the Jewish people because of Moshe and Aharon?

QUESTIONS LEVEL- B

1. What does ערי מסכנות mean? 2. A) How did Hashem appear to Moshe in the desert? B) Why?

QUESTIONS LEVEL- C

2. A) With what emotion did Aharon greet Moshe? B) What was his reward for this?

QUESTIONS LEVEL- D

1. What relationship is there between eating *chazeres* on *Pesach* and the *pasuk* of וימררו את חייהם?

ANSWERS LEVEL- A

1. He thought they would rise up against him in case of war.

2. Shifrah (Yocheved) and Puah (Miriam).

3. The Jewish women did not need mid-wives since they gave birth before they arrived.

4. He couldn't speak well.

5. He made them work twice as hard. They were to produce their daily quota, although he would not give them more straw for making bricks.

ANSWERS LEVEL- B

1. Storage cities.

2. A) In a burning bush. B) To show that He was also suffering with the Jews.

ANSWERS LEVEL -C

1. A) With great joy in his heart, he kissed him. B) He merited to wear the *Choshen Mishpat* over his heart.

ANSWERS LEVEL- D

1. As the *chazeres* is sweet in the beginning and bitter at the end, so the Egyptians acted toward our ancestors. First Pharaoh told Yosef to take the best land; in the end the Egyptians enslaved the Jews with hard labor.

פרשת וארא
PARASHAS VA'EIRA
▶◀

וידבר ה' אל משה ואל אהרן ויצום אל בני ישראל

"And Hashem spoke to Moshe and Aharon, and he charged them to (lead) Bnei Yisrael (6:13)

Rashi explains that Hashem enjoined *Bnei Yisrael's* first "leadership" to guide them gently and patiently. The *Midrash* is more explicit in demanding forbearance from *Bnei Yisrael's* leadership. Regardless of the people's reluctance to obey, even if they respond to their leaders with animosity and impudence, the leaders must, nonetheless, patiently accept their behavior. Community service is demanding and may become demeaning. It can literally destroy a lesser individual. One who cannot maintain his composure in stressful situations is not qualified for a position of community leadership.

Horav Shlomo Wolbe, Shlita, emphasizes that patience and forbearance are necessary attributes for anyone who is involved in community service -- be it teaching, Rabbinics, community service or congregational work. He cites the following practical application relating to the field of education. Prior to being accepted to a certain school, a student is examined to ascertain whether he is suitable for the institution. From the time of the student's acceptance, the true *Torah* educator assumes the responsibility to care for this student, to support him through various situations. This applies even if the student were to do something wrong. How shameful it is that there exists an arrogance among educators to expel a student for an offense which is not in keeping with the dictates of the school! In some instances, expulsion from school is tantamount to a spiritual death sentence.

Horav Wolbe admonishes educators to be cognizant of the words of *Horav Yitzchak Blazer, z.l.,* who stated that even a robber has a *Shulchan Aruch*, It is forbidden to punish him beyond the

79

requirements of the code of Jewish law! Not every infraction of school rules warrants expulsion. A *Torah* educator must emulate the attributes of Hashem. He should be compassionate and gracious, slow to anger, kind and affable, as well as forgiving and merciful.

The ideas stated in this thesis may be adapted to the home, which serves as the family's mini-community. In their leadership role, the parents are charged with raising their children to follow in the path of Hashem. This can only be effected in a home in which pleasant, open communication pervades. The effect of strict disciplinary measures is ephemeral. Nothing erodes the natural heartfelt relationship between parents and children like fear. Through an educative process based on gentleness, patience, understanding and, above all, *siyata dishmaya*, parents will merit to have *Torah nachas* from their children.

***

ואני אקשה את לב פרעה
"And I will harden the heart of Pharaoh." (7:3)

We are taught that every person has before him two paths: the path of good and life, and the path of evil and death. One of our prime tenets of faith is that we the have the freedom to choose between these contrasting paths. Pharaoh was evidently so evil that this opportunity was denied to him. There is a divergence of opinions among the commentaries regarding this denial.

A unique insight offered by *Horav Simcha Zissel, z.l.,* of Kelm sheds light upon this problem. He explains that by increasing Pharaoh's obstinacy, Hashem was revealing the true character of evil-doers who defy Hashem, despite their awareness of Him. As Hashem delivered the plagues, Pharaoh was slowly developing an intimate and profound understanding of the awesome powers of the Almighty. In order to maintain the balance of free-will, Hashem had to harden Pharaoh's heart.

Pharaoh's profundity was balanced by his impudence. *Horav Yaakov Kamenetsky, z.l.,* expanded on this idea in a lecture to *Torah* educators. He explained that the *Torah*'s concept of free-will does not give one license to blindly follow his natural instincts, unconstrained by Hashem's protective counterbalancing influence. To have freedom of choice means to maintain a perspective of balanced alternatives. Where man is subject to his inherent passions, Hashem provides a force to counteract this coercion. If man were not to have Divine assistance, he could not resist the constant temptations catalyzed by his animalistic instincts.

Horav Kamenetsky stated that *Torah* educators are Hashem's vehicle for providing Jewish children with this counterbalance. Jewish education provides the opportunity for a Jewish child to study *Torah* and live a *Torah* way of life, enabling him to experience the balancing alternative to base instincts. Increasing Pharaoh's obstinacy was a favor to him, for it restored his free-will. Jewish education, condemned by the spiritually ignorant as a form of religious coercion, provides in fact, a necessary assurance of a child's spiritual freedom. To deprive a Jewish child of his or her right to a *Torah* education is tantamount to withdrawing his or her freedom of choice.

***

כי ידבר אליכ ם פרעה לאמר תנו לכם מופת ואמרת אל אהרן קח את מטך
והשלך לפני פרעה יהי לתנין

When Pharaoh will say to you. deliver a proof, then say to Aharon; take your staff and cast it before Pharaoh and it will turn into a <u>crocodile.</u>" (7:9)

In the *Midrash*, *Chazal* ask, "Why specifically did this miracle of the staff turning into a crocodile occur?" They respond that Pharaoh is compared to a crocodile. They cite the following *pasuk* in *Sefer Yecheskel (29:3) -* התנים הגדול הרובץ בתוך יאוריו, *A great animal of the sea which rests peacefully in its stream.* Pharaoh said, *"If the son of Abraham will come to me, I shall kill him."* When Moshe came to him, Pharaoh at once became as ineffective as a staff. We suggest that *Chazal's* comparison of Pharaoh to a crocodile, who lies peacefully in the water awaiting its prey, conveys a powerful message. One who stays away from the stream, which is home to the crocodile, is safe from the crocodile's predatory jaws. The Jew should be aware that separatism is not an indication of weakness and that isolationism does not suggest impuissance. Indeed, one needs a great deal of moral courage to assert one's opinion in the face of contending majority.

The *Bais Halevi* writes that whenever Jews attempt to assimilate, Hashem renews the differentiation by filling the hearts of the gentiles with hatred. This incitement accrues to our benefit, for it affirms the distinction between *Am Yisrael* and other nations throughout the generations. The gentiles' antagonism towards the Jew serves to keep the peoples separate and to facilitate our redemption. Alas, due to his alienation from *Torah* and *mitzvos*, the apologetic Jew lacks true pride in his Jewish heritage, cowering in his attempt to assimilate. If such individuals would only realize that the "crocodile" lies in waiting, prepared to devour his naive prey. The "crocodile" is turned into a staff only as a result of Hashem's beneficence, enabling us to exist in peace among the nations of the world.

***

וימתו הצפרדעים מן הבתים ומן החצרות ומן השדות

"And the frogs died out of the houses, out of the courtyards, and out of the fields." (8:9)

The second plague to strike Egypt was frogs which swarmed all over the land. They found their way into every house, into the bedrooms, even into the ovens and kneading troughs. The *Midrash* extolls the virtue of these frogs. Their devotion to serving Hashem at the expense of their own lives has served as a paradigm of exemplary *Kiddush Hashem*. Their willingness to enter the burning hot ovens was totally alien to their natural instincts for survival. Yet, they overcame their very nature to serve Hashem. When the day arrived for that plague to subside, the frogs from all over Egypt died and were gathered into heaps. The whole land smelled from the foul stench.

What happened to the frogs that entered the ovens? Did they also die as the others did? The *Yalkut Shimoni* states that the frogs who entered the ovens <u>did</u> <u>not</u> die. They disappeared somehow, but not by death. They followed Hashem's command, defying nature, and entered the deadly ovens. For this act of self-sacrifice they merited to conquer death. What a lesson in *Kiddush Hashem*! Faith so absolute that defies nature must triumph over death. *Moreshes Moshe* points out that this has been our legacy throughout history. *Torah* observance defies explanation and rationalization. As we face the constant challenges to our faith, we must stand resolute and courageous, prepared to shoulder the burdens against all odds, even if we do not feel we have the means. We will continue to defy the elements as we have always done, as we await that moment of glory and peace that the advent of *Moshiach* will bring.

QUESTIONS LEVEL- A

1. Who were the three sons of Levi?
2. How was Yocheved related to Amram before they were married?
3. What was the first plague?
4. Who struck the earth to produce the third plague?
5. Name the fifth, sixth and seventh plagues.

QUESTIONS LEVEL- B

1. Why did Hashem smite the Nile River for the first plague?
2. Why does the *Torah* use the word צפרדע in the singular?

QUESTIONS LEVEL- C

1. What is the difference between להטיהם with the letter ה and לטיהם without the letter ה?
2. What are the two meanings of נטה ידך על השמים?

QUESTIONS LEVEL- D

1. What is the difference between the prophesy of Moshe and the prophesy of other prophets?

ANSWERS LEVEL- A

1. Gershon, Kehos and Merori.
2. She was his aunt, his father's sister.
3. *Dam* - Blood.
4. Aharon.
5. *Dever, Barad, Shechin.*

83

ANSWERS LEVEL- B

1. Since the Egyptians worshipped the Nile River, Hashem wanted to show them that it is really not a god but rather that it is controlled by Hashem. Hashem always strikes a nation's god prior to punishing the nation.

2. *Rashi* explains that a swarm of frogs in Hebrew is considered a singular unit. He also cites the *Midrash* which states that there really was only one frog which multiplied when it was hit.

ANSWERS LEVEL- C

1. לטיהם is the work of demons and להטיהם is the work of witchcraft.

2. 1) לצד שמים - towards Heaven. 2) Hashem raised Moshe up over the Heaven.

ANSWERS LEVEL- D

1. 1) Moshe saw when he was awake, while others saw in a dream. 2) Moshe spoke directly to Hashem, while others spoke to an angel. 3) Moshe remained relaxed after a prophesy, while others were shaken. 4) Moshe would receive prophesy at any time, while others had specific times.

פרשת בא
PARASHAS BO
▶◄

ויקחו להם שה לבית אבות שה לבית

"And they shall take to them (every) man a lamb for their father's house, a lamb for a household." (12:3)

ושחטו אתו כל קהל עדת ישראל... ולקחו מן הדם ונתנו מן הדם על שתי המזוזות ועל המשקף

"And they shall slaughter it the whole assembly of the congregation of Yisrael... and they shall take of the blood and they shall <u>put</u> it upon the two doorposts and on the lintel." (12:6,7)

In this *pasuk* we note the first *mitzvah* in which *Bnei Yisrael* are enjoined as they prepare for the Exodus from Egypt. It focuses upon the head of the house, while it also embraces the whole family. Even though there is great need for collective communal involvement, the individual is not absolved of his own personal responsibility. We have become so dependent upon communal institutions that we may have forgotten what it means to fulfill our obligations <u>personally.</u> We send the aged to be cared for by the communal organization and the poor to central *tzedaka* funds, while we relegate our children to be brought up and taught by others. As *Bnei Yisrael* approached freedom and eventual nationhood, we were admonished to bear this idea in mind. No nation becomes a nation unless each individual bears his own responsibilities.

Moreshes Moshe observes that Moshe could never impose his will upon the people without their consent. It was necessary for the entire assembly to be actively involved. The Rabbi, the teacher, and the school cannot succeed without the parents' active participation. A Rabbi cannot enforce *Shabbos* observance if it does not exist at home. A teacher cannot impose *tefillah* if it is not modeled at home.

One of the most unique features of the first *Korban Pesach* was the ritual of smearing the blood on the doorposts. When the

Kohanim sprinkled the blood as part of a sacrificial offering, it was referred to as זריקה, *sprinkling,* of the blood. The procedure of ונתנו על שתי המזוזות, they *shall put the blood,* נתינה, contrasts this. To sprinkle means to throw the blood from a distance. Putting the blood on the doorposts, forces one to draw near to them. One cannot be a Jew by proxy or have an observant Jewish home by remote control. One cannot delegate his children's future to the school and divorce himself from their spiritual upbringing. There has to be a תתנו - a total personal involvement.

The great message to be gleaned from this first *mitzvah* is that one must make personal sacrifices at home. An individual cannot rely on others to do his job. When there is obvious personal sacrifice for Jewish idealism, children grow up consciously aware of their heritage, ready to accept their mission.

***

זכור את היום אשר יצאתם ממצרים... היום אתם יוצאים בחדש האביב

"Remember this day (in) which you went out from Egypt. Today you go forth in the month of Aviv." (13:3,4)

We may question the *Torah*'s inclusion of the word הזה - *"this day".* Why is it necessary to emphasize "this" day? There is obviously something unique about that day which must be especially remembered. We may suggest the following thought. The *Torah* seems to accentuate the time of year when the Exodus from Egypt took place. Hence, it is stated, *"Today you go forth in the month of Aviv,"* which refers to the month of *Nissan* or the beginning of spring. This is a time of renewal when the young seedlings are beginning to blossom. It is a time of growth and expansion, a time to go forward with excitement and exuberance. It was also, as *Rashi* remarks, a fitting time for the Exodus to take place. It is neither too hot nor too cold, and there are no rains.

The *Netziv, z.l.,* suggests another insight into the month of *Aviv.* Just as during the spring season seedlings easily germinate and grow with little external support, the great miracles which *Bnei Yisrael* witnessed should inspire them to develop profound levels of faith in Hashem. The lessons garnered from the Exodus should serve as a vehicle for *"emunah,"* faith, in the Almighty.

This is the meaning of היום הזה- "this day." <u>Today</u> you have been privy to such glorious sights that easily convince you to believe. Remember this during moments of trial and travail, when Hashem's Providence is "hidden." All too often we remember only the moments of sorrow and anguish, and we forget those instances in which Hashem's beneficence is publicly revealed. We are enjoined to remember the Exodus not as an abstract historical occurrence, but rather to vividly "relive" this experience as if we had been there. Consequently, we will be imbued with an indomitable and resolute faith in Hashem.

***

והגדת לבנך ביום ההוא לאמר בעבור זה עשה ה' לי בצאתי ממצרים.
והיה לך לאות על ידך... למען תהיה תורת ד' בפיך

"And you shall tell your son on that day saying: It is because of this that Hashem did for me when I went forth from Egypt. And it shall be for you a sign upon your hand... In order that the law of Hashem may be in your mouth." (13,8,9,10)

We may wonder why, particularly in the chapter dealing with consecrating the first-born, the "children" would question our spiritual practice. Indeed, there were other *mitzvos* which they could have found enigmatic. *Horav Nissan Alpert, z.l.,* offers a homiletic appreciation of this *pasuk.* The "children" questioned the need for the first-born to be consecrated from birth, to be immediately inducted in Hashem's service. Would it not have been more appropriate for them first to mature both emotionally and spiritually before choosing to serve Hashem? The response to this question is *"It shall be for you a sign upon your hand."* As *Rashi* explains, this refers to the left hand which is weak.

Horav Alpert applies this concept as an analogy to the young child who is still spiritually weak and deficient. The educative process should begin when the child's mind is impressionable. This is the *Torah*'s message. The spiritual development of a Jewish child begins immediately at birth and is an ongoing process which continues throughout his whole life. This process is a sublime endeavor in which parents are involved by consecrating their children, inducting them into a noble heritage, and charging them with carrying out Hashem's mandate. To paraphrase *Horav S. R. Hirsh, z.l.,* "A *youngster must have learned the ABC's of the moral life at home before the school begins to guide him to the primer and the blackboard of theoretical knowledge, which is much easier to acquire."*

A child is born with a multiplicity of strengths and weaknesses, tendencies and aspirations, proclivities and impulses, which are already integrally etched into his little mind and heart. Any one of these attributes can develop either into a tower of life and happiness or into an abyss of curse and ruin. It depends greatly upon the moral training and guidance he receives at home and later on at school.

The most fortunate children are those whose parents care about their own spiritual and moral development. The respect we show for our own spiritual and moral concerns serves as the most effective incentive for our children to aspire to reach higher goals.

***

והיה כי יביאך ד' אל ארץ הכנעני כאשר נשבע לך ולאבותיך ונתנה לך

"And it shall be when Hashem will bring you into the land of the Canaanites as He swore unto you and your fathers, and He shall give it to you." (13:11)

Rashi explains that *Bnei Yisrael* should feel that *Eretz Yisrael* was being given to them anew on that very day, rather than as an inheritance bequeathed to them by their ancestors. This special appreciation of *Eretz Yisrael* is more than a reflection of our love towards the land. It is also an essential prerequisite for its procurement. As we study *Torah* daily, we are reaffirming our acceptance of it, and we are obligating ourselves to its mandate. We likewise view *Eretz Yisrael* as our land.

Horav Yerucham Levovitz, z.l., remarks that although *Eretz Yisrael* was pledged to our ancestors, it demands our own commitment and loyalty. Consequently, each Jew must affirm his own devotion to *Eretz Yisrael*. As our ancestors merited *Eretz Yisrael* only through *Torah* and *mitzvah* performance under situations of intense pressure, we will only be worthy of its receipt after we indicate our devotion and commitment.

QUESTIONS LEVEL-A

1. Who raised the *mateh* to bring the locust over Egypt?

2. What was the ninth plague?

3. A) Was the *Korban Pesach* a male or female lamb? B) How old may the the lamb be?

4. How did the *Bnei Yisrael* carry their *matzah* as they left Egypt?

5. A) To whom are the first born animals to be given? B) To which non-kosher animal does the law of the first-born apply?

QUESTIONS LEVEL- B

1. A) Did *makas bechoros* kill an Egyptian who was in the home of a Jew? B) Did it kill a Jew in the home of an Egyptian?

2. How many years passed from the *bris bein habesarim* until the birth of Yitzchak?

QUESTION LEVEL- C

1. A) Does one fulfill the *mitzvah* of eating *matzah* with flour of *maaser sheini*? B) From where do we learn this?

2. Why is the donkey the only unclean animal which maintains *kedushas bechor*?

QUESTIONS LEVEL- D

1. A) How many times in the *Torah* is the *Parsha* of *Tefillin* mentioned? B) What are they? (topics of each *parsha*) C)How many *parshios* are there in the *Tefillin*? D) How are they placed in the *shel yad*? E) How are they placed in the *shel rosh*?

ANSWERS LEVEL- A

1. Moshe.

2. *Makas Choshech.*

3. A) Male. B) Less than a year old.

4. On their shoulders.

5. A) *Kohen.* B) Donkey.

ANSWERS LEVEL- B

1. A) Yes. B) No.

2. Thirty years.

ANSWERS LEVEL- C

1. A) No. B) One may fulfill the *mitzvah* only with that type of *matzah* which may be eaten anywhere. However, *maaser sheini* may be eaten only in Yerushalayim.

2. 1) The Egyptian first-born were compared to donkeys. 2) The donkeys helped *Bnei Yisrael* when they left Egypt by carrying the gold and silver which *Bnei Yisrael* took from Egypt.

ANSWERS LEVEL- D

1. A) 4 times. B) קדש לי, והיה כי יביאך, שמע, והיה אם שמע. C) 4 *parshios*. D) They are written on one parchment, rolled up and placed in the *shel yad*. E) One *parsha* is placed in each of the dividers of the *shel rosh*.

פרשת בשלח
PARASHAS BESHALACH
►◄

וירא ישראל את היד הגדולה... ויאמינו בה' ובמשה עבדו

**"And Yisrael saw the great hand (might) of Hashem... and they
believed in Hashem and in Moshe His servant.** (14:31)

What was unique about these miracles that stimulated *Bnei Yisrael's*
faith in Hashem more strongly than did the miracles wrought in
Egypt? What provoked *Bnei Yisrael* to finally express gratitude to
Hashem through the vehicle of *"shirah,"* song of praise? *Horav
Nissan Alpert, z.l.,* offers a profound homiletic response to this
question. Historical events are all part of a great portrait created by
Hashem as the master artist. These seemingly isolated incidents all fit
in to make up a beautifully crafted and brilliantly designed mosaic. In
order to appreciate the total project, man must be able to stand back
and gaze upon this magnificent design from the distance of historical
perspective. Exercised by an intelligent person, this form of
intellectual hindsight creates an awareness of the profound purpose of
each of the specific events. It also sheds light upon the individual and
collective role each plays in the great panorama of history.

One cannot contemplate an historical event and comprehend
it through the limited scope of the finite. It must be viewed as a link in
the chain of a historical continuum. *Rabeinu Yaakov M'Lisa,* the
"Maase Nissim," uses this idea to explain the apparent redundancy in
the famous poem of *"Chad Gadya,"* which we recite annually at the
end of the *Pesach Seder.* He states that each link in the chain of
events which is initiated by this *"gadya,"* goat, is actually symbolic of
an event in *Am Yisrael's* history. The first occurrence was the Exodus
from Egypt, looking forward toward *"Tikun Ha'olam,"* the perfection
of the world, and toward the ultimate "slaughtering of the Angel of
Death." The preceding stanza is repeated in each new verse in order to
emphasize that every historical occurrence is interrelated with the
next.

91

In Egypt, *Bnei Yisrael* saw the *Finger of Hashem* in various events. They did not integrate the divergent events into one framework. At the splitting of the Red Sea, however, they saw the complete *Hand of Hashem*. In other words, they saw the entire picture, the past, present, and future, all at once. Perceiving a global reality enabled *Bnei Yisrael* to appreciate and acknowledge all of Hashem's miracles. The profound insight represented by Hashem's Hand effected the ויאמינו בה', total belief in Hashem.

***

ויאמר ד' אל משה הנני ממטיר לכם לחם מן השמים ויצאו העם ולקטו
דבר יום ביומו למען אנסנו הילך בתורתי אם לא

"And Hashem said to Moshe. Behold I am about to cause to rain for you bread from the Heaven, and the people will go out daily to collect (their daily portion) so that I can test them if they will follow in My Torah or not." (16:4)

The Divine gift of *manna* was essentially the last of the great miracles which surrounded the Egyptian Exodus. These wonders were designed to illuminate our path and guide us in our belief in Hashem. Indeed, *Chazal* view the *manna* as the ultimate miracle which nurtured our *emunah* and stimulated our *bitachon* in Hashem. Hashem brought us through the desert in a long, circuitous way. He nourished us with *manna* from Heaven and water from the Well in order to imbue *Torah* into our bodies and souls.

Relying upon Hashem to provide *"parnasah,"* livelihood, and believing in His "ability" to sustain His children is a challenge. Indeed, precisely at the moment that man is involved in the acquisition of his daily bread, he risks losing his last vestige of human dignity. One who does not place his trust in Hashem often falls prey to an insatiable greed that is unleashed by this desire to acquire his daily sustenance. The more idealistic concepts of working to live, living in sublime serenity, and awaiting the *Shabbos Kodesh* in which man spiritually elevates the whole week are lost in the search for daily bread. As *Horav Shlomo Breuer, z.l.,* writes, "In the struggle for his daily bread, man faces the danger of succumbing and sinking to the level of an animal. Few are those who emerge victorious from this struggle, being able to maintain their human dignity and Divine image."

Horav Breuer derives this thought from this *parsha. Klal Yisrael* witnessed the great miracles of the Exodus and were privy to the splitting of the Red Sea. When they were faced with the daily battle for nourishment, however, they panicked and suddenly forgot all the miracles. In their anxiety, they were even prepared to return to Egypt!

Chazal assert that maintaining the sustenance of man is more difficult than the splitting of the Red Sea. *Horav S. R. Hirsch, z.l.,* defines this hardship as one's deliverance from the foolish notion that the burden of sustenance rests solely upon the shoulders of man. The ability to shoulder the burden of threatening hunger and financial instability develops only through an awareness that man is called upon to do only what Hashem expects him to do.

The ultimate victory over this ominous threat, however, is Hashem's, Who sustains and nourishes all mankind. The most difficult orientation for man to accept is the acknowledgment that he is not in control, not in charge. It is Hashem who sustains and nourishes us. This was the educative lesson of forty years of *manna* sustenance. All the anxiety of the struggle for daily bread must be relaxed while the minds and bodies of *Bnei Yisrael* absorb the miracles and *Torah.* Their human dignity will thus be preserved in this most difficult battle.

We may advance this idea further. *Chazal* state: *Marriage is as difficult as the splitting of the Red Sea.* The anxieties that abound in man's quest for a mate are obvious. There is an aspect of this difficulty, however, which seems insurmountable to some. The added responsibility of a partner for life demands that an individual assume independence and readiness to support and sustain a family. One must place his trust and faith in Hashem, Who has sustained him until this point, to maintain His beneficence.

Unfortunately, a predominant cause of apprehension concerning *shidduchim* does not involve character traits or religious orientation. A major concern focuses on the ability to be sustained during one's tenure in *Yeshivah Kollel* following marriage. The maturation necessary to overcome this anxiety and to transcend material concerns for a spiritual quest is difficult to acquire. How regrettable are those who acknowledge Hashem's "ability" to split the

Red Sea, but deny His capacity to support one who devotes himself to *Torah* scholarship. Those who embark on the road to matrimony, be it parents or young men and women, should trust that Hashem, Who miraculously redeemed us from Egyptian bondage, split the Red Sea, rained *manna* for forty years, and has sustained us throughout our tumultuous history, will continue to support and nurture those who have faith in Him.

***

"And Amalek came and (he) battled with Yisrael in Refidim."
(17:5)

The *Ramban* writes that when *Bnei Yisrael* went forth to wage war with Amalek, Moshe feared the worst. He prayed intensely to Hashem on their behalf. The *Ramban* questions Moshe's concern. Had not Hashem performed miracles for them? Was there any reason for Him to neglect them at this stage of their redemption?

The *Ramban* explains that Moshe feared Amalek particularly because he was Eisav's grandson. Eisav had been assured of the blessing of *"by your sword you shall live."* This blessing accorded him great physical might, which assured him of success in his battles. This blessing was the source of Yaakov's fear. His response was based upon his own blessing from his father *"The voice is the voice of Yaakov (and the hands are the hands of Eisav)."* Yaakov was blessed with the power of *tefillah*, prayer. Yaakov had the ability to conquer Eisav's "hands" by using his "voice".

Horav Yecheskel Levenstein, z.l., points out that keeping this concept in mind, we should reflect upon the power of prayer. Each prayer intrinsically contains the blessing of Yaakov. Every time we stand before Hashem and entreat Him through prayer, we are able to use *"Birkas Yaakov"* as a vehicle to ascend the loftiest spiritual heights in order to attain our request. How often do we neglect this blessing and pray without feeling and concentration? How many of life's trials and tribulations could be mitigated through this unique blessing? We should bear in mind that prayer is more than good advice; it is a unique gift bequeathed to the descendants of Yaakov.

QUESTIONS LEVEL- A

1. From which direction did Hashem send a strong wind?

2. When the *Yam Suf* split, what happened to the water?

3. What happened to the Egyptians when they tried to cross the *Yam Suf*?

4. A) Did everyone receive an equal portion of *manna*? B) How did this happen?

5. Who led *Bnei Yisrael* in their fight against Amalek?

QUESTIONS LEVEL- B

1. Why wasn't *Baal Tzafon* destroyed?

2. How did *Bnei Yisrael* know that the Egyptians had died in the sea?

QUESTIONS LEVEL- C

1. What did the pillars of fire and cloud "do" when the Egyptians entered the sea?

2. Why does the *Torah* specify that *Bnei Yisrael* arrived at *Midbar Sin* on *Iyar 15*?

QUESTIONS LEVEL- D

1. A) How many times did *Bnei Yisrael* test Hashem in the desert? B) Which of these tests are mentioned in this *parsha*?

ANSWERS LEVEL- A

1. From the east.

2. It stood up like a wall.

3. They all drowned.

4. A) Yes. B) Miraculously, everyone ended up with an equal portion.

5. Yehoshua.

ANSWERS LEVEL- B

1. In order to fool the Egyptians into thinking that Hashem could not destroy it.

2. The *Yam Suf* spit their bodies out on the shore in front of *Bnei Yisrael*.

ANSWERS LEVEL- C

1.The pillar of cloud descended and made the ground like clay, and the pillar of fire heated it, causing the hoofs of the Egyptian horses to be dislocated.

2. On that day they finished their supply of cakes which they brought from Egypt. They now needed the *manna*. This teaches us that they ate from the remains of the dough for 61 meals.

ANSWERS LEVEL- D

1. A) Ten times. B) Seven. 2 at the *Yam Suf*, 2 regarding the lack of water at Marah , 2 regarding the *manna* and one regarding the *slav*.

פרשת יתרו
PARASHAS YISRO
►◄

וישלח משה את חתנו וילך לו אל ארצו

**"And Moshe sent away his father-in-law, and he (Yisro) went his
way to his own land."** (18:27)

Rashi states that Yisro returned home solely in order to convert the
remainder of his family to Judaism. The *Maharal* interprets the words
"And Moshe sent" to imply that Moshe gave his blessings to this
return. *Horav A.H. Lebovitz, Shlita,* poignantly extols the supreme
sacrifice that Yisro made by leaving *Bnei Yisrael* and returning to
Midyan. *Bnei Yisrael* had been privy to a unique miraculous
existence. Sustained by *manna*, protected by the Clouds of Glory and
a Pillar of Fire, *Bnei Yisrael* had experienced the most intense
spiritual moments of all time. Under the tutelage of the greatest
teacher, Moshe *Rabbeinu*, they shared the consummate environment
for unparalled spiritual growth.

It would have required a formidable reason for Yisro to
withdraw from this idyllic environment in order to return to heathen
surroundings, antithetical to *Torah* world view. Moshe felt it
worthwhile that Yisro leave at this time, so that he would return and
inspire his countrymen.

Horav Lebovitz states that we can certainly learn from Yisro
regarding our responsibility to reach out to our alienated brethren. If
Yisro was willing to perform this task, how much more so are we
obligated to reach out to our fellow Jews even when it forces us to
make personal sacrifices. The spiritual and physical welfare of our
brethren is a responsibility which we must shoulder with love,
devotion, and pride.

Horav Moshe Feinstein, z.l., provides specific guidelines for
those whose overwhelming concern for their fellow Jew draws them
into the field of *kiruv*, reaching out. Although he perceives *kiruv* to be

a great *mitzvah*, he states that one must first strengthen his own commitment to *Torah*. The focus of one's concentration during the formative years in *yeshivah* should be self-improvement. During one's youth, *Torah* study should be his all-encompassing occupation. An inner striving towards greatness in *Torah* will effect positive results. One can assume responsibility for others only after he has developed his own potential in *Torah* learning.

This sequence is reflected in our daily prayers when we ask Hashem to give us the ability to *"learn and to teach"*. First we must learn; this will enable us to teach others.

Especially in contemporary times in which the yearning for *Torah* observance is growing, it is incumbent upon us to reach out to our brethren. One must acknowledge, however, the risks incurred through involvement in more worldly circumstances. It is proper to issue words of caution in this regard, as well as words of encouragement. Perhaps the most important safeguard for one who hopes to bring others close to *Torah* is that he make *Torah* the primary focus of his own life. When one follows the way of life prescribed by the *Torah*, he is indeed protected from all harm by Hashem. He is granted the *siyata dishmaya* to succeed in his spiritual outreach.

***

ואתם תהיו לי ממלכת כהנים וגוי קדוש

"And you will be to Me a kingdom of Kohanim (priests) and a holy nation." (19:6)

A *Kohen* is one whose life is devoted to the service of Hashem. The title *Kohen* also implies "scholar". As it is written in *Shmuel II 8:18* - ובני דוד כהנים היו, which means that they were *Torah* scholars. Hence, the prime pursuit of *Am Yisrael* is the study of *Torah*.

Horav Avigdor Miller, Shlita, observes that this *pasuk* does not merely state Hashem's promise of *Am Yisrael's* future reward. It is an aspect of Hashem's covenant with us which responds to our acceptance of the *Torah*. When we responded with the נעשה ונשמע, *"We will do and we will hear,"* we thereby obligated ourselves to be a kingdom of *Kohanim* and a holy nation. Every *Ben Yisrael* was to become a *"Kohen"* in regard to his obligation to study *Torah* and live a life of holiness. Although many people have gone on to other pursuits, the study of *Torah* has remained a lifelong goal. Indeed, throughout our history we have always distinguished parts of the day, week, month, or year for *Torah* study and scholarship, reflecting the fact that this endeavor is our lifelong occupation.

The second aspect of this tribute is *kedushah,* holiness. The quality of *"kedushah"* is not perceived simply as an aspect of our relationship with Hashem, the source of all *kedushah*. It is actually a component, emanating from Hashem, which is imbued in the object of this *kedushah*. Thus, the term "holy people" signifies a unique meta-physical distinction, albeit invisible, in the person. An object charged with electricity is physically different, even though its appearance has not been transformed. Similarly, various inconspicuous physical changes may exist within an object. When *Bnei Yisrael* execute Hashem's mandate, they are transformed into different beings, even though their superficial physical appearance has apparently not been altered.

***

אנכי ה' אלקיך

"I am Hashem your g-d." (20:2)

The *Aseres Hadibros*, the Ten Commandments, have been described as the fountainhead of Jewish law. Indeed, it is the most sublime synopsis of human duties; it will never be antiquated. The *Aseres Hadibros* comprised the first compendium of laws which Hashem gave to *Am Yisrael*.

Contemporary man distinguishes between his visible actions (i.e., the things we do and don't do) and the actions that are in the back of his mind (i.e., the things that we think of and do not do). We tend to discern between the things we do and the motive behind these actions. This unfortunate situation plays a pivotal role in shaping society. There is a significant storehouse of literature dedicated to the observance of practical duties, but there is very little written concerning the duties of the heart and soul which are not overtly expressed. The conduct that goes on in a man's mind and heart is no less important than his actions.

Moreshes Moshe observes a noteworthy insight from the

specific order of the *Aseres Hadibros*. The first and last of these commandments do not seem to be connected with any particular code of practical conduct. In contrast, the second through the ninth commandments include duties which focus on the fulfillment of specific acts. They must be stimulated into operation, to be actively regarded or disregarded.

Let us momentarily reflect upon the first and last commandments. The first consists of a single sentence, which states simply that Hashem took us out of Egypt. It is a confirmation of faith. It is a commandment to believe in the existence of Hashem, to be heard in our hearts and souls. The last of the commandments is again a simple statement, *"Do not covet."* Neither imperative can be translated into practice. Its focus is the heart and mind, the impulses and the desires. These two commandments deal with an inner state of mind. If one believes in Hashem, the first commandment, then the rest follows naturally. The last commandment represents faith in oneself, mastery over desires, control over impulses, and discipline of the mind. If this step is attained, the other *mitzvos* will follow automatically.

These two commandments comprise the framework of the entire Decalogue. The condition of one's faith shapes his mind and character. It is the determining factor in successful fulfillment of the *Torah*. Although they may seem superficially impressive, pious talk and meritorious deeds do not always disclose the truth. A smile does not necessarily indicate friendship, nor does a good deed always reflect devotion. The motive, the sincerity of mind and heart, mirrors the truth. Holy instincts and pure character, combined with righteous conduct, are the hallmarks of a *Torah* Jew.

QUESTIONS LEVEL A

1. Whom did Yisro bring with him to the desert?

2. With whom did Yisro sit down for a meal when he came to the desert?

3. In which month did *Bnei Yisrael* arrive at *Midbar Sin*?

4. Where did *Bnei Yisrael* camp when they came to *Midbar Sin*?

QUESTIONS LEVEL- B

1. State two meanings for the phrase ויחד יתרו.

2. Why did Yisro leave the desert to return to Midyan?

QUESTIONS LEVEL- C

1. A) What day is referred to by ויהי ממחרת? B) Is this the correct place in the *Torah* for this *parsha*?

2. A) To what type of stealing does לא תגנוב refer? B) What is the punishment for this sin?

QUESTIONS LEVEL- D

1. Which different *mitzvos* are represented by the *pasuk* והודעת להם את הדרך ילכו בה ואת המעשה אשר יעשון?

ANSWERS LEVEL- A

1. Tziporah and her two sons.

2. With Aharon and the Elders, while Moshe served.

3. The third month, *Sivan*.

4. Opposite *Har Sinai*.

ANSWERS LEVEL- B

1. 1) And Yisro rejoiced. 2) His flesh became a mass of prickles and cuts, (he grieved over the destruction of Egypt).

2. He went back to convert his family.

ANSWERS LEVEL- C

1. A) This was the day after *Yom Kippur*. B) No, This episode happened after *Matan Torah*.

2. A) Kidnapping. B) Death.

ANSWERS LEVEL- D

1. והודעת להם - teach them a livelihood. את הדרך - acts of kindness. ילכו- visiting the sick. בה - burying the dead. את המעשה ־ justice. (לפנים משורת הדין) ־אשר יעשון - going beyond the letter of the law.

פרשת משפטים
PARASHAS MISHPATIM
►◄

וכי יריבון אנשים... אם יקום והתהלך בחוץ... רק שבתו יתן ורפא ירפא

"And if men quarrel... if he rise again and walk outside... only he must pay the loss incurred by absence from work and cause him to be throughly healed.' (21:18,19)

The *Talmud Brachos 60a* interprets the repetition of the word healing ורפא ירפא as granting permission to the physician to heal. *Rashi* extends the words of the *Talmud* by asserting that Hashem smites and man heals. Thus, he implies that a special biblical dispensation sanctioning human healing is necessary. (We are not focusing here upon the issues of trust in Hashem -- or lack thereof -- which relate to human healing.)

The *Chofetz Chaim, z.l.,* however, presents an interesting insight into the problem of human healing and the role of doctors in the healing process. He questions the *Talmud's* "searching" to find an authorization for the physician to perform acts of healing. Does this concept infer justification for the physician to abdicate his professional expertise and not provide proper health care for a patient? He responds simply by saying that Hashem, for whatever reason, precipitates a human being's illness. Does man have the right to intervene and heal this person? This intriguing question is one of the fundamental theological and philosophical difficulties that abound regarding human healing.

Horav Eliyahu Lopian, z.l., explains that, although Hashem has indeed decreed the illness, He has, nonetheless, given permission to the physician to heal. *Horav* Lopian makes one very important stipulation regarding this authorization. The physician must be acutely aware that the illness he is attempting to cure is one that was inflicted by the Almighty, Who has granted him license to heal. Such a physician heals in accordance with the *Torah* perspective. With the help of the Almighty, his efforts are crowned with success.

ויבן מזבח תחת ההר ושתים עשרה מצבה לשנים עשר שבטי ישראל

"And he built an altar at the foot of the mountain, and twelve monuments for the twelve tribes of Yisrael." (24:4)

Even though this altar was dedicated in the name of the entire nation, each of the twelve tribes was individually represented by a separate monument. Thus, each tribe became obligated to accept total responsibility for the fulfillment of the entire *Torah*, rather than sharing that responsibility with the other tribes. Hashem has chosen to maintain the individuality of each tribe, so that each one continues to view itself as sustainers of the Covenant with Hashem.

Horav Avigdor Miller, Shlita, suggests two additional reasons for maintaining the distinct status of each tribe. First, Hashem imbued each tribe with unique characteristics, which constituted its own contribution to the perfection of *Klal Yisrael.* Each maintained its own territory and asserted its own identity. Each tribe intermarried within that tribe thus enhancing its particular personality traits. By sustaining its distinctiveness, the tribes aimed to achieve greater perfection of the entire collective unit, *Bnei Yisrael.*

Another advantage of preserving the individual status of each tribe was to exclude the influence of dissidents. A united people may be vulnerable to the seductive powers of a charismatic innovator. For example, when Yeravam *ben* Nevat seized power over the Ten Tribes, the remaining tribes of Yehudah and Binyamin continued to be loyal. They, therefore, endured until today, even after the others were lost. This was possible only because these tribes possessed independence as a result of their individual status and territorial integrity.

***

ויראו את אלקי ישראל ותחת רגליו כמעשה לבנת הספיר וכעצם השמים לטהר

"And they saw the G-d of Yisrael; and under His feet there was a form of a sapphire brick, like the very Heaven for clearness."
(24:10)

The above sentence is complex. Undoubtedly, the unimaginable notion of "seeing" Hashem refers to some aspect of Divine Glory, as the commentaries have already expressed. The allusion to the *"brick of sapphire"* begs for explanation. Why does the *Torah* mention this? The *Targum Yonason* cites a *Midrash* which sheds light on this enigma. This brick is a reminder of the wretched slavery to which

103

Bnei Yisrael were subjected. The Jewish men and women worked side by side, trampling and treading the mortar. One delicate young woman in the advanced stage of pregnancy miscarried as she was treading upon the mortar. The stillborn child became mixed into the brick mold. The terrible wailing of the mother ascended to the Heavenly throne, whereupon the angel Gavriel was dispatched to retrieve this "brick" and bring it up to Heaven. It was placed next to Hashem's throne as a memorial.

A profound lesson can to be derived from this story. No incident is relegated to oblivion. Hashem records every horror, regardless of who is affected. No tragedy suffered by His children is considered insignificant. Amid all of the tension and shouting, one young woman pathetically cried out. The angel made a brick from the unborn child, and Hashem had it placed near His seat. Indeed, as the *Midrash* continues, that very night Hashem smote all of Egypt's first-born. The sapphire memorial was the most fitting tribute to this young *neshamah*, and, perhaps, a consolation for the mother. With this concept in mind, we may begin to confront some of the horrifying tragedies, we have experienced, both as individuals and as members of *Am Yisrael*.

An amazing *Chazal* expresses a similar idea. The *Talmud* in *Avodah Zarah 3B*, questions, What does Hashem do in the fourth part of the day? The response is: Hashem studies *Torah* with little children! *Rashi* explains that this refers to children, who had died when they were yet young!

Horav S. Schwab, z.l., applies this *Chazal* in a most poignant way. Imagine for one horrifying moment, the one and one half million Jewish children whose lives were so brutally snuffed out during the Holocaust. They were tragically sacrificed just as they were at the threshold of life. They are presently studying *Torah* with Hashem, Himself. They have a personal *chavrusa* with the Almighty! This is perhaps the meaning of the "sapphire memorial." Hashem perennially remembers those who have experienced more than their share of anguish in life.

In a homiletic exposition, *Reb Yitzchak Bunim, z.l.,* compares the *Yeshivah* Day School movement to the angel Gavriel in ancient Egypt. When the European Jews arrived in America "en masse," they immediately began working, kneading "clay" and making "bricks" in order to build an economic base for their families. They toiled to provide their families with material sustenance, but, unfortunately, many forgot to provide their children with spiritual sustenance. The Jewish soul was tragically becoming stillborn! The soul that should hold its head up high, filled with pride and joy, was being buried in the "bricks" of materialism.

Just as Gavriel scooped up the stillborn child out of the lime and clay to bring it to the heights of Heaven, so, too, have our *Torah* day schools, through their devoted teachers, taken the souls of the young out of the materialistic milieu and provided them with the opportunity to ascend to the throne of glory. The Jewish spirit is stimulated only through a proper education under the auspices of a *Torah* day school, staffed by teachers who exemplify the true essence of *Torah*. Through this endeavor, Judaism will not be stillborn, but will live, thrive and endure.

QUESTIONS LEVEL- A

1. Can a Jewish girl be sold as a maidservant?
2. If a master kills an *eved Knaani* who dies immediately, what punishment does he get?
3. When is a *shoel* not obligated to pay?
4. Was anyone permitted to go up on *Har Sinai* with Moshe?
5. What did Moshe sprinkle over *Bnei Yisrael*?

QUESTIONS LEVEL- B

1. Which death is given to one who wounds his parents?
2. The *Torah* refers to a person who digs a pit as the *baal h'abor*. Does he really own it?

QUESTIONS LEVEL- C

1. May the master give a *shifcha Kenanis* to an *eved Ivri* who is single?
2. How much is *mohar*?

QUESTIONS LEVEL- D

1. Why does the *Torah* refer to a Jewish slave as *eved Ivri* and not *eved Yisrael*?

ANSWERS LEVEL- A

1. Yes.

2. Death (by a sword).

3. 1) In case the owner is with the *shoel*. 2) If the borrowed object is damaged due to a normal work load.

4. No.

5. Blood.

ANSWERS LEVEL- B

1. *chenek*.

2. No, because it is in a public domain; but since he dug the pit the *Torah* holds him responsible for it as if he is the owner.

ANSWERS LEVEL- C

1. No.

2. Fifty *Shekalim*.

ANSWERS LEVEL- D

1. 1) The term *Yisrael* implies strength and holiness. The *Torah* does not want to associate slavery with this term. 2) The term *Yisrael* is a reference to the Jews before *matan Torah*. This Jew, by selling himself as a slave to someone else besides Hashem, acted as if he didn't hear what Hashem said during *matan Torah*.

פרשת תרומה
PARASHAS TERUMAH

ויקחו לי תרומה

"That they take for Me a Terumah." (25:2)

The *Baal Shem Tov* notes that *Parashas Terumah*, which contains the *mitzvah* of donating toward the building of the *Mishkan*, immediately follows *Parashas Mishpatim*, which ends with the receiving of the *Torah*. He explains that the command to build the *Mishkan* was Hashem's way of telling *Bnei Yisrael* to substantively actualize their acceptance of the *Torah*. It isn't sufficient to proclaim נעשה ונשמע, *"We will do and we will hear,"* and then return to our daily lives as if nothing had transpired. It is imperative to stimulate the potential of our statement into action. If it remains dormant, eventually it will lose its spirit and vibrance.

We may apply this concept to other forms of spiritual inspiration. Often one listens to a charismatic speaker deliver a profound lecture or participates in a heightened spiritual experience, only to let the effects dissipate. Beyond the change one experiences at the initial encounter, one must seek to sustain the original feelings. This form of emotional response is reinforced through *Torah* study. One who is spiritually inspired, but does not continue on to *Torah* study, will unfortunately remain spiritually crippled. The effort one expends in immortalizing his moments of spiritual elevation will be reflected in his personal growth and development.

***

מאת כל איש אשר ידבנו לבו תקחו את תרומתי... זהב וכסף ונחשת

"An offering from everyone whose heart motivates him to give... gold, silver, and copper." (25:2,3)

Each of these metals is of different value. They are, nonetheless, included together and considered of equal importance. For, this is *"an offering of the heart,"* regarding which it is stated: *Whether one gives more or less, it is meaningless, as long as his thoughts are focused for (the honor of) Heaven." (Berachos 5b).* How much one gives is not important. Rather, it is the motivation for his donation which is of critical value. Thus, gold, silver, and copper can be perceived equally.

***

ועשו ארון עצי שטים

"And they shall make an Aron of shittim wood." (25:10)

Bnei Yisrael were enjoined to build the *Aron Hakodesh* prior to the *Mishkan* itself. Why was this? *Horav M. Gifter, Shlita.* suggests the following reason for this. The *Aron*, which held the *Torah*, represents the *Torah* as the foundation of our people. Because we have the *Torah*, Hashem chooses to rest the Divine Presence in our midst. Consequently, we must orient our priorities in accordance with the *Torah*.

Horav Gifter notes that the *Aron* was built even prior to the *Mizbayach*, Altar. The *Mizbayach* denotes sacrifice and its derivative, *mesiras nefesh,* self-sacrifice for Hashem and His *mitzvos.* He explains that only through *Torah* can the parameters of *mesiras nefesh* be clearly defined. The clarity of vision which evolves from total *Torah* study and scholarship structures one's perspective concerning self- sacrifice. Without *Torah's* guidance, intelligence and reason give way to the irrational and absurd. Thus, self-sacrifice can become an act of murder and destruction.

This idea may be extended to all areas of endeavor. The *Torah* perspective must guide all of activity, even concerning *mitzvos* which are "humanitarian" in nature. *Horav Chaim Mordechai Katz, z.l.,* used to explain the *Mishnah* in *Peah*, which crowns *Torah* study above all *mitzvos*, including wonderful acts of lovingkindness. The *Mishnah* enumerates many noble *mitzvos,* such as honoring parents, doing acts of kindness, coming to the *Bais Hamedrash* on time, and visiting the sick. It ends with the phrase ותלמוד תורה כנגד כולם *"and Torah study is "equal" to all."* The word כנגד, actually is translated as "opposite" rather than equal.

In light of this, *Horav* Katz explains that every *mitzvah* must be "held up" opposite and performed in light of the *Torah. Torah* must mold the personality and total perspective of a Jew. His philosophy of life must coincide with the *Torah's* philosophy of life! Only then does he satisfy the mandate of ‫ותלמוד תורה כנגד כולם.‬

***

‫ועשו ארון עצי שטים וצפית אתו זהב טהור מבית ומחוץ תצפנו‬

"And they shall make an Aron of shittim wood... and you shall cover it with pure gold from within and without." (25:10,11)

Although in the eyes of the beholder, the *Aron* appeared to be made completely of gold, it is a well known fact that this was only an overlay. The actual *Aron* was made of wood, sandwiched between outer and inner layers of gold. This seems enigmatic. It would be appropriate that this most sublime vessel, which housed the *Torah*, consist entirely of gold. Certainly gold would more readily reflect the magnificence and majesty of the Almighty. *Horav Dovid Feinstein, Shlita,* who raises this question, offers the following lesson to be derived from this "wooden" *Aron*. Wood is a living substance which grows and reproduces. In contrast, gold, which captivates its beholder with its beauty, is inanimate. Which one would make a more suitable repository for the *Torah*?

The *Torah* was given to human beings, who are made of flesh and blood. They are subject to the seductive influence of their *yetzer hora*, evil inclination, and must exert amazing strength to avoid falling prey to its constant blandishments. Nonetheless, this is life. One must live and grow in order to overcome these obstacles. Thus, a wooden *Aron* teaches us that the *Torah*, a tree of life, was not to be contained by the cold inert gold, regardless of its beauty. Rather, the *Torah* was given to living breathing, growing, human beings in order to enable them to attain eternal life.

Why then, asks *Horav* Feinstein, is the *Aron* covered from within and without with gold? The answer is that while a *Torah* scholar is subject to the same weaknesses as others, he must, nonetheless, attempt to purify himself to the greatest extent possible. Although he is human, he should aspire to reach the purity of an angel. Thus, the gold is also within to teach us that, even in privacy, a *ben Torah* should be pure. In the innermost parts of his private life, he should mirror the virtue he has achieved though *Torah* study. The gold within and without serves as the structure for the inner growth of the *Torah* scholar.

***

ועשית את הקרשים למשכן עצי שטים עומדים

"And you shall make the boards for the *Mishkan* from shittim wood standing upright." (26:15)

The *Midrash* questions the specific use of *shittim* wood for the beams of the *Mishkan*. *Chazal* respond that Hashem has chosen to teach a lesson regarding the proper *derech eretz* one must model when building a house or when undertaking any endeavor which affects others. Hashem chose *shittim* wood which comes from a barren tree. Likewise, when we build, we should use wood which originates from a tree which does not produce fruit.

This *Midrash* is noteworthy. The *Mishkan* is the major source of holiness in this world. Yet, its construction may not affect any other form of "life," even inanimate life. How much more so should we be considerate of the sensitivities of others when we embark upon a new venture. When building an edifice for *Torah*, whether it be a place for *Torah* study or prayer, we should construct it of components which do not infringe upon others. The money and materials must originate from reputable sources. One should never identify himself or his activities with financial sources of questionable repute.

***

והבריח התיכון בתוך הקרשים מבריח מן הקצה אל הקצה

"And the middle bar in the midst of the boards shall pass from end to end." (26:28)

The *Targum Yonason* explains that this middle bar originated from Avraham's famous "inn" from which he would provide food and drink for wayfarers. The angels cut it down and threw it into the sea, where it floated until it was retrieved by Moshe. *Horav E. Muller, Shlita*, notes the significance of this statement. Everyone was requested to contribute their heartfelt donation towards the construction of the *Mishkan*. In order to maintain this structure, however, it was essential to have as the middle bar a pole which was derived from a house which exemplified the highest level of *chesed*.

The *Mishkan*, in which the *Shechinah* "rested," was built from and maintained upon *chesed*. We should take serious note of this ethical lesson. The *Mishkan* depicted the type of sanctity required of *Klal Yisrael*. All of the vessels served to demonstrate the various attributes which should combine to produce the *Torah* Jew. A person imbued with such noble qualities must exemplify the *middah* of *chesed* in order to maintain them.

QUESTIONS LEVEL- A

1. What were the dimensions of the *Aron*?

2. What was the purpose of the *badim*?

3. What were the dimensions of each *yeriah*?

4. Including the corners, how many *kerashim* were there on the western wall?

5. What were the dimensions of the *chatzer Ha'Mishkan*?

QUESTIONS LEVEL- B

1. What is the meaning of the phrase מבית ומחוץ תצפנו?

2. How high was the *Mishkan*?

QUESTIONS LEVEL- C

1. From where did they get the dye for the *tcheleis*.

2. How high was the *Mizbayach Ha'nechoshes*?

QUESTIONS LEVEL- D

1. Why was the *kapores* called by this name?

ANSWERS LEVEL- A

1. 2.5 cubits in length, 1.5 cubits in width, and 1.5 cubits in height.

2. To carry the *Aron*.

3. 28 cubits long and 4 cubits wide.

4. Eight.

5. 100 cubits long and 50 cubits wide.

ANSWERS LEVEL- B

1. The wood of the *Aron* shall be covered with gold from inside and out. *Chazal* comment that the *Aron* was made of three boxes. A gold box was placed into a wooden box which in turn was placed into another gold box.

2. 10 cubits.

ANSWERS LEVEL-C

1. From the blood of the *Chalazon*.

2. The *Torah* says the *Mizbayach* should be 3 cubits high. However, R' Yosi says in the *Talmud* that this only refers to the top section (above the *karkov*). The *Mizbayach* was 10 cubits high.

ANSWERS LEVEL- D

1. *kapores* is derived from the word *kaparah*, which means "to atone." It atones for the Sin of the Golden Calf.

פרשת תצוה
PARASHAS TETZAVEH
▶◀

ואתה תצוה את בני ישראל

"And you shall command *Bnei Yisrael.*" (27;20)

Moshe's name is not mentioned in this *parsha.* The *Baal Ha'Turim* states that Moshe entreated Hashem on behalf of *Klal Yisrael* after they sinned with the Golden Calf. He pleaded, *"Erase me from Your Book."* In accordance with Moshe's emphatic statement, Hashem chose one *parsha* in which Moshe's name would not be recorded. We may wonder why *Parashas Tetzaveh* was chosen to be the *parsha* from which Moshe's name was excluded.

Horav Nissan Alpert, z.l., suggests that the word *"tetzaveh,"* which means command, alludes to *Am Yisrael's* leadership. The function of leadership is to command and guide the people. In order that leaders be able to successfully execute their duty, they must realize that they are merely vehicles of Hashem for motivating *Am Yisrael's* positive response. They must transcend their own egotism, so that the people perceive them simply as agents of Hashem.

Horav Alpert amends this idea with an emphasis on the word ואתה, *"and you".* The אתה represents the leader's unique personality. His behavior should serve as a role model for the populace so that they are encouraged to serve Hashem by "your" example. The *pasuk* would then be defined in the following manner: ואתה תצוה. The אתה, your total demeanor, should be an example to *Bnei Yisrael* in observing Hashem's *mitzvos.*

Modeling by both parents and teachers, is an effective pedagogic tool. *Chazal* tell us that when Yosef was faced with the most difficult test of moral fortitude to confront a young man, he was saved from downfall by visualizing the image of his father, Yaakov, before him. This vision brought Yosef back to his senses and made him recoil from the temptation to sin with Potiphar's wife. Thus,

Yosef was able to regain control over his passions, so that he was saved for the great spiritual destiny that had been intended for him.

Likewise, parents should be cognizant of the moral and spiritual image which they imprint upon the hearts and minds of their children. This image personifies an example of moral and spiritual purity. If a child is imbued with a positive imprimatur, it will reach into the deepest recesses of his or her innermost being.

Horav S.R. Hirsch, z.l., states that parents and teachers are appointed to act as the moral and spiritual guides for their children. Their words and their actions have a powerful effect upon the impressionable souls of their children. Inappropriate behavior performed by parents or teachers can poison the souls of the children entrusted in their custody. To paraphrase *Horav* Hirsch, "*To be a father or a teacher means to be above reproach in one's own morals and actions."* A child who has just cause to criticize the speech or conduct of his parents or teachers will be less inclined to obey them. The child's obedience will always be in direct proportion to the respect he has for the personality of his parent, teacher or guardian. The moral consistency of a parent or teacher is their key to a child's conformity to the role model's expectations.

***

ועשית בגדי קדש לאהרן אחיך לכבוד ולתפארת
"And you shall make sacred garments for Aharon your brother for glory and majesty." (28:2)

The *Torah* devotes an entire *parsha* to the preparation of the priestly vestments. Indeed, the *Torah* apportions more space to the *"Bigdei Kehunah"* than to the sacred vessels which were used in the *Mishkan.* Although the priestly vestments were not an inherent part of the actual service, the service could be performed only when the *Kohen* was wearing them. It seems apparent that the *Bigdei Kehunah* performed a sublime role.

The *Chizkuni* explains that בגדי קדש, sacred garments, is the key phrase which defines the moral and spiritual striving represented by the priestly garb. The beauty manifested by these vestments was not of a mundane nature, but rather constituted a sanctified beauty. Clothing is a symbol of man's higher nature. By distinguishing

114

between man and animals, clothing gives man special dignity. The *Kohanim* were, therefore, required to dress consistently with their exalted position, reflective of man's higher calling.

Horav M. Gifter, Shlita, suggests the following insight to be derived from the *Bigdei Kehunah.* Every virtue which man possesses is valued according to the individual's ability to "clothe" himself in this characteristic. Man's essence must mirror these qualities. The moral attributes, *"yiraas shomayim,"* and character refinement manifested by the *Kohen* should be inherent throughout his entire essence. It should be reflected externally, as well. If these traits are not externally apparent, the *Kohen* is not suitable to entreat Hashem on behalf of *Am Yisrael.* The service of atonement demands one who personifies perfection.

Horav Gifter extends this idea to include all members of *Bnei Yisrael.* Every Jew is obligated to affirm himself as a member of a *"kingdom of priests and a holy nation".* This "appellation" is to be *Am Yisrael's* distinctive feature. To fulfill this noble goal we must invest ourselves with the "clothing" of a holy nation: *middos tovos* (pure moral characteristics), *Torah,* and *mitzvos.* Analogous to the *Kehunah,* our worthiness of the mantle "holy nation," is symbolized by our being "clothed" in our holy merit.

***

ועשית ציץ זהב טהור והיה על המצנפת והיה על מצח אהרן ונשא אהרן
את עון הקדשים

"And you shall make a showplate of pure gold... and this shall go over the turban... and it shall be on Aharon's forehead, and so Aharon shall do away with the transgressions of the holy things."
(28:36,37,38)

Chazal state that the *"tzitz"* atoned for the sin of impudence exhibited by the people. This seems enigmatic. How does Aharon's wearing of the *tzitz* atone for a generation's brazenness and lack of courtesy? Does the *Kohen Gadol's* wearing of the *tzitz* give one license to be impertinent? *Horav Reuven Katz, z.l.,* resolves this difficulty in the following way. One who secretly sins will be embarrassed if his baneful act is publicized.

115

In contrast, one who is impudent defies criticism and publicly flaunts his evil in the most arrogant manner. Atonement for a sin is effected through the balance of *"middah k'neged middah,"* measure for measure. The punishment will be meted consistent with the form and type of evil, and forgiveness will result. Consequently, the recommended method for atoning this sin is to employ the identical tactics, but in reverse. By proudly raising up our heads in defiance, not submitting to those who would slander the *Torah* by ridiculing its adherents, we will overcome the evil of impudence.

This concept is especially applicable in contemporary times, when the *Torah* community has been virulently criticized by those who differ with the *Torah* way of life. Even though we should not seek to propagate dispute, we nonetheless are not obligated to accept the negative statements spoken or written against the *Gedolei Yisrael, Torah* leaders. We are responsible to voice vigorous protest. We are duty bound to repudiate those distortions expressed against the *Torah* and its luminaries. We do not have license, however, to demean ourselves by hurling insults or making derisive personal attacks. We must maintain our dignity, while we stalwartly carry forth the banner of *Torah* Judaism.

***

והיה המזבח קדש קדשים

And the altar (of copper) shall be a sanctuary for sanctuaries"
(29:37)

It seems peculiar that the *Torah* twice refers to the copper altar, which was situated outside of the *"Heichal,"* as *"kodesh kodoshim."* This is in contrast to the altar of incense , which was placed opposite the *Aron Hakodesh* and is described merely as *"kodesh." Horav Moshe Feinstein, z.l.,* suggests the following homiletic interpretation. The placement of the altars, inside or outside, symbolizes the *Torah* scholar when he is inside or outside of the *Bais Hamidrash.* A *Torah* scholar should be cognizant that while he is "holy" in the *Bais Hamidrash,* he must be "doubly holy" when he leaves this sheltered environment.

In the course of time, the *Torah* scholar will certainly come in contact with people of unfavorable repute who would sway him from the path of *Torah*. His virtue should be so well developed that it

116

the path of *Torah*. His virtue should be so well developed that it inspires whomever he meets. One who is considered "holy" in the *Bais Hamidrash* by his peers is viewed by people in the "outside" world as special as well. Every action he performs is amplified because of his exalted image in the eyes of others. One who is *"kodesh"* in the *yeshivah* should remember that he is viewed as *"kodesh kodoshim"* by others, and he must project this image in all of his interactions with people.

QUESTIONS LEVEL- A

1. What type of oil was used to light the *Menorah*?
2. What was the *cheisehv Ha'eifod*?
3. What was inscribed on the *Choshen*?
4. What was the *Meil* made of?
5. Where was the *Tzitz* worn?

QUESTIONS LEVEL- B

1. How was the "pure olive oil" prepared?
2. Why was the *Choshen Ha'mishpat* called by this name?

QUESTIONS LEVEL- C

1. What is the difference between the oil used for the *Menorah* and the oil used for the *Menachos*?
2. How many letters were there on each of the *Avnei Shoham*?

QUESTIONS LEVEL- D

1. Using the definition of the word *"Kehunah"*, what is the loftiest level of *Avodas Hashem*?

ANSWERS LEVEL- A

1. Pure olive oil.
2. It was the belt which was a part of the *Eifod*.

4. *Techeiles.*

5. On the forehead.

ANSWERS LEVEL- B

1. This oil came from the first pressing of an olive. It was not ground on a millstone in order to prevent any sediment from getting into it.

2. 1) It atoned for mistakes in judgement. 2) It had the *Urim V'etumim* which was clear and faithful.

ANSWERS LEVEL- C

1. The oil used for the *Menorah* was from the first pressing and had no sediment or impurities in it whatsoever, while, in contrast, the oil used for the *Menachos* was ground on a millstone and had some impurities in it.

2. There were twenty-five letters on each stone.

ANSWERS LEVEL- D

1. *Rashi* defines *Kehunah* as "to serve." The greatest level of spirituality is the level of *Kehunah,* which means that one is there only to "serve" Hashem. Moshe was referred to as the servant of Hashem.

פרשת כי תשא
PARASHAS KI-SISA
►◄

וישכימו ממחרת ויעלו עולות ויגישו שלמים וישב העם לאכול ושתו ויקומו לצחק

"And they arose early on the morrow, and <u>they</u> <u>offered</u> <u>burnt</u>
<u>offerings,</u> and <u>they</u> <u>brought</u> <u>peace</u> <u>offerings</u>, and the people sat
down to <u>eat</u> <u>and</u> <u>to</u> <u>drink,</u> <u>and</u> <u>they</u> <u>rose</u> <u>up</u> <u>to</u> (play) <u>make</u>
<u>merry</u>." (32:6)

The Golden Calf incident was *Am Yisrael*'s first deviation from the
Torah path. This was the first time that *Bnei Yisrael* supported ideals
antithetical to *Torah* values. The relationship between the ideology of
these historical sinners and their actions is typical of those who have
espoused distorted thinking throughout the generations. The visions
and their behavioral consquences are the same today. It is only the
names and places which have changed.

Horav Y. Galinsky, Shlita, notes the progressive deterioration
of *Bnei Yisrael's* values from the sequence of events portrayed by the
pasuk. First it states, *"They offered burnt offerings."* A burnt offering
is a donation totally devoted to the Almighty, since the whole animal
is burnt upon the altar. In the beginning, *Bnei Yisrael* maintained
complete dedication to their ideals. They demonstrated neither
self-serving interests nor self gratification. After a while, the spark of
their enthusiasm dissipated. It was replaced by a pervasive attitude,
represented by the phrase *"They brought peace offerings."* They
affirmed their devotion towards the Divinity, but it was no longer with
the same zeal. They were gradually submitting to their personal vested
interests. This sterile form of service gave way to a routine approach,
reflected in the words *"They sat down to eat and drink"*. The facade of
spirituality was destroyed. Their true intentions were revealed. The
deception of piety and spiritual concern was unmasked. Now they
were prepared for the total deacadance, indicated by the final phrase of
the *pasuk, "They rose up to play and make merry"*.

119

The truth overcomes the sham. The sham of false idealism and the deception of insincere religious enthusiasm are ultimately exposed. Hashem had granted us a *Torah*, which presents the prescribed blueprint for an integrative lifestyle. Deviation from the *Torah*, as expounded by *Chazal*, even in the name of religious idealism is tantamount to blasphemy.

***

וידבר ד' אל משה לך רד כי שחת עמך... סרו מהר מן הדרך...

עשו להם עגל מסכה... ראיתי את העם הזה והנה עם

קשה ערף הוא.. ועתה הניחה לי ויחר אפי בהם ואכלם

"And Hashem spoke to Moshe... go descend, for your people have become corrupt... they made for themselves a Golden Calf... and Hashem said to Moshe: I have seen these people and behold they are a stubborn people... and now leave Me be and let Me vent My anger and annihilate them." (32:7,8,9,10)

The *Torah* lists the sins transgressed by *Bnei Yisrael*. They corrupted themselves, and they made a Golden Calf. They replaced service to a Divine G-d with the worship of a molten image. Hashem did not choose to destroy them, however, for these sins. Only after they are described as an obstinate people does Hashem seek to decimate them. *Horav Meir Chadash, z.l.,* notes that stubbornness is an evil which must be totally eradicated. Obstinacy, by its very nature, is the antithesis of free will. One who doggedly refuses to accept guidance and reproach, who continues upon his chosen path of evil even in defiance of punishment, is a person who is obsessed with performing evil. He is powerless to act by the dictates of his own conscience. Such a person cannot rationally choose between right and wrong. Therefore, he is unable to repent his ways.

A necessary prerequisite for *teshuvah*, repentance, is recognition of a misdeed. There is a natural inclination to deny one's own wrongdoing. When one justifies his negative actions, he is preventing himself from pursuing the road to *teshuvah*. Indeed, the more we legitimize our wrongdoing, the more we are likely to to believe that what we are doing is right, perhaps even meritorious.

Klal Yisrael are referred to as *"a stiff necked people."* This description is intrinsically a blessing in disguise. Being "stiff necked," we have been able to muster the moral courage to stalwartly maintain our faith in Hashem. Despite the pain, sorrow, and suffering which have accompanied us throughout history, we have held our heads high. To misinterpret the blessing of "resolve and determination" as "stubbornness," a trait which promotes evil, is reprehensible. This type of repulsive behavior enabled the people to participate in the progressive sin of the Golden Calf and resulted in Hashem's tragic decree.

***

ויהי כאשר קרב אל המחנה וירא את העגל ומחולות

ויחר אף משה וישלך מידיו את הלוחות וישבר אותם תחת ההר

"And it came to pass when he came near to the camp, that he saw the calf and (the) dancing that Moshe's anger arose, and he threw from his hands the Luchos and he broke them." (32:19)

We must endeavor to understand what transpired when Moshe approached the camp that precipitated his angry reaction. Did he not already know the extent of *Bnei Yisrael's* transgression? The *Abarbanel* questions Moshe's intentions in bringing the *Luchos* down only in order to break them. He responds that Moshe desired to accentuate *Bnei Yisrael's* travesty and its consequences. Therefore, he broke the *Luchos* blatantly in front of them. The text, however, seems to imply that it was only after Moshe "came near" the camp and actually saw their conspicuous transgression that he reacted in such an intense manner. We may also question the wording of the text. The *Torah* states, *"He saw the calf and dancing."* This is not a single vision! It is two distinct spectacles. The *Torah* should have written, *"And he saw the calf and (he saw the) dancing."*

Horav Yaakov Kamenetsky, z.l., suggests the following interpretation. Upon descending the mountain, Moshe sought a merit upon which to vindicate the Jews' tragic sin. Perhaps they made the calf as a result of severe depression or hardship. Possibly it was an inevitable outcome of their being deprived of Moshe, their leader. When he approached, however, he saw the people dancing with the calf. His anger mounted as he recognized their joy in partaking in this sinful act. The calf alone did not cause Moshe's reaction. Rather, the Jews' audacious exalting in their sinful act catalysed his response.

121

ויעמוד משה בשער המחנה ויאמר מי לד' אלי

"And Moshe stood in the gate of the camp and he said (called out) whoever is with Hashem (should come) to me!" (32:26)

As a young man, *Horav S. Schwab, z.l.,* had the occasion to spend a *Shabbos* with the *Chofetz Chaim, z.l.,* On Friday morning, the *Chofetz Chaim* questioned him regarding his lineage, whether he was a *Kohen* or a *Levi. Horav* Schwab responded in the negative. The *Chofetz Chaim* remarked, "What a pity! *Moshiach* is coming, and the *Bais Hamikdash* will be rebuilt. If you are not a *Kohen*, you will be unable to perform the *Avodah*, priestly service."

The *Chofetz Chaim* continued, "Do you know why? Because 3,000 years ago, during the incident of the Golden Calf, when Moshe called out *"Whoever is with Hashem should come to me,"* my grandfather came running to serve, but your grandfather did not respond to the call! This is the message," he continued. "Every Jew has moments during his lifetime in which he hears that inner voice calling out מי לד' אלי. Listen! When you hear that sound, respond immediately, while the opportunity still exists."

How often does the occasion arise when we hear this inner voice reverberating within us, imploring us to go forth to act for *Torah*? Alas, in the frenzied pace of our everyday routine, only those few who dedicate their lives to *Torah* hear the plaintive cry. We may suggest that this "voice" refers to any moment of opportunity. Often in our daily endeavor we come across opportunities for spiritual growth in the form of a charitable undertaking, a special *mitzvah*, or a chance to study in a class or with a study partner. These seemingly innocent incidents are echos reverberating from Heaven, availing us of a chance to grow. We should heed the words of the *Chofetz Chaim* by being in the forefront of those responding to the call.

QUESTIONS LEVEL- A

1. How were *Bnei Yisrael* counted?

2. What was unique about the way in which the *Luchos* were inscribed?

3. Who moved his tent out of the Jewish camp?

4. How many times a year should a Jew go up to Yerushalayim?

5. When is the *Korban Pesach* supposed to be slaughtered?

QUESTIONS LEVEL- B

1. Why was the *chelbenah* (which had a bad odor) mixed with the other spices in order to produce the *Ketores*?

2. From which species of grain does one have to give *Bikurim*?

QUESTIONS LEVEL- C

1. In what order did the *Kohanim* wash their hands and feet??

2. What reasoning did Moshe use to permit himself to break the *Luchos*?

QUESTIONS LEVEL- D

1. For how long did the *Shemen Ha'mishchah* that Moshe made continue to be used?

ANSWERS LEVEL- A

1. Individuals were to give a half-*shekel* each, and then the money was counted.

2. They were inscribed on both sides.

3. Moshe *Rabbeinu*.

4. Three.

5. After all the *chametz* has been disposed of.

ANSWERS LEVEL- B

1. To teach us that when we either fast or say our *teffilos*, we should include all *Bnei Yisrael*, even the wicked.

2. The seven species.

ANSWERS LEVEL- C

1. The *Kohen* would place his right hand on his right foot and his left hand on his left foot, then water would be poured on them at one time.

2. He reasoned that if *Korban Pesach*, which is only one of the *mitzvos* of the *Torah*, is prohibited to be brought by a *ben naichar,* one who is strange to the ways of Hashem, surely the entire *Torah* may not be given to a nation when everyone is a מומר. Therefore, he broke the *Luchos*.

ANSWERS LEVEL- D

1. It continued to be used until the destruction of the *Bais Hamikdash*. It was then hidden until the coming of *Moshiach,* who will restore it.

123

פרשת ויקהל
PARASHAS VAYAKHEL
►◄

והמלאכה היתה דים לכל המלאכה לעשות אתה והותר

"And the stuff they had was "sufficient" for all the work to make it with some "left over." (36:7)

The text of this *pasuk* seems enigmatic. The word "sufficient" implies an accounting of materials for a precise purpose, for which an accurate amount is necessary. "Left over," on the other hand, denotes a surplus of these materials.

Horav M. Shapiro, z.l., offers a novel approach to resolving this apparent "contradiction." Every Jew contributed towards the *Mishkan*, each according to his own means. Some individuals wanted to donate more than their resources permitted, but were not allowed to do so. There were also probably individuals who had procrastinated, intending to give more before the call came to cease the donations. The *halachah* regarding the latter case is clear. When one plans to donate to *"hekdesh",* sanctuary, the intended object becomes sanctified even if the individual had not uttered a word of affirmation. We note that thoughts are accepted as binding. What happens to these thoughts and worthy intentions? They surely do not vanish into oblivion!

Horav Shapiro deduces that these holy thoughts are transformed into deeds. This is consistent with the statement of *Chazal* that one who has been prevented from performing an intended *mitzvah* is viewed by the *Torah* as having performed it. Responding to the above problem, he states that the actual donations were sufficient to serve the concrete needs of the *Mishkan* and its vessels. The "left over" refers to the surplus of good will and intentions, the unrealized aspirations of those who had hoped to go beyond the letter of the law, but missed the opportunity. These donations remained a separate phenomenon, hovering above humanity in the spiritual realm.

The airspace surrounding the Sanctuary was also holy, despite its intangibility. How did it receive sanctification if it had no corporeal form? How could the air, which has no tactile properties, become as consecrated as the actual place? *Horav Shapiro* responds that this unique holiness was a direct result of the yearnings and strivings of the people whose intended donations had become ensconced in the air of the *Mishkan*. We may advance this thought further. When one studies *Torah* or performs another *mitzvah*, he creates a metaphysical form of sanctity for which he will be rewarded. The attitude with which he approaches this *mitzvah* performance is also a source of *kedushah*, holiness. The resulting *kedushah* becomes an intrinsic part of the place in which he performs this deed.

For example, one who studies *Torah* in a certain room creates an atmosphere of *kedushah* in that room. We suggest that the quality of the of *kedushah* in that room is consistent with the enthusiasm he applies and the holiness he attributes to his *Torah* study. The level of *kedushah* in a given place correlates highly to the attitude towards the *mitzvah* performance in that place. If the *Torah* study is cold and insipid, the place will maintain that same sterile form of spirituality. If the *Torah* study is a manifestation of one's love for and devotion to Hashem's *Torah*, it will be reflected in a sublime form of sanctity that can be intuitively felt when one enters the room.

QUESTIONS LEVEL- A

1. What type of wood was used in the *Mishkan*?

2. What were the *Avnei Milluim* used for?

3. Were there enough donations for the *Mishkan*?

QUESTIONS LEVEL- B

1. Define the word ארגמן.

2. Define the words קרסי המשכן.

QUESTIONS LEVEL- C

1. A) How many major kinds of work are prohibited on *Shabbos*? B) What are they called in *Lashon Ha'kodesh?*

2. Which *Yerios* are considered the actual *Mishkan?*

QUESTIONS LEVEL- D

1. Why was *shitim* wood used for the *Mishkan?*

ANSWERS LEVEL- A

1. *Shittim* wood.
2. The *Choshen*.
3. Yes.

ANSWERS LEVEL- B

1. Purple wool.
2. Fasteners, clasps.

ANSWERS LEVEL- C

1. A) Thirty-nine. B) 39 *avos melachos*.
2. The lower ones, y*erios Ha'Mishkan*.

ANSWERS LEVEL- D

1. Since the Jews would sin in *Shittim*, this wood was chosen to protect and atone for them.

126

פרשת פקודי
PARASHAS PEKUDAI
►◄

ויכל משה את המלאכה

"And so Moshe finished the work." (40:33)

The *parsha* concludes with the final account of the erection of the *Mishkan*. It mandates the precise placement of the *Shulchan,* table, the *menorah*, and the *Aron Hakodesh.* The entire *parsha* is a study in detail, providing the exact description of each vessel and the specific verbs used to describe each activity necessary for creating these vessels. Examples include: *"and he gave;" "and he placed;" "and he brought;" "and he spread out;" "and he screened."*

Horav Moshe Swift, *z.l.,* notes the *Torah*'s emphasis on each activity. Every man has his own job to perform. One cannot be a silent partner in Jewish affairs. Each person must perform his endeavor of choice to his fullest potential. Some individuals must give, and some must take. Those who can work for the community are mandated to do so.

Everything in Jewish life has its own specified place. The *Shulchan* in the *Mishkan* was the place for the "bread." Bread symbolizes physical needs. The *Menorah*, alluding to faith, was their source of light. The *Aron*, which housed the *Torah*, was representative of *Torah* study and observance. There are so many functions to fulfill in a community. Each member should aspire to develop his G-d given potential to its fullest. Each one must occupy his own unique position within the community structure.

When individuals choose to cross the boundaries of their own designated role, discord arises. The *Chashmonaim*, who descended from the tribe of Levi, were to serve as the spiritual progenitors of *Klal Yisrael.* Instead, they chose to enter the field of monarchy, a position which was designated for the tribe of Yehudah. This resulted in their tragic decimation.

127

How unfortunate is it that in the field of Jewish education everyone perceives himself as the educator par excellence. The unsophisticated and ignorant offer the educator instructions in his profession! Were this to happen in any other profession, the person would be ridiculed. If each of us would seek to excel in our own field of potential, not trespassing the role of others, we would be much happier and more productive members of the community.

***

כי ענן ד' על המשכן יומם ואש תהיה לילה בו לעיני כל בית ישראל
בכל מסעיהם

"For the cloud of Hashem (was) upon the *Mishkan* by day and used to be on it (by) night, before the eyes of all the House of Yisrael throughout their journeys." (40:38)

The importance of the words, *"before the eyes of all Yisrael,"* is indicated by their placement at the end of *Sefer Shemos*. Similarly, at the end of *Sefer Devarim* we find a comparable statement, which concludes the entire *Chumash*. The emphasis is placed upon the fact that this generation has served as eternal witnesses to attest to Hashem's wondrous glory to all future generations. Today we view events of the past through the eyes of that generation. Hashem's power, might, and miracles were demonstrated before a whole nation, not in an isolated place before a select group of witnesses. Consequently, their false spiritual mentors reported many miracles which they claimed were shown to them in private. *Klal Yisrael*, however, was able to identify Hashem's miracles which were performed *"before the eyes of all Yisrael"* -- not in a single incident, but *"throughout all their journeys."*

Horav Avigdor Miller, Shlita, notes that all that happened to that generation has served to guide the ensuing generations with one significant difference. Those acts which were performed publicly for this historic generation were performed secretly in future generations. Hashem is with us wherever we go. The Cloud of Glory and the *Shechinah* are aspects of our relationship with Hashem. What was "seen" by that generation constitutes a model for future generations. Hashem's protective influence over His people will never cease to be a guiding influence. If one only focuses his sense of vision, he will perceive what is obvious.

QUESTIONS LEVEL- A

1. Who was in charge of giving out the different jobs associated with taking care of the *Mishkan* during *Bnei Yisrael's* travels in the desert?

2. What was the first vessel to be brought into the *Mishkan*?

QUESTIONS LEVEL- B

1. Define the words ארבעה טורי אבן?

2. Define the words מכתב פתוחי חותם?

QUESTIONS LEVEL- C

1. How many silver *adanim* were there altogether?

2. On which day of the *miluim* were Moshe and the *Kohanim* sanctified together?

QUESTIONS LEVEL- D

1. A) How many times does the *Torah* mention the name of בצלאל בן בן אורי בן חור? B) Why?

ANSWERS LEVEL- A

1. Isamar ben Aharon.

2. The *Aron*.

ANSWERS LEVEL- B

1. Four rows of stones.

2. Engraved like a signet ring.

ANSWERS LEVEL- C

1. 100, 96 for the *kerashim* and 4 for the *Paroches*.

2. Eight.

ANSWERS LEVEL- D

1. A) Three times. B) To correspond with his 3 attributes: *chachmah, binah,* and *daas.*

ספר ויקרא
Sefer Vayikra

Dedicated by

Steven DeFren
& Daughter Rachel

In loving memory of his mother
Ethel DeFren
עטיל בת שמואל ז"ל

נפ' י"ח שבט תשנ"ג

How does one pay tribute to a mother,
Who lived for others,
Without demanding anything for herself?
She suffered debilitating pain,
But always had a smile for everyone.
Her life was her family,
Her pride was her son,
Her joy was her granddaughter.
Her kindness and sensitivity is a cherished memory.
Her warmth and affection is sorely missed.

May the furtherance of Torah study
be an eternal merit for her soul.

פרשת ויקרא
PARASHAS VAYIKRA
▶◀

ויקרא אל משה
"And He called unto Moshe." (1:1)

The *Midrash* states that Moshe was actually known by ten different names, each describing a different aspect of his multi-faceted personality. Each name depicted a specific trait not implied by the others. Of all the names mentioned, however, the name Moshe, given to him by Bisya, the daughter of Pharaoh, was the one by which Hashem addressed him. A name is an appellation which characterizes a person's personality, a single word which uniquely encapsulates an individual's entire essence. We must, therefore, endeavor to understand why Hashem selected the name Moshe to reign supreme over all the other names. Indeed, the name Moshe is merely a description of the fact that Bisya saved Moshe from drowning. How does this name describe Moshe's essence?

Horav Chaim Shmulevitz, z.l., explains that it is apparent that Moshe's rescue was attributed to Bisya's *mesiras nefesh,* self-sacrifice. She defied her father's decree in order to save a life. Since Moshe's survival was accomplished through Bisya's act of self-sacrifice, this attribute became thoroughly imbued in him. It became an intrinsic part of his personality. Thus, the most fitting description of Moshe's essence was "Moshe," a name which refers to Bisya's selfless act.

There can be no name more suitable for a *Torah* leader than one which conveys the attribute of *mesiras nefesh.* Self- sacrifice for the *Klal,* general population, as well as for each individual, is the crucial attribute essential for successful leadership of *Am Yisrael.* This quality was strongly manifest by Moshe throughout his tenure as *Am Yisrael's* leader.

***

133

(1:1) ויקרא אל משה וידבר ה' אליו מאהל מועד

"And He called unto Moshe, and Hashem spoke to him out of the Ohel Moed."

Rashi explains that this "voice" ceased at the boundaries of the *Ohel Moed*. He adds that this was not because the voice was weak, since it was an amazingly powerful sound. Hashem intercepted this sound so that it would not be heard outside of the *Ohel Moed*. Why did Hashem create such a powerful voice only to miraculously disrupt its emanation?

Horav Y. Neiman, z.l., offers a profound insight into this matter. This voice was not miraculously intercepted, rather, one is required to be within the confines of the *Ohel Moed* in order to hear the voice of Hashem. The sanctity of the *Ohel Moed* provided a unique atmosphere for increased spiritual growth. Consequently, only Moshe -- and not all of *Bnei Yisrael* -- was worthy of this special opportunity. Hashem's voice exists everywhere. One must be attuned to it. The *Ohel Moed* symbolizes any place or any time in which one involves himself in *Torah* study. The holiness emanating from this lofty endeavor so thoroughly permeates one's essence that he is transformed into another person with unique capabilities. He is able to hear the sounds of holiness and to process the Divine message of the Almighty.

***

(1:2) אדם כי יקריב מכם קרבן מן הבקר ומן הצאן תקריבו את קרבנכם

"If a man among you desires to bring a sacrifice near to Hashem, from the cattle, from the herd, and from the flock shall you bring near your sacrifice."

In the *Midrash*, *Chazal* explain the *Torah's* choice of the word "אדם" rather than "איש". They state that one's *korban* must be similar to that of אדם הראשון. As he was the rightful owner of his possessions, his sacrifice was pure and untainted by the stigma of theft. We, too, must take care not to offer a sacrifice which is taken from anything which was unlawfully acquired. This statement is problematic. Obviously, *Chazal* do not use the word "theft" in the usual sense of the word. This meaning could have been derived from the last word of the verse, "your sacrifice." Indeed, the *Talmud* in *Baba Kamma 6b* notes, *"Your sacrifice and not that which is derived unlawfully."* The *Torah* must, therefore, be alluding to a different form of unlawful acquisition -- one which disqualifies the sacrifice, even though the source seems to be trivial.

Horav S. R. Hirsch, z.l., suggests that the word *"adam"* does not refer to man as being "earthborn." This characteristic is applicable to all creatures. *Adam* is related to הדום, *hadom*, which means footstool. This word portrays man as the footstool of the Almighty, the executor of the Divine Glory on earth. As אדמה, the earth is beholden to man whose responsibility it is to guide the earth to its Divinely appointed destiny. Nature's destiny is distorted and doomed to decay if man does not fulfill his task. Although heaven and earth were fully created, the earth remained *"void and empty"* until man, אדם, was to come and stimulate אדמה towards its ultimate perfection.

In his farewell to *Am Yisrael*, Moshe implored the people to be conscious of responding to Hashem's demands. He perceived that his people were in possession of material plenty. He admonished them to take note of the source of the abundance, Hashem. Moshe saw the disaster which would befall those who considered themselves master over their possessions and lords over their own destiny. If the awareness of Hashem's supreme leadership fades from our consciousness, we forfeit our relationship with Him.

Horav Shlomo Breuer, z.l., explains that the delusion of כחי ועוצם ידי - human strength and power - as the source of human possession is blasphemous and ultimately destructive. A person driven by this delusion manifests a form of robbery which, if allowed to germinate, will poison his religious consciousness. The *korbanos* demand that we bring Hashem closer into our lives. This goal is realized when we rid ourselves of the false image of כחי ועוצם ידי. Hashem's proximity arouses the constant awareness within us that *"He is the one who provides your strength."* If we sacrifice that which is "ours," we are actually offering to Hashem that which is "stolen." We cannot pursue Hashem's nearness using material goods which we have "unlawfully acquired" through misguided arrogance.

Hashem demands *korbanos* like Adam's, completely untainted by personal vanity and delusions of power. *Korbanos* are designed to renew the relationship which, at the beginning of Creation, intimately bound man to Hashem. Thus, we understand the admonition at the prelude to the law of sacrifices, אדם כי יקריב. You must seek My nearness by affirming your belief in the source of all material plenty, just as Adam, the bearer of Divinity, did.

***

נפש כי תחטא בשגגה מכל מצות ד' אשר לא תעשנה

"If any one shall sin through error from all of the mitzvos of Hashem that they not be done." (4:2)

This *pasuk* seems enigmatic! This individual transgressed only one sin. Yet, the *Torah* views this infraction as if he had transgressed numerous sins! *Horav Nissan Alpert, z.l.,* suggests the following approaches to this question. One who has attained spiritual nobility, even one who has reached the acme of *Kehunah*, priesthood, the *Kohen Gadol*, is still vulnerable to spiritual transgressions. Such an individual who sins, even in error, reflects that he is yet lacking in spiritual perfection. He is deficient in performing all the *mitzvos* of Hashem. During his moment of spiritual decline, he indicates that he is capable of sinking to the nadir of corruption. When one has not developed spiritually in all *mitzvos*, then he is susceptible to danger. This is the *Torah's* message.

Horav Alpert suggests another interpretation for the *Torah's* use of such all-inclusive terminology. When an individual who serves as a paradigm for others sins, his malevolent actions cause severe repercussions beyond his immediate surroundings. When people see a great man sin, regardless of the particular "sin," they are adversely influenced.

Horav Alpert applies this thesis to explain the sequence of the pasuk, *"If the anointed Kohen shall sin, so as to bring guilt on the people."* The essence of the *Kohen's* sin is its effect on the people and the resulting *chillul Hashem*, desecration of Hashem's Name. Consequently, he must publicly indicate his repentance by personally bringing his *korban* to the opening of the *Ohel Moed* and sprinkling the blood seven times before Hashem. This emphasizes the idea that since his sin was "before Hashem," it can only be purged through public *Kiddush Hashem.* When one is seeking penance for his wrongdoing, he should simultaneously consider the effect his actions had upon others. Only then will his *teshuvah* be complete.

QUESTIONS LEVEL- A

1. The procedure of scooping out the flour is called _____.

2. Which spice is used for a *Minchah*?

3. What must be done to all *korbanos* before being placed on the *Mizbayach*?

4. What type of animal is brought for a *Korban Asham?*

QUESTIONS LEVEL- B

1. Why is the term אדם used regarding the offering of a *korban*?

2. May *melikah* be performed with a knife?

3. Must the pouring of the oil and the mixing with the flour, be performed by a *Kohen*?

QUESTIONS LEVEL- C

1. In which place was *semichah* not permitted?

2. Which *korban* consisted of *chametz*?

3. Which *korban* consisted of *devash*?

QUESTIONS LEVEL- D

1. What are three differences between the *Minchas Bikurim* and the other *menachos*?

ANSWERS LEVEL- A

1. *Kemitzah.*

2. *Levonah.*

3. They must be salted.

4. *Ayil (ram).*

ANSWERS LEVEL- B

1. Just as *Adam Ha'rishon* did not offer a *korban* from something which was stolen (since everything belonged to him), so, too, when one offers a *korban*, it should be only from his own property.

2. No.

3. No.

ANSWERS LEVEL- C

1. On a *Bamah.*

2. The *Shtei Ha'lechem.*

3. The *Bikurim.*

ANSWERS LEVEL- D

1. מנחת חובה, מנחת צבור, שעורים - מנחת ביכורים.

מנחת נדבה, מנחת יחיד, סולת - מנחות.

פרשת צו
PARASHAS TZAV
▶◀

צו את אהרן ואת בניו
"Command Aharon and his sons." (6:2)

Throughout *Sefer Vayikra* we find the expressions, *"Aharon and his sons"* or *"the sons of Aharon"* constantly recurring. Rarely do we find Aharon mentioned seperately. Yet, the *Kohanim* have been able to trace their lineage directly to *Aharon Ha'Kohen.* It was never just Aharon alone; it was always Aharon together with his sons, preserving the link in the chain of our heritage. This is more noteworthy in *Sefer Vayikra* (more appropriately called, *Toras Kohanim*), the book which explains the laws concerning the priestly sacrifices. Sacrifice stands at the foundation of our people. It is at the root of the Jewish family. When we have made the necessary sacrifices, we have been consequently blessed with the successful preservation of our heritage. The father's willingness to sacrifice for his son has been a critical force of endurance for our People.

The *Moreshes Moshe* advances this idea further. There is no purpose in building a *Mishkan* if the Divine command does not apply to father and son alike. The Divine directives are charged to the present and future generations, father and son alike. Of even greater importance is the *parsha's* final *pasuk, "And Aharon and his sons did all the things that Hashem commanded by the hand of Moshe."* It does not say ויעשו - *they did*, in the plural, but ויעש - *he did*, in the singular. It implies that each individual, father and son, on his own initiative did as he was commanded. When Aharon was no longer able to carry out his duty, his sons continued the service.

There comes a time in everyone's life when his activity slows down and eventually ceases. Continuity, however, can be maintained through a successful transmission of the reins from generation to generation. This passage is successfully effected by maintaining a constant relationship between generations, a sharing of thought, spirit and activity. Children do not merely grow up, they are brought up. This "bringing up" of Jewish children is represented by the historic *"olah,"* sacrifice, the burnt offering whose fire has continued to burn on throughout the everlasting night of Jewish history. This fire has been and will continue to serve as our constant source of illumination until the advent of the light of *Moshiach.*

***

והרים את הדשן אשר תאכל האש

"And he shall take up the ashes which the fire consumed the burnt offering on the altar and he shall place them beside the altar." (6:3)

The first task assigned to the *Kohen* every morning in the *Bais Hamikdash* was the removal of the ashes of the previous day's sacrifices from the altar. *Horav M. Shapiro, z.l.,* explains that these ashes were removed, because their cooling effect on the embers prevented the new fire from burning properly. It is prohibited to wield iron on the *Mizbayach*, because iron shortens life, while the *Mizbayach* lengthens it. Likewise, it was necessary to remove anything that smothered the fire which was designated to burn constantly. This also applies to the *Menorah*, whose residue was cleaned out in order to allow a clean bright flame to burn.

Horav Shapiro derives a profound moral lesson from this daily service. A *Kohen*, a descendant of Aharon, was charged with the prime task of reaching out to his Jewish brethren in order to bring them closer to their Father in Heaven. When a person sins, he must bring his sacrifice to the *Bais Hamikdash* where the *Kohen* offers it to Hashem. The sprinkling of the blood, combined with the eating of the *korban's* flesh, helps the person to atone for his sin. Indeed, this is the source of the appellation, *"korban."* It brings a person "closer," *"karov"* to Hashem.

Every Jew has within him a spark of heavenly spirituality. In some individuals this spark is buried beneath many layers of superficial physical domination, repressed by man's base material desires. That small measure of spirituality, the tiny spark of *kedushah*, nonetheless anchors the Jew to Hashem, ultimately enabling him to return from iniquity. Every single Jew harbors that tiny spark of *kedushah.* Everyone has some redeeming quality which constitutes an ember of holiness, waiting to be stoked to eternal brilliance.

The *Kohen* is enjoined to seek out that *"pintele Yid,"* to fan the spark to life. His sensitivity avails each individual the opportunity to pursue eternal bliss. This idealistic goal can only be achieved if the *Kohen* is able to remove the cold ashes of apathy in order to stimulate the Jewish heart and soul, so that the flame from within will burn pure with vigor and brilliance.

***

ולבש הכהן מדו בד

"And the Kohen shall put on his fitted linen garment." (6:3)

Rashi explains that the vestments should fit correctly on the *Kohen*. If they are either too long or too short, they are inappropriate for ritual purposes. *Horav M. Sternbuch, Shlita,* suggests that this concept also applies to other areas of spiritual endeavor. The external garment should be suitable and consistent with the stature of its wearer. The *Rambam* states that those designated elite who dedicate their entire life to *Torah* study are included as honorary members of the tribe of *Levi*. Their devoted service to Hashem represents the loftiest pursuit, parallel to the dedication of the *Leviim.*

Therefore, the *Torah* scholar should be cognizant of his manner of dress. He should refrain from clothing himself in inappropriate attire. His outer garments and grooming should be in consonance with his station in life. Clothing himself in apparel not worthy of his position creates a *chillul Hashem.* Dressing in an arrogant manner demonstrates a haughtiness which is the result of insecurity and diffidence.

We may advance this idea further. Every individual has his own unique characteristics. Consequently, each individual is best suited for those particular positions in life in which he can realize his greatest potential. When someone rejects his own potential by pursuing a profession removed from his stronger qualities, he is denying his G-d-given direction. This could harm the individual, as well as those around him.

People should seek to develop their individual personality to its fullest extent. They should be careful not to assume another's role.

141

Kohanim have a predetermined occupation for which they are specifically suited, as a result of their descendance from *Aharon Ha'kohen*. They are charged to "clothe themselves" in the attire befitting them by remaining dedicated to their Heavenly ordained vocation.

Horav Sternbuch states that the word בד is closely related to the word לבד, which means "alone." This alludes to the *talmid chacham's* mission. He stands alone. He should be aware of the *Torah's* demands upon him and not allow himself to be influenced by those who seek to alter his opinion on a given matter. He must remain resolute and uncompromising in his commitment to Hashem and His *Torah*.

***

ויתן על תנוך אזן אהרן הימנית ועל בהן ידו הימנית ועל בהן רגלו הימנית

"And (Moshe) placed some blood on the right earlobe of Aharon and on his right thumb and on his right big toe." (8:24)

The *Torah* refers to the thumb as *bohen*, while *Chazal* refer to it as the *gudal* because of its thickness (as implied by the word גדול which means large). *Rabbeinu Bachya* notes the specific names which *Chazal* have given to each finger of the hand. He cites *Rashi's* commentary on the *Talmud, Kesubos 5b*, which explains the reason for the name of each finger. Each reason is based upon the finger's specific function reflected in holy endeavor. It is amazing that when *Chazal* identified each finger, they named it in accordance with its holy function. Most people who use each finger for a different holy function are not *Kohanim* Should not a name be given according to its primary use, which is for mundane matters?

The *Mesilos Chaim* explains that the spiritual function of an object is evidently the determining factor in its name. The reason for this is simple. Everything is created for a single purpose, to serve Hashem. Man is here to serve the Almighty and to sanctify His Name with all of his organs and faculties. Consequently, the name of the fingers correspond with their spiritual potential.

PENINIM   *Parashas Tzav*   פנינים

QUESTIONS LEVEL- A

1. After the ashes are removed from the *Mizbayach*, where are they taken?

2. Is the *Korban Chatas* slaughtered in a different place than the *Korban Asham*?

3. What type of *korban* is a *Korban Todah*?

4. What are the *Yi'mei Ha'Meluim*?

5. How many rams were sacrificed in the *Yi'mei Ha'Meluim*?

QUESTIONS LEVEL- B

1. A) What is a *Mincha Chareivah*? B) Who offers it?

2. In which directions is *tenufah* made?

QUESTIONS LEVEL- C

1. What are the four types of bread that are brought with a *Todah*?

2. What is *pigul*?

2. Does the *cheilev* of a *nevailah* become *tamei*?

QUESTIONS LEVEL- D

1. What are the four new *dinim* concerning *Korban Minchah* which are mentioned in this *parsha* which have not been mentioned in *Parashas Vayikra*?

ANSWERS LEVEL- A

1. Outside of the camp.

2. No.

3. A *Korban Shelamim*.

4. The seven days when Aharon and his sons were inaugurated for *Kehunah*.

5. Two.

143

ANSWERS LEVEL- B

1. A) A *minchah* that has no oil. B) A poor man who can't afford a *chatas* (for certain sins only).

2. Back and forth, up and down.

ANSWERS LEVEL- C

1. .מאפה תנור, מאפה תנור רקיקים, חלות רבוכות, לחם חמץ

2. One that brings a *korban* with the intent of eating it after its prescribed time.

3. No.

ANSWERS LEVEL- D

1. 1. It may not be made *chametz*.

2. It must be eaten in the *chatzer Ohel Mo'ed*.

3. It must be eaten by male *Kohanim*.

4. The *dinim* concerning the touching of the *minchah* by any food.

פרשת שמיני
PARASHAS SHEMINI
▶◀

ויהי ביום השמיני קרא משה לאהרן ולבניו

"And it was on the eighth day, Moshe summoned Aharon and his sons." (9:1)

Horav E. Munk, z.l., poignantly explains the significance of that glorious day, the eighth day of the inauguration services. It was *Rosh Chodesh Nissan*, the day the *Mishkan* was erected, a day crowned with ten crowns of distinction. On this particular day, *Klal Yisrael* was to attain an unprecedented level of communion with the Divine Presence. Moshe, however, knew that this exalted state of intimacy would require strict discipline from every member of the nation, especially its leadership. The slightest act of desecration would be punished, even if it were committed by those who were closest to Hashem. The *Mishkan* would be consecrated by a public manifestation of Divine Glory.

Moshe prepared for this moment by taking all necessary precautions. Indeed, the *Midrash* states that Aharon and his sons were sequestered in their quarters for seven days. This was a time for meditation and contemplation. In effect, a ritual parallel to the seven day *shiva* mourning period was observed prior to the death of Nadav and Avihu. Induction into leadership requires concentrated deliberation about its awesome responsibilities. These seven days, a melange of joy and sadness, were to drive home the awesomeness of their next undertaking.

In this mixed atmosphere of trepidation and joy, fear and excitement, the eighth day began for Moshe. The *Torah* denotes these mixed feelings with the word ויהי, which the *Midrash* tells us indicates anxiety and distress. It is the harbinger of bittersweet joy and mixed emotions. The *Midrash* observes that once again the *Torah* illustrates that the righteous are not permitted to savor their happiness here on this earth.

Horav Munk suggests a novel appreciation of the significance of the "eighth" day. He cites *Horav S.R. Hirsch, z.l.*, who, in a thesis on *Bris Milah*, explains that the day following a seven day period has a special meaning. He explains that the number six represents the limited material and physical nature of creation, while the number seven denotes the superiority of the spiritual dimension over the physical. Hence, the number eight suggests the notion of combining the physical with the spiritual into a harmonious relationship. This is the ideal of Judaism: the symbolic merging of the physical and the spiritual in which the physical is totally dedicated to the advancement and growth of the spiritual.

In the present context, the seven day waiting period for the *Kohanim* comprised their preparation for the climax of their lives. The seven day period ended the physical phase of their lives. With the advent of the eighth day, they ceased to be private citizens. They had now attained a higher level of existence, which demanded their consecration to Hashem and His people. On this exalted day, particularly, the *Shechinah* was to appear.

***

ותצא אש מלפני ד' ותאכל אותם

"And there came forth a fire from before Hashem and devoured them (Nadav and Avihu)." (10:2)

The *Midrash* explains that the death penalty had previously been decreed against Nadav and Avihu at the time of *Matan Torah*. At that time, Nadav and Avihu, together with the elders, ascended *Har Sinai* to receive the revelation of the *Shechinah*. Upon experiencing this unique revelation, however, they derived personal pleasure from it and did not respond with proper reverence. They were all judged to be guilty by Hashem. Hashem refrained from meting out their punishment immediately. One reason suggested is that Hashem bestows prophecy only on one who is happy and at peace. Had a national tragedy such as the death of Nadav and Avihu occurred prior to *Matan Torah*, the Jews would have been incapable of experiencing *Matan Torah* in the appropriate manner which they did. Therefore, Hashem postponed their deaths until a later date.

We may question this. Why did Hashem mar the inauguration of the *Mishkan*? Is there not also a requirement for joy during this auspicious occasion? What difference is there between *Matan Torah* and *Chanukas HaMishkan*, when the *Shechinah* came to repose amidst *Klal Yisrael*? *Horav Y. Feigelshtok, Shlita,* responds that in order for *Matan Torah* to have occurred, the quintessence of joy must have pervaded, untainted by even the slightest blemish of sadness. *Torah* study is the most sublime endeavor. Through Torah study, the Jew has the privilege to indulge in Hashem's greatest gift, the lifeblood of our people, the *Torah*. One who studies *Torah* with the appropriate attitude transcends pain, suffering, and frustration. His total immersion in *Torah* study liberates him from the vicissitudes of life and adds to his enduring happiness.

***

ויקחו בני אהרן נדב ואביהוא... ויקריבו לפני ד' אש זרה אשר לא צוה אתם וימותו לפני ד'

"And the sons of Aharon, Nadav and Avihu, took... and they brought before Hashem an alien fire that He had not commanded them." (10:2,3)

The catastrophe which befell Nadav and Avihu is one of the great tragedies of the *Torah*. It begs for explanation. Each in his own way, the various commentators offer an orientation for understanding their sin and its ensuing punishment. *Horav S.R. Hirsch, z.l.,* suggests that they had acted on impulse, in an outburst of enthusiasm. This impassioned act of pride in approaching the altar proved fatal to them.

Joyful emotions, regardless of their sincerity, may not be used to serve as a pretext to break the discipline established by law. Alteration of Hashem's law cannot be tolerated, especially on the part of a *Kohen*. We are not to presume to judge Hashem's *mitzvos* and independently determine the best manner for performing them. To do so would be to disregard Hashem's own guidance as prescribed by His *Torah*. Our duty is to strive to understand His mandate and to apply all of our strength and enthusiasm in order to observe His dictates.

The sons of Aharon were to manifest the epitome of discipline. Had their sin been committed by a less significant person, it would have been perceived as less offensive. One of the hallmarks of a leader is self-discipline and obedience to *Torah* law. When leaders deviate, their sin is much more pronounced.

In a similar vein, the *Chidushei Ha'Rim* shows that the most noble intentions cannot mitigate an act not dictated by Divine command. Although the sons of Aharon thought they were performing a *mitzvah*, it was in fact not commanded by Hashem- אשר לא צוה אותם. A *mitzvah* becomes consecrated by the fact of its Divine origin. Thus, when we perform a *mitzvah* we recite the words אשר קדשנו במצותיו, *"Who has sanctified us with His mitzvos, and commanded us."*

This idea may be extended further. Only *Bnei Yisrael,* who are enjoined to perform these *mitzvos,* will become sanctified through their performance. A humanitarian act of loving kindness elevates the Jew who executes it, because he was ordained by Hashem to perform this act. One who acts out of his own sense of humanitarism, although he may be an honorable person, does not become sanctified through his deed.

***

וכל כלי חרש אשר יפל מהם אל תוכו כל אשר בתוכו יטמא ואתו תשברו

"Any earthenware utensil into whose interior one of them will fall everything within it shall become contaminated and you shall break it." (11:33)

An earthenware vessel can contract impurity only through internal ritually unclean contact. *Horav E. Munk, z.l,.* cites *Rav Mendel Mi'kotzk* who distinguishes between a metallic vessel, whose intrinsic value is based upon the metal from which it is made, and an earthenware vessel, whose value is based upon what it contains. This is the reason that an earthenware vessel is contaminated only from the inside and cannot be purified by immersion in a *mikveh,* as a metallic vessel can. Consequently, an earthenware vessel which has become *tamei,* ritually contaminated, must be broken.

The vessel is like a man formed from the *"dust of the earth."* When man expresses his penitence before Hashem, he perceives himself כחרס הנשבר, to be like a broken earthenware vessel. Man's value comes from what is inside him, his inner essence. A man who renders his soul unclean can effect its purity only through contrition, humility, and a broken heart.

We may advance this idea further. Man serves as a vessel whose intrinsic value is based upon what he contains within him which he shares with others. He is like a pipe which transports goods from one place to another. Man's success in this world is measured by the degree of which he has been a vessel, to serve others. As Hashem is the essence of *"chesed,"* pure altruism, so should man aspire to attain sublime heights of selfless devotion to others. Man, who was fashioned from the earth, should strive to be the ultimate vessel for service to his Creator and his fellow man.

QUESTIONS LEVEL- A

1. What laws was Aharon commanded concerning his hair and clothes?

2. What were the *Kohanim* commanded not to drink before doing the *avodah*?

3. Which two signs must every kosher animal have?

4. How many kosher insects are mentioned in this *parsha*?

QUESTIONS LEVEL- B

1. Why was it necessary for Moshe to prod Aharon to go to the *Mizbayach*?

2. Why is the חסידה given this name?

QUESTIONS LEVEL- C

1. Does the law of נבלה apply to all parts of an animal?

2. When is it prohibited for a person to touch a נבלה?

QUESTIONS LEVEL- D

1. What are the three *Brachos* of the *Kohanim*, and how do they correspond with *korbanos*?

149

ANSWERS LEVEL- A

1. He (and his remaining children) could not do the *avodah* with torn clothes. Also they could not let their hair grow long.

2. Wine (and other alcoholic beverages).

3. Split hooves and chews its cud.

4. Four.

ANSWERS LEVEL- B

1. Because Aharon felt himself unworthy to be the *Kohen Gadol*.

2. Since it performs acts of חסד with members of its own specie.

ANSWERS LEVEL- C

1. No, only to the parts which are edible.

2. During the days of the שלש רגלים, when one comes to Yerushalayim, he must remain on a high level of *kedusha*.

ANSWERS LEVEL- D

1. חטאת - יברכך. עולה - ד' יאר .שלמים - 'ישא ד

פרשת תזריע
PARASHAS TAZRIAH
▶◀

אדם כי יהיה בעור בשרו שאת או ספחת או בהרת... והובא אל הכהן

When a man shall have in the skin of his flesh an intensely white spot, or one nearly so, or a shiny white one... then he shall be brought to the Kohen. (13:2)

The *Netziv. z.l.*. cites the *Zohar*, which states that the word *"adam"* refers to one who is dignified and respected. This statement seems enigmatic. *Tzara'as* is an affliction visited upon one who has spoken *lashon hara* and slandered others. Indeed, *Chazal* say that the word *"Torah"* is written five times regarding *tzara'as,* to teach that one who speaks *lashon hora* transgresses the five *chumashim* - or the entire *Torah!* Why then would the *Torah* refer to this person as an *"adam chashuv"*?

Horav *Nissan Alpert, z.l.,* suggests the following resolution to this question. The *Talmud* provides great detail describing the causes of *tzara'as* in man, clothing and the home. The *Torah,* however, hardly alludes to its etiology. This seems puzzling. Should not the *Torah* have emphasized the root of the sin, so that man would refrain from the dysfunctional forms of behavior which precipitate *tzara'as?* It is even more striking that the sin of *lashon hora* is not even mentioned until *Parshas Kedoshim!*

The greatness of a man is apparently not assessed by whether or not he is plagued with *tzara'as.* Man's stature is commensurate with his ability to learn from his mistakes and to do whatever he can do to rectify his wrongdoing. One who studies proficiently, but does not change his baneful *middos*, achieves nothing. An *"adam"*, man, is esteemed if, when he is stricken with a plague in his body, goes to the *Kohen* for guidance. One who subdues his ego and goes to the spiritual mentor of *Bnei Yisroel*, the *Kohen,* manifests his own respectability. A person's response to punishment is the determining factor of its efficiency.

וראה הכהן בעור הבשר

And the Kohen shall look at the plague in the skin of the flesh
(13:3)

Tzara'as, which is inappropriately translated as leprosy, was actually a spiritual affliction. One who had transgressed certain sins, such as speaking *lashon hora* was inflicted with *tzaraas.* This affliction appeared on one's body, his clothes, even the walls of his home. One who suspected himself of being a victim of this disease would go to the *Kohen* in order to be examined. Only after the *Kohen* declared him a *metzora* would he be considered *tamei* and consequently subject to all of the laws of *tzara'as.*

Horav A. H. Lebovitz, Shlita, cites the *Midrash* which relates a story about an impoverished *Kohen* who chose to leave *Eretz Yisroel* in order to seek a livelihood. After telling his wife about his intentions, he began teaching her the laws regarding *tzara'as,* so that she could substitute for him during his absence. He told her to check the hairs of the afflicted person. Each hair on a person's body is nurtured by its own follicle, which is created particularly by Hashem to sustain the individual hair. If the hair has withered it indicates that the source beneath has dried up. Upon hearing this, his wife exclaimed, "If Hashem sustains each and every hair of the human body, surely He will provide sustenance for you." This naive, but profound, admonishment caused the *Kohen* to reconsider and remain in *Eretz Yisroel.*

Horav Lebovitz questions this *Midrash.* Obviously, the *Kohen* was aware of Hashem's omnipotence, nonetheless, he chose to abandon *Eretz Yisroel* to seek a livelihood elsewhere. What did his wife tell him that precipitated his change of mind?

He explains that one can be aware of a certain truth and even teach it to others, yet still neglect to follow his own teaching. People can acknowledge a reality for others, but fail to apply this knowledge to themselves. The *Kohen* was aware of Hashem's constant providence, yet he did not integrate his reality fully into his life. Had he done so, he would have practiced what he taught.

Why is this? How can someone who is a mentor to others, a ceaseless fountain of knowledge, who is empowered to transmit *Torah* to others fail to reflect upon his own teachings? How often do we inspire others to perform deeds and activities, while we personally are lax in their performance? How do we implore others to believe, trust, and hope for sustenance and salvation, while we are personally diffident?

Perhaps the solution lies in the manner in which one views the vocation and responsibility of teacher. An individual who devotes himself to transmitting the ideals of Hashem's *Torah* to others is a conduit to bring these truths to his people. One can be a vehicle for transmission in one of two ways. He can be like a hollow pipe through which the liquid flows effecting no change upon the conduit; alternatively, he can be like a sponge, into which the liquid is absorbed and subsequently "squeezed" out. The *Torah* one teaches must be completely infused into the teacher. In order to inspire others, he must be a paradigm for his own teachings. His teachings must be reflected in his demeanor, so that one can be properly transmitted to others.

QUESTIONS LEVEL-A

1. Two _____ hairs are a sign of impurity for a *metzora*.
2. A bald spot from the middle of the head until the back of the neck is called _____.

QUESTIONS LEVEL-B

1. How may *yemai tohar* are there after the birth of a boy?
2. How does the *Torah* refer to the spreading of the *nega*?

QUESTIONS LEVEL-C

1. What actions must a *metzora* take that are a signs of mourning?

QUESTIONS LEVEL-D

1. In the *parshios* of *negaim* the word *"Torah"* is mentioned five times. What is the significance of this?

ANSWERS LEVEL-A

1. White.
2. *Karachas.*

ANSWERS LEVEL-B

1. Thirty-three days.
2. *pisyon.*

ANSWERS LEVEL-C

שאילת שלום, כיבוס, עוטה בגדו על שפמו, פריעה, פרימה.

ANSWERS LEVEL-D

1. It corresponds to the five *chumashim* to teach us that one who speaks *lashon hora,* which causes *tzara'as,* transgresses the five *chumashim.*

פרשת מצורע
PARSHAS METZORAH
▶◀

ובא אשר לו הבית והגיד לכהן לאמר כנגע נראה לי בבית

**And the one to whom the house belongs shall come, and he shall
tell the Kohen saying, something like a plague had appeared to
me in the house. (14:35)**

The *Torah* relates a form of disease which can afflict the Jewish
home. The *Torah* refers to this disease as *tzara'as*, a sort of spiritual
leprosy within the walls of the house. The *Torah* details specific
instructions for the *Kohen* and the owner of the house regarding the
procedure for dealing with this "affliction". *Chazal* emphasize the
Torah's choice of the word in the house. Indeed, as they note, *"tumah
is declared only if the rot appears inside the house."* One's internal
life is expected to be in order.

The hypocrisy to which children are sensitive must not exist.
There must be honesty between man and Hashem, between husband
and wife, and between sons and daughters. Children emulate what
they see. What the father does, the son will do. That which the father
refrains from doing, the son will likewise refrain from doing. The
tznius which is reflected in a mother's demeanor will be mirrored by
the daughter. If the inside of the house is strong and pure, no outside
disease will be able to penetrate its walls. The disease only
contaminates from *within,* not from *without.*

To advance this idea, *Moreshes Moshe* notes the opening
pesukim of *Parashas Tazriah,* which deal with childbirth. We notice
that the *Torah* does not initially refer to children as sons or daughters.
Rather they are described as male or female. It is only after the days of
(the mother's) purity are fulfilled, that they become sons or daughter.
In those homes in which charity, prayer, Torah study and community
involvement are the accepted norm, the children are truly the "heirs"
to their parents. When these sublime spiritual endeavors are not
observed in a home, the children remain male and female without any

155

link to the previous generation. Relationships dissipate, and the link is broken. If this does not occur immediately, then it will in due time. When the home is internally pure, our children will continue to remain "our" children.

***

והזרתם את בני ישראל מטומאתם

And you shall separate Bnei Yisrael from their contamination.
(15:31)

The word והזרתם, you shall separate, from contamination is derived from the word נזר, crown. The crown distinguishes its wearer from the masses. The *Sfas Emes* explains, that similarly, *Bnei Yisrael* distinguish themselves by separating from the moral contaminants which abound. It is the true hallmark of *Bnei Yisrael's* majesty that they rise above earthly contamination in order to devote themselves to serving Hashem. Those who dedicate their lives to this endeavor are truly worthy of Hashem's crown.

QUESTIONS LEVEL - A

1. a) How many birds must a *metzora* bring, upon becoming *tahor*? b) How many are slaughtered?

2. a) For how long is the house quarantined the first time? b) What is done if the *nega* has spread?

QUESTIONS LEVEL-B

1. What "good news" was there for the *Bnei Yisroel* regarding *tzara'as habayis*?

QUESTIONS LEVEL-C

1. The *Kohen* is told to place the oil on the מקום דם האשם. What does this mean?

2. What is the meaning of the word והזרתם?

156

QUESTIONS LEVEL-D

1. The *nigei bayis* did not take affect until they came to *Eretz Yisrael*. When did the *nigei adam* start?

ANSWERS LEVEL-A

1. a) Two. b) One.

2. a) Seven days. b) The section of the house that contains the *nega* is removed and new earth and stone is placed instead.

ANSWERS LEVEL-B

1. The Emorim hid their money in the walls of their homes. Since the law of *tzara'as habayis* sometimes require the tearing down of the house these treasures would be found by the Jews coming into *Eretz Yisrael*.

ANSWERS LEVEL-C

1. On the place where blood should be, whether it is there or not.

2. You shall be separated.

ANSWERS LEVEL-D

1. While the Jews were still in the desert.

פרשת אחרי מות
PARSHAS ACHREI MOS
▶◀

כתנת בד קדש ילבש

"A sacred linen tunic he shall wear."

Upon entering the *Kodesh Hakadoshim*, Holy of Holies, the *Kohen Gadol* divested himself of his ornate priestly vestments and clothed himself in simple, white linen. In public, the *Kohen* was responsible to maintain the dignity appropriate to his noble station in life. When he went into the Holy of Holies to confess the sins of *Am Yisrael*, to entreat Hashem on behalf of His people, he entered dressed as an ordinary *Kohen*. At the spiritually heightened moment, the most solemn of the year, the most venerated of men became a simple mortal. The facades of dignity and station in life no longer distinguished him from any other person. This was his moment of truth. All human devices are valueless when man comes in face-to-face confrontation with his maker. This awesome feeling affected the *Kohen Gadol's* entire being, mirrored in his external clothing.

These "sacred" vestments are worn by each Jew as he is placed in his "final" resting place. The body is clothed in white linen shrouds in preparation for the ultimate day of judgment. Before Hashem, all men are the same. The only distinguishing characteristics are the merits of *Torah* study and *mitzvah* performance which an individual has accrued during his lifetime.

***

דבר אל בני ישראל ואמרת אליהם אני ד' אלקיכם

Speak to the Bnei Yisroel and say to them I am Hashem your G-d. (18:2)

These three words, אני ד' אלקיכם *"I am Hashem your G-d,"* preface the chapter which relates the laws of morality. The primary objective of the laws contained in *Sefer Vayikra* is to raise *Am Yisrael* to the

158

spiritual level of a *"kingdom of priests and a holy nation."* Hashem had already mandated laws regarding holiness in the ritual service, man's diet, and spiritual purity. In this chapter, He continued with laws dealing with moral purity.

Horav Eli Munk, *z.l.,* notes that moral legislation, like other types of legal directives, is not based upon social order, physical hygiene, or the instinct for self-preservation. These decrees are presented purely as the will of Hashem. In this spirit, the words, *"I am Hashem your G-d,"* serve as the imprimatur to the beginning and end of the chapter. These words constitute the ultimate justification for the fundamental dictates of moral purity.

Horav S.R. Hirsch, *z.l.,* explains that marital legislation originated in the *mitzvah* of פרו ורבו - *be fruitful and multiply.* Even though our natural physical inclinations would engender the fulfillment of this command, it is nonetheless essential to express it as a <u>Divine</u> command. Marriage is thereby revealed to be far more than a simple sanctification of our instincts. It is elevated to the degree of a national institution, which is far more holy than the mere expression of physical drives. Hashem has commanded us to contribute to the moral development of His world. The guidelines for the successful accomplishment of this task are spelled out by Hashem in this *parsha.*

The *Torah* calls upon *Bnei Yisrael* to divorce themselves from the abominable practices of Egypt and Canaan. *Am Yisrael* receives its most noble distinction specifically in the area of morality. The citizens of the greatest civilization of those times lived completely unrestrained in areas of moral behavior. Indeed, they viewed discipline as an intolerable anathema to freedom of natural expression. For the first time, man was mandated to submit his natural instinct to a higher moral discipline. This discipline serves to consecrate the physical by elevating it to a sublime standard. Progressive spiritualazation of the physical is the essence of *kedushah,* holiness.

***

ושמרתם את חקתי ואת משפטי אשר יעשה אתם האדם וחי בהם

"And you shall guard My laws and My social laws, which if a man will do, he will live thereby, I am Hashem." (18:5)

Horav M. Elan, *z.l.,* offers a novel interpretation of this *pasuk.* The daily routine and lifestyle of some individuals are not consistent with their level of profundity in *Torah* law. They expound great scholarship, citing insightful thought and philosophy, but their actual behavior is consistent with one who is ignorant of the law. The true goal of every person should be that his conduct be commensurate with his degree of sophistication in *Torah* awareness. This is the *Torah's* message. Your shall guard My laws and live by them. Your lifestyle shall reflect your knowledge.

This is especially true when one is seeking to inspire others, particularly children. Nothing is as reprehensible as the sanctimonious exposition of *Torah*. Young people revolt against double talk. One must practice that which he preaches, if he wants theory to extend beyond the hypothetical to become reality.

QUESTIONS LEVEL-A

1. On what day of the year was Aharon commanded to do all of the *avodos* that are described in this *parsha*?

2. a) What must be done to the blood of a beast or a fowl after *shechitah*? b) What reason does the *pasuk* give for this?

QUESTIONS LEVEL-B

1. Which sin was atoned for by the שעירי חטאת?

2. What does the *Torah* imply by saying אני ד'?

QUESTIONS LEVEL-C

1. Where did the *tevillos* that the *Kohen Gadol* performed on *Yom Kippur* take place?

2. In which situation may one who divorced his wife marry her sister?

QUESTIONS LEVEL-D

1. The numerical value of השטן is _____? What does this represent?

ANSWERS LEVEL-A

1. *Yom Kippur.*

2. a) One must cover their blood. b) Since the *nefesh* is in the blood.

ANSWERS LEVEL-B

1. It atoned for those who mistakenly entered the *Mikdash* while they were in a state of *tumah*.

2. I am trusted to pay each person the reward which they deserve.

ANSWERS LEVEL-C

1. The first *tevilah* was done in the "*chayl*" outside of the *Azarah*. The next four *tevillos* had to be made in a *makom kadosh* on the roof of the *Bais Ha'paravah*.

2. Only after his ex-wife's death.

ANSWERS LEVEL-D

1. The numerical value of השטן is 364 which represents the days of the year that the שטן is מקטרג. On *Yom Kippur* the *Satan* has no power to do harm to the Jews.

161

פרשת קדושים
PARASHAS KEDOSHIM
►◄

דבר אל בני ישראל ואמרת אליהם קדושים תהיו

"Speak to the entire assembly of Bnei Yisrael and say to them be holy." (19:2)

Rashi explains that this *parsha* was proclaimed *"b'hakhel"* because the majority of the fundamental laws of the *Torah* are dependent upon it. All of *Klal Yisrael* assembled to read this *parsha*, while many other *mitzvos* focus on specific groups, such as *Kohanim, Leviim,* firstborns, or males, the principle of *kedushah,* holiness, pertains to all members of the Jewish community. Each member of *Bnei Yisrael* is enjoined to work towards this goal to the best of his capabilities.

Horav E. Munk, z.l., advances this idea. The presence of the entire community signifies that the ideal goal of holiness can be achieved only through the collective efforts of all *Klal Yisroel.* Although each individual is able to ascend to a high degree of holiness, his personal effort is of only relative importance. The majority of the basic laws of the *Torah* require the participation of the whole community. These *mitzvos* include the communal *korbanos,* the duties of social welfare to the community, *Shmittah, Yovel,* and the gatherings of Jews during the three *Yamim Tovim.* Members of *Klal Yisrael* cannot achieve perfection in isolation or solitude: it requires interaction with one another. *Horav Y. Neiman, z.l.,* offers another approach to understanding the need for the entire assembly to gather for the proclamation of קדושים תהיו. He cites the *Zohar* which states that this *parsha* was a source of great joy to the scholars who studied it. Why? He responds that one may think that only select individuals have the opportunity to ascend to the lofty degree of holiness expected by the *Torah.* This is not true! Everyone has the potential to achieve this apex. One must work and toil to reach for this goal. This is the reason that all of the Jews assembled together. The message is clear and applicable to everyone. One must only endeavor for this goal, and he will attain it.

QUESTIONS LEVEL-A

1. What reason is mentioned in the *Torah* for the command that the Jews be holy?

2. What is the meaning of the word מדה?

QUESTIONS LEVEL-B

1. What is a *shifchah charufah*?

2. a) May one walk into the *Mikdash* with dirt on his foot? b) From where do we learn this?

QUESTIONS LEVEL-C

1. What is the deeper meaning of ולפני עור לא תתן מכשול ?

2. What specific form of persecution does the *Torah* mean when it says regarding a *ger*?

QUESTIONS LEVEL-D

1. Which negative commandment in this *parsha* corresponds with the ninth commandment of the *Aseres Hadibros*?

ANSWERS LEVEL-A

1. Since Hashem is holy He wants the Jews to also be holy.

2. Measurement.

ANSWERS LEVEL-B

1. A women which is half a *shifchah* and a half a *bas chorin* who is betrothed to an *eved Ivri*.

2. a) No. b) It says "*one should fear the Mikdash*" and treat it with respect.

ANSWERS LEVEL-C

1. Do not give improper advice.

2. Do not poke fun of him or remind him of his past.

ANSWERS LEVEL-D

1. לא תלך רכיל בעמך - לא תענה

פרשת אמר
PARSHAS EMOR
▶◀

ויאמר ד' אל משה אמר אל הכהנים בני אהרן ואמרת אליהם
לנפש לא יטמא בעמיו

"And Hashem said to Moshe speak unto the Kohanim, the sons of Aharon, and say unto them, none shall make himself unclean through contact with the dead." (21:1)

The *Kohanim* were admonished not to come in contact with the dead, since this would render them unfit to perform the *avodah*. This rule was relaxed only in a situation which involved close relatives. *Chazal* explain the redundancy of the word אמר ואמרת by stating that it was a special directive to the *Kohanim* that the adults must instruct the young. It seems enigmatic that the *Torah* places emphasis upon teaching the young, while specifically discussing contact with the dead.

We suggest that there is a special message to be gleaned from this *pasuk*. During moments of personal grief one tends to become absorbed with the loss he has sustained. This proclivity is recognized by the *Torah*. Human weaknesses and personal sentiments often take over our entire perspective on life during moments in which we confront human mortality. We may be inclined, however, to forget about the living during such times of emotional stress. We may become less focused upon the children and deprive them of adult supervision, while we attend to our own immediate needs.

We have a propensity to be so involved in burying the dead that we neglect to maintain control over the living. We tend to say *"Kaddish"* for the deceased and neglect to say *"Kiddush"* for the living. We spend money for monuments, rather than on education of the young children. This is the *Torah's* message: even in your deepest grief, do not neglect the young. We must never fall victim to the clutches of depressive reactiveness. Our devotion to *Torah* should highlight our commitment to provide for the future.

164

This idea is especially relevant during these days of *Sefiras Ha'omer*. *Rabbi Akiva's* twenty four thousand students perished during this period. The terrible disaster would have destroyed a lesser man than *Rabbi Akiva*. His life's work, his academies of *Torah* learning, the ultimate future of *Klal Yisrae*l, were all destroyed! The *Torah* was virtually in danger of being forgotten! Who would be the *Torah* teachers? The world would be in a tragic state.

Moreshes Moshe explains *Rabbi Akiva* did not allow himself to become a victim of despondency. He did not accept that it was all over. He moved to the south to establish new schools and to develop new students, who would bring the beacon of *Torah* to the world. The greatest fear of our people has been that *Torah* might be forgotten. Ignorance has always been an even greater fear than oppression. If ignorance and illiteracy prevail, we will have a beautiful world with no character and no structure, a beautiful home with neither moral values nor ethical standings. We will become a people who neither pray nor study, who have no sense of direction or self-control.

Rabbi Akiva did not surrender to his grief. He went forward to build for the future. This was the same force which drove those who came to these shores to build *Torah* schools from the ashes of the European Holocaust. These heroes, whose indomitable spirits helped them to transcend their grief and reestablish *Torah* study, brought with them new light into the overwhelming darkness of Jewish life. The commitment of parents to *Torah* education during those critical times can well serve as an inspiration for their children and grandchildren today. When pleasures were rare and comforts scarce, they managed to gather whatever monies were required to pay for their children's *Torah* education. We, too, must endeavor to ensure that the *Torah* will reign eternal throughout the vicissitudes of life, so that our future, the young children, will be guaranteed a strong and vigorous Jewish community.

***

וספרתם לכם ממחרת השבת ...שבע שבתות תמימות תהיינה

"And you shall count for you from the morrow after shabbos seven complete sabbaths (weeks) it shall be." (23:15)

Horav S.Y. Zevin, z.l., offers a novel homiletic exposition of this *pasuk.* When one counts something, he indicates his esteem for the particular object. Indeed, at the beginning of *Sefer Bamidbar, Rashi* states that *Hashem* counted *Bnei Yisrael* a number of times because of His great love for them. The days and years of one's life should likewise be important in one's eyes. One should value every moment of life and appreciate its true meaning, *"so that we do not struggle in vain nor produce for futility" (Isaiah 65:23).* Those moments which have passed are no longer accessible to us. Therefore, every moment should be reckoned and cherished.

   "Seven complete sabbaths it shall be." This *pasuk* alludes to the days of our lives, as stated in *Tehillim 90:10 "The days of our years, among them are seventy years."* Consequently, one should "count" his days to demonstrate his respect for the passage of time. There are, however, two ways to count. One can count his own money, or he can count money which belongs to another person. Obviously, one who counts his own money does so with concern and excitement, since he is dealing with his personal property. One who counts another's money, however, will do so complacently, without emotional attachment, because he has not contributed to this wealth, it has no meaning or value to him. Man can count the days of his life apathetically or he can count them prudently, conscious of their value and worth. We are enjoined to *"count for you,"* as if this counting is for you and no one else. We must show our appreciation of the greatest gift from *Hashem,* life itself, and seek to take advantage of every moment granted to us by dedicating our days to the service of *Hashem.*

***

ולא תחללו את שם קדשי ונקדשתי בתוך בני ישראל

"And you shall not desecrate My holy Name, and I should be sanctified among the Bnei Yisrael." (22:32)

The *pasuk* contains the solemn admonition against profaning Hashem's Name, as well as the positive precept to sanctify His Name. The *Torah* commands us to sanctify and exalt Hashem's Name by the very nature of our moral conduct. The passive application of *"Kiddush Hashem"* through martyrdom is also implied. We are mandated to sanctify His Name through life and through death. This *mitzvah* is to become an inherent component of our personality. Such supreme

166

dedication to Hashem had been a beacon of inspiration to us throughout the generations.

In our own times, during the period of the Holocaust, the spiritual resistance to the bestial decrees of the sadistic Nazis, the courage expressed by our people in living as well as dying with dignity, should be recorded and remembered in detail. The dedication of the believing Jews, who summoned up an incredible and invincible reservoir of commitment to *Hashem* and His *Torah,* was the true "Jewish resistance." Because of their total devotion to Judaism, their sense of pride in being the *Am Ha'Torah,* these individuals were able to face life and death in the ghettos with dignity and serenity. *Halachah* encompassed every aspect of their life. Even in their last moments, they confronted death with an amazing sense of *emunah* and ecstasy as they performed *"Kiddush Hashem. "*

The Piazesner Rebbe, *z.l.,* observed that he who is murdered in *Kiddush Hashem* does not suffer at all. His anticipation of dying *"al Kiddush Hashem"* elevates all of his senses to the point that his material being is dissolved of itself. He, therefore, feels not pain, but rather the joy of fulfilling this *mitzvah.* In the *Sefer Kedoshim,* the *Slonimer Rebbe* cites the *Zohar,* observing that *Hashem* dyes His "garment" in the blood of martyrs who perish *"al Kiddush Hashem."*

Horav N. Alter, *z.l.,* emphasized that the imperative of *Kiddush Hashem* may assume various forms, but central to this *mitzvah* is the admonition not to degrade ourselves before the gentiles. A Jew must live life and face death with the dignity becoming one who is cognizant of the Divine component in man. This awareness stimulates the Jew's trust in *Hashem* and inspires him with the courage to carry on, despite all odds, the heritage and legacy bequeathed to him.

***

ויצא בן אשה ישראלית והוא בן איש מצרי... ויקב בן האשה הישראלית

את השם ויקלל...ושם אמו שלומית בת דברי

"And the son of an Israelite woman went out... and he was the son of an Egyptian man. And the son of an Israelite woman pronounced the Name of Hashem and blasphemed... and the name of his mother was Shlomis Bas Divri..." (24:10,11)

Horav S.R. Hirsch, z.l., notes that the *Torah* mentions the mother's name only after the son had sinned. Prior to his sin, he is referred to simply as *"the son of an Israelite woman."* The *Torah* mentions the mother's prior immorality in light of the sin performed by the son. Without the mother's immoral behavior, such an outbreak of un-Jewish depravity would never have occurred. Shlomis' anonymity would have been secured. After her son's transgression, however, it became evident that only the mother's immoral relationship with an Egyptian could have nurtured such miscreant behavior among *Klal Yisrael.* The horror of the son's crime provided evidence that the mother was the actual source of this evil.

How piercing are these words! One can go through life performing evil, scorning and ridiculing the framework of *Torah* law, only to have his illicit behavior highlighted in his child's dysfunctional behavior. One may think he has deceived the world by veiling his actions with a facade of piety. His iniquities, however, will become apparent through his child's baneful activity, which will return to haunt and castigate him.

On a more positive note, our good deeds and proper behavior transmit valuable attitudes to our children. They learn to replicate our blessed ways. Although it may not always be readily obvious, a parent's exemplary devotion to *Torah* and *mitzvos* will be imbued in his children enabling them to carry on his legacy.

QUESTIONS LEVEL- A

1. What is the *halachah* regarding a *Yisrael* that eats *Terumah b'shogeg*?

2. May a Jew bring a blemished *korban*?

3. Which two *matnos aniyim* are mentioned in this *parsha*?

4. What type of oil was used for the *Ner Tamid?*

QUESTIONS LEVEL- B

1. If a *Kohen* marries a women that is forbidden to him, their child will be a _____.

2. What is done with a *baal mum* that can not be sacrificed?

QUESTIONS LEVEL- C

1. Is the removal of *peyos ha'zakan* with a tweezer or scissors prohibited?

2. A) May a *Kohen onan* eat *Terumah?* B) From where do we derive this?

QUESTIONS LEVEL -D

1. Why does the *Torah* not state לדורותיכם regarding the fast of *Yom Kippur?*

ANSWERS LEVEL- A

1. He must pay *keren v'chomesh.*

2. No.

3. *Leket, peah.*

4. Pure olive oil.

ANSWERS LEVEL- B

1. *Chalal* or *Chalalah.*

2. It is used as a *nedavah* for the *bedek habayis.*

ANSWERS LEVEL- C

1. No, only a razor is prohibited.

2. A) Yes. B) It says, *"Only a zar is excluded from Terumah."*

ANSWERS LEVEL- D

1. Since at the *chanukas ha'bayis* of the first *Bais Hamikdash* they didn't fast.

פרשת בהר
PARASHAS B'EHAR
►◄

שש שנים תזרע שדך ושש שנים תזרע כרמך...
ובשנה השביעית שבתון יהיה לארץ

"Six years you shall sow your fields and prune your vineyards...
but on the seventh year there shall be a solemn Shabbos for the
earth." (25:3)

We may note the *Torah's* sudden change in focus. It begins by
addressing its words towards the individual farmer, but closes with an
admonition directed generally towards the entire Jewish people. We,
as a nation, must see to it that the *Shmittah* mandate is observed.
Indeed, we can derive multi-faceted lessons from *Shmittah*.

Horav Shimon Schwab, z.l., observes that *Shmittah*
symbolizes *mesiras nefesh,* self-sacrifice. It personifies the apex of a
Jew's courageous dedication to Hashem's command. A man who owns
a parcel of land becomes intimately attached to it. He toils in
back-breaking work in order to eke out his living from it. Yet,
suddenly he is asked to divest himself of this source of livelihood for
an entire year, in order to allow all Jews and all animals to "trespass"
on his pride and joy. Why? Because it is Hashem's command. This is
true heroism!

Second, *Shmittah* attests to the entire Jewish People's belief
that Hashem "owns" the land. We demonstrate publicly that we are
surrendering our control and ownership of the land. We must even
renounce whatever outstanding debts are owed us. Through *Shmittah*
observance, we indicate our faith and trust in Hashem. We do not
worry while the land lies fallow. Our trust is resolute, our faith
unshaken.

Third, *Shmittah* is a testimonial to *Klal Yisrael's* uniqueness.
Hashem has established a covenant with *Klal Yisrael,* elevating them
to a unique stature. From the *Shmittah* experience, we perceive the

exceptional relationship we are privileged to have with Hashem. Throughout every aspect of our laws, we sense the Divine providential protection accorded to us. How true are the words of the *pasuk*, "*Who can be compared to Your nation Yisrael, one people on the earth (DH1 17:21)?*" Our relationship with Hashem is like that of no other nation. We should remember that this holy alliance brings with it monumental obligations for trust and faith in Hashem.

***

וקראתם דרור בארץ לכל ישביה

"You shall proclaim freedom throughout the land to all its inhabitants." (25:10)

This *pasuk* refers to the *mitzvah* of freeing Jewish slaves at the beginning of *Yovel*. The *Torah*, however, does not seem to address only the slaves. The enjoinment quite clearly speaks about all inhabitants. The vast majority of Jews were not slaves! The *Pnei Yehoshua* suggests the following idea. One who enslaves others is himself a slave. He is subservient to his own egotistical desire to dominate others. This is alluded to by the statement in the *Talmud Kiddushin 20a*, "*One who purchases a Jewish slave in reality acquires a master for himself.*" He who enslaves others, becomes enslaved himself. Consequently, one who emancipates his slave is, in reality, freeing himself.

One must respect the rights of others and not attempt to encroach upon their freedom. One who attempts to control others reflects his own negative self-image. The need to malign others is a desperate attempt to mask one's own insecurity. The need to obtain a feeling of superiority is manifest by those who surround themselves with individuals inferior to themselves. It is truly a sad statement about an individual, if the only way that he can maintain his self-esteem is through the subjection of others who are powerless to defend themselves.

The *Torah* teaches us that true freedom is effected only when all men are free, when the dignity of all people is respected by all, and when the underprivileged are not disdained and violated.

171

QUESTIONS LEVEL- A

1. Where did Hashem instruct Moshe in the laws of *Shmittah*?

2. A) Does an *eved Ivri* go free during *Yovel*? B) Does an *eved Canaani* go free during *Yovel*?

3. Which sin does the *Torah* discuss at the end of the *parsha*?

QUESTIONS LEVEL- B

1. A) How many cities comprised the *Arai Ha'Leviim*? B) What other name did "some" of these cities have? C) How many of these cities were also called by the second name?

2. A) What is the meaning of the phrase להשתחוות עליה? B) Is this type of *avodah* permitted when it is done for Hashem?

QUESTIONS LEVEL- C

1. If the various *Shmittos* were not observed, is the *Yovel* still declared?

2. From where is the term *Yovel* derived?

QUESTIONS LEVEL- D

1. Why were the *Arai Miklat* part of the *Arai Ha'Leviim*?

ANSWERS LEVEL- A

1. Har Sinai.

2. A) Yes. B) No.

3. *Avodah Zarah.*

ANSWERS LEVEL- B

1. A) 48 cities. B) *Arai Miklat.* C) Six.

2. A) This is an *avodah* consisting of laying down on the ground and stretching forth one's hands and feet. B) This *avodah* is permitted only in the *Bais Hamikdash*.

ANSWERS LEVEL- C

1. Yes.

2. It is derived from the blowing of the *shofar* at the beginning of the fiftieth year. The word *Yovel* means horn.

ANSWERS LEVEL- D

1. It is only logical that a city which is inhabited by such holy people as the *Leviim* should be an appropriate place for refuge and atonement for the unintentional murderer. Furthermore, in a city in which the temperament reflects mercy and peace, forgiveness and sympathy, the refugee will be more readily accepted.

פרשת בחקתי
PARASHAS BECHUKOSAI
▶◀

ואשבר מטת עלכם ואולך אתכם קוממיות
"And I have broken the bars of your yoke and made you go upright." (26:13)

Rashi cites the *Midrash* which explains this blessing with two words, with בקומה זקופה, "erect stature." *Horav M. Shternbuch, Shlita,* expounds on this concept. There are individuals who, although they are observant, tend to deny their compliance with Hashem's *mitzvos.* Consequently, they mask their *mitzvah* performance and attempt to conceal their allegiance to the *Torah.* These individuals disguise authentic observance with artificial excuses. They are moral cowards who lack the courage of their convictions, demonstrating a lack of pride in their heritage. They are fearful that, due to their commitment to Judaism, they will be viewed as different. This perception might taint their social status. The *Torah* teaches us that *mitzvos* must be performed with dedication. When *Klal Yisrael* discharges *mitzvos* properly, they will merit a sense of worth to stand dignified, exalted in transmitting the banner of *Torah.*

***

להפרכם את בריתי
"To break My covenant." (26:15)

Rashi explains this refers to כופר בעיקר, one who will eventually deny the basic tenets of religion or the existence of Hashem. This commentary does not seem consistent with the sequence of the text. After the *Torah* enumerates various punishments to befall those who sin, it states: *"And if after all this you will [still] not listen to Me and walk contrary to Me (בקרי)"* (26:27). *Rabbeinu Yonah* characterizes קרי as one who dismisses the punishments as "accidental" happenings, which are not relevant to him at all. According to the text, this sin is even more egregious than the previous ones. This seems enigmatic! Is there a more reprehensible sin that denying the existence of the Creator? One who denies Hashem's existence will surely dismiss His punitive measures as merely random occurrences!

Horav Yechezkel Levinstein, z.l., suggests that the concept of כופר בעיקר applies to anyone who deviates from total dedication to the Divine. A Jew must place his complete trust in Hashem and not in any other ideology. This was indicated by the sin of the Golden Calf. *Bnei Yisrael* were seeking an intermediary to replace Moshe. The concept of an intermediary is blasphemous. Hashem is a personal G-d, Who responds directly to each individual without any displacement.

Anyone who does not have absolute total faith in Hashem is tainted by the stain of כופר בעיקר. Thus, one who dismisses Hashem's punishments is essentially reinforcing his blasphemous beliefs.

***

לא מאסתים ולא געלתים לכלתם

"I will not have been revolted by them, nor will I have rejected them to obliterate them." (26:44)

The *Zohar Hakadosh* suggests a special meaning for this phrase. Instead of the word לכלות, "to obliterate," he reads it as the word כלה, "bride," drawing the following analogy. A wealthy man was seen walking through a very poor section of a hostile land. When questioned regarding his whereabouts, he responded that he was searching for his bride-to-be. Indeed, when she appeared, the whole street took on a different appearance in his eyes. Even the air took on a sweet fragrance for him. So, too, Hashem will not reject us when, like an impatient bride, we await Him during our exile in strange lands.

QUESTIONS LEVEL- A

1. A) What is the *erech* of a male between the ages of twenty and sixty years old? B) What is the *erech* of a female between the ages of twenty and sixty years old?

2. What is done in the event the *ma'arich* is poor and does not have the required amount for the *arochin*?

3. A) How is the value of a *sadeh mikneh* estimated? B) Must the owner add a *chomesh* upon redeeming this type of field?

QUESTIONS LEVEL- B

1. When is it necessary to confess the sins of one's father?

2. A) What does one have to add to the value of *maaser sheni* when he redeems it? B) Does this apply when one redeems a friend's *maaser sheni*?

QUESTIONS LEVEL- C

1. To what does the phrase ושברתי את גאון עזכם refer?

2. What is the *halacha* regarding one who is *makdish* the leg of an animal as an *olah*?

QUESTIONS LEVEL- D

1. When the *Torah* mentions the blessing of rain, what is the meaning of גשמיכם "your rain"?

ANSWERS LEVEL- A

1. A) Fifty *shekalim*. B) Thirty *shekalim*.

2. We place the one to be evaluated before the *Kohen* and he is evaluated according to the means of the giver.

3. A) According to the value of the harvest to be expected for the remaining years until *Yovel*. B) No.

ANSWERS LEVEL- B

1. When the sons continue in their father's way of doing *avairos* and follow his example.

2. A) He must add a *chomesh*. B) No.

ANSWERS LEVEL- C

1. The destruction of the *Bais Hamikdash*.

2. The animal must be sold as an *olah*, and the monies realized by its sale are *chullin* and are returned to the owner with the exception of the value of the leg.

ANSWERS LEVEL- D

1. It is a reference to the rain of *Eretz Yisrael* that it will be blessed while the surrounding lands will suffer from drought, thus forcing them to purchase food from *Bnei Yisrael*.

ספר במדבר
Sefer Bamidbar

Dedicated by
Charles and Debbie Zuchowski and Family

in loving memory of his mother
Sara Zuchowicki

שרה בת לייב ע"ה
נפ' י"ג אב תשנ"ה

Her sensitive smile would light up a room.
Her indomitable faith would overcome
the greatest obstacles.
Her warm personality touched everyone
who knew her.
Her encouragement gave us the
confidence to perservere.
Her guidance directed us on the right path.
She was our mother, our mentor
and our best friend.

May her legacy of love and faith for Yiddishkeit
remain forever imbued in our children.

פרשת במדבר
PARASHAS BAMIDBAR
▶◀

וידבר ד' אל משה במדבר סיני

"And Hashem spoke to Moshe in the wilderness of Sinai." (1:1)

The *Midrash* states that the *Torah* was given through the media of fire, water, and wilderness. The commentators differ in communicating the message of this *Midrash. Horav M. Shapiro, z.l.,* suggests that these three elements reflect the magnitude of *Klal Yisrael's* devotion to Hashem to the point of their self-sacrifice.

Fire alludes to the fiery caldron into which Avraham *Avinu* was thrown because of his staunch belief in Hashem. This, however, only illustrates self-sacrifice on the part of the <u>individual</u> Jew. Water, which symbolizes *Klal Yisrael's* passage through the Red Sea, represents our unwavering devotion to Hashem as a <u>whole nation.</u> Yet, these two examples alone still do not provide sufficient proof of *Klal Yisrael's* loyalty. Surrounded by threatening animals, *Klal Yisrael* travelled in a wilderness devoid of nourishment for forty years. Throughout this period, they displayed their <u>constant,</u> unstinting love for Hashem. *Mesiras nefesh,* which is demonstrated by this threefold pattern of individual, collective, and constant devotion to Hashem, is evidence of the strength of our nation's bond to Hashem.

***

וידבד ד' אל משה במדבר סיני

"And Hashem spoke to Moshe in the wilderness of Sinai." (1:1)

Chazal note an integral relationship between the *"midbar,"* wilderness, and the *Torah*. Much of the *Torah's* narrative takes place in the wilderness. The *Torah* itself was given in the wilderness, a point which *Chazal* emphasize frequently. It is, therefore, appropriate that the *Torah* reading immediately prior to *Shavuos*, the festival of the giving of the *Torah*, is *Parashas Bamidbar*. *Chazal* suggest many explanations for this connection.

Horav S.R. Hirsch, z.l., expresses a simple, but profound, idea regarding the *Torah's* ideology in forming the framework of each Jew individually and *Klal Yisrael* as a unified entity. Hashem chose the barren, free pastures of the unclaimed wilderness, yet untainted by human involvement, for *Matan Torah.* Far removed from the decadent societies of nations and cities, the wilderness set the model stage for the new foundation, which was to be supported solely by Hashem. In the desert, unencumbered, Hashem gave the *Torah* to *Klal Yisrael.* In the desert, where everything was structured from the ground up, *Klal Yisrael* received their mandate and mission.

Torah law is to be the basis of a Jew's whole essence, his entire perspective, his every movement. It is not sufficient for the *Torah* to reach man when he has attained maturity -- or society when it has already been established. The work of *Torah* begins at the origin for all earthly existence. Its sphere is the entire process of planting and nourishing nature. From its inception, all of human nature must be engendered, sustained and nurtured to fulfill the Divine requirements of morality and justice. Thus, human nature will develop the capacity to serve Hashem in purity and holiness.

The place which Hashem designated for the giving of the *Torah* communicates an important message regarding the *Torah's* status in the life of its people.

***

וימת נדב ואביהוא לפני ד' בהקריבם אש זרה... ובנים לא היו להם

"And Nadav and Avihu died before Hashem when they offered a strange fire ... and they had no children." (3:4)

The *Midrash* states that had Nadav and Avihu taken wives and had children, they would not have died. The *Chasam Sofer* explains that innocent children have the need to receive proper guidance from their parents. It would, therefore, have been in the children's merit that Hashem would have granted the parents life. *Chazal,* however, state other reasons for Nadav and Avihu's tragic deaths. Two reasons which are emphasized are: Nadav and Avihu's entrance into the *Mikdash* after having drunk wine; and their inappropriate rendering of a *halachic* decision in the presence of Moshe, their *rebbe.* These latter two reasons do not seem to coincide with the above stated *Midrash*!

The *Chasam Sofer* suggests that, indeed, the reasons can be reconciled. In fact, Nadav and Avihu's lack of sensitivity in showing proper reverence to the *Mikdash* and to their *rebbe* was a direct result of not having had children. In order for one to become sensitive to a specific orientation, he needs to experience it. One does not truly grasp the essence of respect for one's father and *rebbe* until he himself fathers children or teaches them. Only then can he comprehend the importance of proper esteem for a parent and mentor. A parent's reaction to his child's lack of respect delivers a message in terms of the parent's own self-evaluation. Nadav and Avihu had not yet been availed the opportunity to learn first-hand the significance of respect. Consequently, this inexperience led to their own insensitivity towards Hashem and Moshe.

Heightened sensitivity regarding one's children can sometimes have a negative effect. Some parents delude themselves by attempting to relive their own lives via their children. Negative feelings and experiences one has had as a youth can have a traumatic influence. This effect can be transferred to children via the parents' demands of them. Parents have an awesome responsibility in raising children. They must inculcate positive feeling and aspirations into their children, while allowing them to mature unencumbered by the parents' own inadequacies and negative self-images.

***

ויפקד אתם משה על פי ד'

"And Moshe counted them according to Hashem's word." (3:16)

Horav Moshe Swift, z.l., notes a disparity between the census of *Bnei Yisrael* and that of *Bnei Levi. Bnei Yisrael* were counted from age twenty and over, thereby facilitating an easy count. *Bnei Levi,* who were counted from age one month upwards, demanded a more difficult count. The *Midrash* emphasized this by noting that Moshe asked, *"How can I enter their tents to determine the number of babies in each family?"* Hashem responded, *"You do your share, and I will do mine."* The *Midrash* continues that Moshe stood at the doorway of each tent. The *Shechinah* preceded him, and a Divine voice emanated from each tent stating the number of babies therein. This is the hidden meaning of our *pasuk*. Hashem's word facilitated Moshe's census.

There is a profound message to be gleaned from this *Midrash*. In order for Moshe to count *Bnei Yisrael* <u>outside</u> <u>of</u> the house, the *Shechinah* must first have penetrated inside the house. If Jewish children are to be included, if they are to be numbered as the ones who carry the yoke of *Torah* on their shoulders, then the *Shechinah* must precede each child's birth. The voice of Hashem must be heard from within the home. The *Shechinah* must totally permeate the atmosphere of a child's upbringing. This begins with his parents' own personal relationship, which should be ensconced in sanctity and purity. It continues on in a home in which prayer, *Torah* study, and *mitzvah* performance are integral components of the lifestyle. The establishment of such a home is the only guarantee that the children will continue to be counted as proud members of *Klal Yisrael*.

***

אלה משא בני קהת

"These things are the burden of the Bnei Kehas." (4:15)

The *Midrash* illustrates the moral superiority of the *Leviim* by citing the difference between the footwear each wore. While members of the other tribes wore sandals, the *Leviim* who were responsible for carrying the *Mishkan* and its vessels, walked barefoot. *Chazal* also observe that the virtuous *Bnei Kehas,* the actual transporters of the *Aron*, walked backward, so that they did not turn their back on the *Aron*. This *Midrash* demands explanation. While walking barefoot and backward are noble ways to express reverence to the *Aron*, these acts do not demonstrate the *Leviim's* unique virtue.

In order to clarify this *Midrash*, comments *Horav Y.A. Sher, z.l.,* we must first comprehend the rationale behind the divergent practices exhibited by the *Leviim*. We note that the imperative to perform the service while standing barefoot applied only to the *Kohanim*, in order to eliminate the separation between them and the floor of the *Bais Hamikdash*. Indeed, the *Leviim*, who carried the *Aron* in the desert, were permitted to wear sandals. The *Leviim* chose, however, to go barefoot because of their extreme sensitivity regarding the honor due the *Aron*. For example, if during the transporting of the *Aron* a strap on a sandal tore, the individual would unwillingly be compelled to halt his service in order to fasten his strap. It was devotion such as this that was the hallmark of the *Leviim's* virtue. When *Bnei Kehas* walked backward, they similarly exhibited a sense of trust and faith in the *Aron's* "ability" to transport its supporters (והארון נושא את נושאיו). The moral superiority of the *Leviim* originated in their boundless devotion to the service of Hashem.

QUESTIONS LEVEL- A

1. What were the heads of each tribe called?

2. Which two words does the *Torah* use to designate a tribe?

3. Which tribes camped to the west of the *Mishkan*?

4. How many *Leviim* were counted?

5. Who covered all the vessels of the *Mishkan* prior to their being transported by the *Leviim*?

QUESTIONS LEVEL- B

1. How were the Jews counted?

2. What was the punishment for a Jew who came forth to do the *avodas Ha'Leviim*?

QUESTIONS LEVEL- C

1. Who carried Yaakov *Avinu's* coffin on the east?

2. A) Which tribe was counted while yet in the womb? B) Why was this?

QUESTIONS LEVEL- D

1. A) Whose *degel* combined the colors of all the *degalim*? B) What was his emblem?

ANSWERS LEVEL- A

1. *Nasi.*
2. *Shevet, Mateh.*
3. Ephraim, Menashe, Binyamin.
4. 22,000.
5. Aharon and his sons.

ANSWERS LEVEL- B

1. By means of a half-*shekel.*
2. מיתה בידי שמים.

ANSWERS LEVEL- C

1. Yehudah, Yissachar, Zevulun.
2. A) Levi. B) Yocheved who was born while Yaakov's family entered the gates of Egypt, was nonetheless counted among the seventy souls who came to Egypt.

ANSWERS LEVEL- D

1. A) Binyamin. B) Wolf.

פרשת נשא
PARASHAS NASO
▶◀

והתודו את חטאתם

"And they shall confess their sins." (5:7)

The *mitzvah* of *"viduy,"* confession, is the prime prerequisite for performing *teshuvah*, repentance. Indeed, without *viduy* the *teshuvah* process has no value. It is puzzling that the *Torah* chooses to mention the *mitzvah* of *viduy* specifically at this point, in reference to the sin of stealing.

The *Chidushei Ha'Rim* explains that actually every transgression committed by man consists of a form of theft. We have been granted life, health, and the ability to perform actions, so that we may serve the Almighty. To employ these G-d given abilities in behavior which violates *Torah* law is tantamount to theft. Not only do we demonstrate ingratitude for all that we enjoy, but we also disdain its true purpose. This is the reason that the *Torah* inserts the requirement of *viduy* in the *pesukim* dealing with theft. While repenting for any violations of the *Torah*, we must concurrently recognize that we have illegally made use of Hashem's gifts to us. With this awareness in mind, our resolution for the future will be realistic, so that proper *teshuvah* can be effected.

***

והביא האיש את אשתו אל הכהן והביא את קרבנה עליה עשירית האיפה
קמח שעורים לא יצוק עליו שמן ולא יתן עליו לבונה

"And the man shall bring his wife to the Kohen and shall bring her offering for her, the tenth part of an eifah of barley meal, he shall not pour upon it any oil, nor pour frankincense on it."
(5:15)

Rashi cites the *Talmud Sotah 12a*, which explains the reason for the specific ingredients of this *korban*. Meal was used instead of fine

185

flour, barley rather than wheat. This modification was due to the repulsiveness of the *sotah's* immoral act; because she acted like an animal, her offering is the food of an animal. Oil is not poured over the meal, since oil symbolizes light and the *sotah* acted in darkness. Frankincense is not placed on the *korban*, since the Matriarchs are referred to as *"levonah,"* frankincense, and she deviated from their paths.

Horav B.Z. Baruk, z.l., makes a noteworthy observation from this *Talmudic* statement. Man thinks that one who serves Hashem in a lackluster manner will be indicted by the Heavenly Tribunal according to his level. Hashem, however, will not admonish him for not attaining the lofty heights reached by *Torah* luminaries. One does not demand of an individual who desecrates *Shabbos* or eats non-kosher that he become like the *Chofetz Chaim*!

This perspective is entirely misdirected! Regardless of one's abysmal degree of spirituality, Hashem will judge him not only for his repulsive transgressions, but also for not attaining the sublime degree of service to Hashem evidenced by the Patriarchs! Man has the ability to reach the loftiest heights of spirituality, to climb to the zenith of *mitzvah* performance and *avodas* Hashem. He will ultimately have to answer for his lack of compliance.

This is *Chazal's* message. On the one hand, the *sotah* is reprimanded for acting as an animal. At the same time, however, she must answer for not being like the Matriarchs! This is consistent with the *Rambam's* statement in *Hilchos Teshuvah,* "Every one must say, 'When will my actions reach those of Avraham, Yitzchak, and Yaakov?'" How fortunate is one whose spiritual aspirations exceed his grasp.

***

וזאת תורת הנזיר ביום מלאת נזרו

"And this is the law of the Nazir, on the day of the completion of his vow." (6:21)

At the conclusion of term of the *Nazir's* vow, he must bring a *korban*. The reason for this *korban* is enigmatic. Is not a *korban* of this nature brought as penance for a specific sin? Rather than the *Nazir* be lauded for his great deed, he is seemingly castigated! *Rabbeinu Bachya* explains that this *korban* is necessary, since it appears as if the *Nazir* is departing from his previous lofty relationship with Hashem. For a significant period of time, he was removed from the pleasures of this world, only to return to his previous lifestyle. Although his lifestyle had been respectable, it was not to the same standards as a *Nazir*. This is unacceptable, from an appearance orientation. Therefore, a *korban* is mandated.

Horav A.H. Lebovitz Shlita, derives a profound insight from the above explanation. We see that even when our actions are definitely within the framework of *Torah* law, the mere semblance of impropriety is in itself a sin. *Rabbeinu Bachya* teaches us that behavior which seems wrong, although in reality may not be, is still improper and demands penance.

This concept reveals a new perspective regarding the far-reaching effect of our every action. Everything we do leaves its impression upon us. If one performs with even the slightest impropriety, it will eventually harm him. As the *Am Hashem*, our mandate is to be an *Am Kadosh*. In order to achieve that goal, everything we do, the way we speak, our manner of dress, and how we eat, must reflect consistency with our aspired station in life.

***

ביום השני הקריב נתנאל בן צוער נשיא יששכר ...הקריב את קרבנו

"On the second day did offer Nesanel ben Tzuar, the Nasi of (the tribe of) Yissachar . . . he presented for his offering." (7:18,19)

Rashi notes the redundancy of the word הקריב, offered, regarding the tribe of Yissachar. In contrast, it is not doubly stated in reference to any of the other tribes. *Rashi* cites different explanations to resolve this question. *Horav M. Wolfson, Shlita,* offers a novel response. Nesanel represented the tribe of Yissachar, which was noted for total devotion to *Torah* study. Indeed, this was their vocation. Their material support came from the tribe of Zevulun, their "partners" in *Torah* endeavor. This "partnership" could easily cause the ignorant bystander to think that Yissachar, in fact, did not possess anything of his own. Everything which was his, in reality, came from his brother.

The *Torah* seeks to correct this misperception by placing an emphasis on the ownership of Nesanel's *korban*. The *Torah*, therefore, repeats the phrase, *"He offered his korban."* Nesanel offered his own *korban.* One must be cognizant that everything originates from Hashem. He gives more to some individuals as a deposit until the time has come for him to share it with his friend. Zevulun, who so nobly supports Yissachar, is actually "returning" Yissachar's portion. That which Yissachar offers to Hashem is truly his own, which Zevulun has been safeguarding for him.

This concept is extremely important to reflect on, especially for those *Bnei Torah* who have chosen to devote their life to *Torah* study and dissemination. An almost paranoid feeling regarding their lifestyle pervades many *Torah* scholars. They feel that, since they are being supported by others, they do not have the privilege to enjoy a lifestyle even remotely similar to that of their supporters. This is utter nonsense! The Yissachar-Zevulun relationship is the paradigm for a partnership in which each member has his individual responsibility. Yissachar must devote his time and energy to *Torah* study, while Zevulun takes care of his material needs. Undoubtedly, Yissachar must be acutely aware of his obligations to devote all of his efforts to *Torah* study as his part of this partnership. The success of the relationship is nurtured in the mutual respect these two partners have for one another and their unique reciprocal obligations to each other.

***

ובבא משה אל אהל מועד לדבר אתו וישמע את הקול מדבר אליו

"And when Moshe went into the Ohel Moed that he might speak with Him, and he heard the voice speaking to him." (7:89)

Rashi points out that the word מדבר, "speaking," is similar to מתדבר, "in the *hispa'el"* form (reflexive form of the intensive stem of the Hebrew verb), implying that Moshe heard the voice of Hashem speaking to Itself. The *Sforno* expands on this idea, suggesting that Hashem *"makes it known to Himself"* and that the voice heard by Moshe was in reality an "overflow" of Hashem's words. This is similar to the voice which every *Navi* receives, each according to his own individual level of perception. Although the words of the *Sforno* are of a profound nature, an important lesson can be derived from this mode of communication between Hashem and Moshe.

Horav E. Shach, Shlita, suggests the following lesson to be derived from the *Sforno*. Anyone who imparts knowledge, be it a parent or teacher, must first become thoroughly imbued with this knowledge. Only after one is diligent in personally acquiring the information and making it an integral part of his own life can the lesson which he imparts leave an everlasting impression upon the student. An exemplary example is that when our *Torah* leaders impart *mussar* they preface their talk by saying that they are also speaking to themselves. This is the *Torah*'s perspective on the true manner of teaching.

QUESTIONS LEVEL- A

1. The *Leviim's* service was from age _____ until age _____.

2. Is a female who has *tzaraas* sent out of the three camps?

3. How does the *Torah* refer to the water which the *sotah* must drink?

4. Which tribe offered the second *korban* for *Chanukas Ha'mishkan*?

QUESTIONS LEVEL- B

1. Which individual who is *tameh* is excluded only from *machane Shechinah*?

2. Why isn't *levonah* put on the *Minchas Sotah*?

QUESTIONS LEVEL- C

1. A) Who was in charge of *Bnei Kehas*? B) Who was in charge of *Bnei Gershon* and *Bnei Merari*? C) What was the reason for this change?

2. Do the *halachos* regarding a *sotah* apply to a woman whose husband is blind?

QUESTIONS LEVEL- D

1. A) Which *parsha* has the most *pesukim*? B) Which *parsha* has the least *pesukim*? C) Which *perek* in *Tehillim* has the most *pesukim*? D) Which *maseches* in *Talmud Bavli* has the most *dafim*?

ANSWERS LEVEL- A

1. 30, 50.
2. Yes.
3. Bitter water.
4. Yissachar.

ANSWERS LEVEL- B

1.One who is *tameh nefesh.*
2. The Matriarches are referred to as *levonah*, and the *sotah* deviated from their path.

ANSWERS LEVEL- C

1. A) Elazor. B) Isamar. C) Elazor was in charge of anything pertaining to the *Kodesh Ha'kadoshim*, while Isamar supervised everything else.
2. No.

ANSWERS LEVEL- D

1. A) *Naso.* B) *Va'Yelech.* C) *Perek* 119. D) *Bava Basra.*

פרשת בהעלותך
PARASHAS BEHA'LOSECHA
▶◀

על הצר הצורר אתכם והרעתם בחצצרת

"Because of the enemy that beseiges you you shall sound the trumpets." (10:9)

The *Rambam* in *Hilchos Taanios (1:1-3)* states that it is a positive *mitzvah* to cry out to Hashem and sound trumpets in response to any disaster which befalls a community. He cites the above *pasuk* as the source for this *mitzvah*. This reaction to tragedies is, in fact, one of the first steps leading to effective *teshuvah,* repentance. We are enjoined to contemplate our troubles, since they are a vehicle by which Hashem communicates His message to us.

In his famous thesis on the Holocaust, *Horav Y. Schwartz, Shlita,* states that this command to search our ways renders it incumbent upon us to explore the recent annihilation of a third of our nation. This terrible tragedy was by no means just another disaster!

He writes that the *mitzvah* of contemplation is a fundamental one, which is one of the *Yesodos Ha'Emunah,* foundations of our faith. He cites the *Rambam* in *Perush Ha'mishnayos*, introduction to *Perek Chelek,* who teaches that Hashem not only knows our deeds, but He is also intimately involved in our affairs. To contemplate our daily events means to delve into the way Hashem involves Himself and interacts with us. This deliberation into *Hashgachas Ha'Boreh,* Divine Providence, strengthens our faith in Him.

In matters of *emunah* it is not sufficient to simply acquire intellectual awareness which may be incompatible with the logistics of life. In matters of faith, abstract knowledge is not sufficient. Rather, one's faith must permeate every facet of his daily perspective. Complacency can drain the lifeblood of our faith. A Jew must believe wholeheartedly that every occurrence of his life is ordained and controlled completely by Hashem. Nothing is coincidental or attributable merely as a part of the natural order of the world. This perception is developed through a total immersion in Hashem's *Torah*, through which one becomes intimately aware of Hashem's Divine Providence.

Since it is our obligation to seek out a rationale for every harsh decree which befalls us, it certainly behooves us to contemplate the Divine decree of the Holocaust. To deny its significance is a *chillul Hashem*, desecration of Hashem's Name. It is not within the scope of this thesis even to attempt to reflect upon this travesty. The purpose is only to emphasize our obligation to come to grips with the tragedy -- not to ignore its message because of the drastic ramifications. We can only study the narrative of the unspeakable events that occurred. By viewing them through the perspective of Divine Providence, we will begin to grapple with their implications. Thus, we will be able to internalize this realization into our psyche, so that our trust in Hashem will be strengthened.

***

ויסעו מהר ד'

"And they travelled from the mountain of Hashem." (10:33)

In *Shabbos (116a)* the *Talmud* interprets this *pasuk* to mean, *"They ceased to follow after Hashem and veered away."* *Tosfos* explains that they left *Har Sinai* *"like a child who races from the classroom at the end of the day."* This seems enigmatic! Were they not to follow the *Aron Ha'Kodesh* when it travelled? What was their sin? Indeed, the *Ramban* states that had this not happened, they would have merited immediate entrance into *Eretz Yisrael*. Certainly, the mere fact of departing from *Har Sinai* was not considered inappropriate. On the contrary, they were travelling towards their goal, entrance into *Eretz Yisrael*.

Horav M. Gifter, Shlita, offers a profound insight into the concept of one's total immersion in *Torah* study. This explanation sheds light upon *Bnei Yisrael's* sin in leaving *Har Sinai* with the wrong attitude. *Bnei Yisrael* were camped before *Har Sinai* as one would be firmly esconsed in a *Bais Ha'Midrash*. When they were commanded to leave their encampment, they should have risen up and left reflecting the same spiritual intensity with which they sat studying

Torah in Hashem's "classroom." In contrast with their sublime level of exposure to Hashem, however, their attitude in leaving *Har Sinai* was indicative of a *"child running from the classroom."* A child is excited as he waits to leave the disciplined framework of the classroom. He eagerly awaits the moment when he is dismissed to go outside to play. When he returns, it is a new beginning. The learning is not the same as before the interruption.

This is the *Torah's* message. A *Ben Torah* must take the *Bais Ha'Midrash* with him wherever he goes. There is no "recess" from *Torah* study. Even a momentary relaxing of the strict discipline of *Torah* immersion can lead to a spiritual downfall, as noted from the subsequent sins committed by *Bnei Yisrael*. Had they not been guilty of this "lighthearted" attitude when turning away from Hashem, they would have been worthy of entering *Eretz Yisrael* immediately. We should be careful to make the fiery passion which burns within us in the *Bais Ha'Midrash*, the discipline and self-control which governs us in the *shul*, an integral part of our lives wherever we go.

***

ויהי העם כמתאננים רע באזני ד'... ותבער בם אש ד' ותאכל בקצה המחנה

"And the people were as murmurers in the ears of Hashem... and the fire of Hashem burned among them and consumed them at the edge of the camp." (11:1)

והאספסף אשר בקרבו התאוו תאוה וישבו ויבכו גם בני ישראל

"And the mixed multitude that was among them lusted and there wept again also the Bnei Yisrael." (11:4)

The *Torah* attributes two sins to *Bnei Yisrael*. There is a definite relationship between the מתאננים act and the ensuing sin of the אספסף Indeed, *Chazal* interpret the *pasuk "Bnei Yisrael began to weep again"* to teach us that the participants in the *"misonenim,"* evil, were also *Bnei Yisrael*. *Horav S. Breuer, z.l.,* examines these two sins and discuss their connection with one another.

The one word, *"k'misonenim,"* *"as murmurers,"* seems to encapsulate the entire scope of their sin. *Chazal* offer two views of this travesty which seem to result from the concept of *"k'misonenim."* *Rashi* explains that *"misonenim"* represents *Bnei Yisrael's* excuse to sever their allegiance to Hashem. Proponents of the alternate view

193

posit that they were mourning their "terrible" lot in life. These two perspectives employ contrasting orientations. Regarding the sin of *"asafsuf,"* the *Torah* states that fire consumed "*at the edge of the camp.*" Once again, *Chazal* express two views. One perspective suggests that the members of the lower social realm were consumed, and the second approach indicates that the fire consumed the rich and noble. We suggest that these two opposing views regarding the nature of the *"asafsuf"* correspond with the divergent opinions regarding the interpretation of the *"misonenim."*

Regarding the search for an excuse to defect from Hashem, *"misonenim"* refers to the lowest among the people as the active perpetrators of the act of desertion. During the course of Jewish history, many movements have arisen which have attempted to seduce the people away from Hashem. These traitors have never attempted to reveal their contempt for Judaism by overtly propagating rebellion against Hashem. Such an open display of treason was never an abject fear for Judaism. The rebellious movements have always concealed their disdain with "excuses." These hidden motives have served to attract their fellow Jews to their "cause" without revealing the true nature of their destructive plans. This was also true regarding the *"misonenim."*

The view which presents the *"misonenim"* as complainers who sought excuses attributes their characteristics to the lowest level of the people. These abysmal characters hid their goal. Their influence was based completely upon their ability to conceal their true objective, total abandonment of Hashem and the way of life He chose for us. The Divine fire which consumed the *"edge of the camp"* was, therefore, directed toward the lowest of the Jews.

The other interpretation presents *"misonenim"* as a form of mourning over oneself and one's lot. Although Hashem's loving care freed the people from worry concerning their daily sustenance, their trek in the desert deprived them of many of the comforts which make life attractive. This obviously refers to the rich and noble who had been accustomed to material pleasures and complained about their deprivation. They were weary of their constraints and "mourned" over their fate. Their selfish and immature attitude was reflected by the act of *"asafsuf."*

האנכי הריתי את כל העם הזה

"Have I conceived this entire nation?" (11:12)

The *Sforno* explains Moshe's statement in the following manner. A father can guide his sons even when their opinions differ. This is due to the sons' perception that their father love's them. Therefore, the sons attribute positive motivations to the fathers' leadership. *Klal Yisrael,* however, did not trust Moshe. They were suspicious of his behavior. This lack of trust undermined Moshe's attempts to effectively lead *Bnei Yisrael.* In his unparalled humility, Moshe reinforced his perception of his shortcomings and inability to evoke *Klal Yisrael's* trust.

The *Sforno* offers an invaluable lesson in education, which is applicable both to the home and the classroom. Evoking the trust of a child is an indispensable prerequisite for success. There is no surrogate for love and the reciprocal respect it engenders in a child towards his mentor. Indeed, the honor we owe our children and pupils is vital. The educator who dismisses a child as "bad" restricts his ability to help make the child a better person. One who does not harbor a good opinion of his charges will reflect his personal conviction in his interaction with them, compromising his chances for success.

Horav S.R. Hirsch, z.l., writes that gentleness and kindness enable the development of the firmness needed to guide a child. Teachers who show no consideration for the personal dignity of their pupils and who demand respect by coercion will quickly watch their efforts result in a failure. A child has a mind of his own and seeks to assert his individuality.

We must always demonstrate the love we maintain for our children and pupils. Their moral frailties must be viewed as temporary weaknesses, which can be overcome. When we give up our aspirations for our students, they will certainly lose hope, too. Our own courage can stimulate their courage, and our hope can uplift them. Our cheerfulness can inspire within them the serenity which can alone foster mental and spiritual growth. This can only occur when the child senses that his mentor loves and respects him.

QUESTIONS LEVEL- A

1. Which word does the *Torah* use to describe the act of "lighting" the *Menorah*?

2. How did Moshe know the correct design for the *Menorah*?

3. Whom did the *Leviim* replace in serving in the *Mishkan*?

4. A) What "covered" the *Mishkan*? B) How did this appear at night?

5. A) How many *chatzotzros* were there? B) Of which material were they made?

QUESTIONS LEVEL- B

1. Why did the *Leviim* bring a *Korban Chatas* upon their induction?

2. Which event precipitated the *bechorims'* consecration to Hashem?

QUESTIONS LEVEL- C

1. After the age of ___ the *Levi* was to cease performing the *avodah*. What was he still permitted to do?

2. What was Eldad and Meidad's prophesy?

QUESTIONS LEVEL- D

1. A) The *Torah* is divided into _____ books? B) What are they?

ANSWERS LEVEL- A

1. בהעלתך.

2. Hashem showed it to him.

3. *Bechorim.*

4. A) Pillar of cloud. B) Fire.

5. A) Two. B) Silver.

ANSWERS LEVEL- B

1. To effect penance for the *bechorim* who sinned with the Golden Calf.

2. Killing of the first-born in Egypt.

ANSWERS LEVEL- C

1. 50, closing the gates, singing, and loading of the wagons.

2. They said, "*Moshe will die and Yehoshua will be the next leader.*"

ANSWERS LEVEL- D

1. A) Seven. B) *Bereishis, Shemos, Vayikra, Bamidbar* until *Vayehi-Binsoah*, the *parsha* of *Vayehi-Binsoah*, after *Vayehi- Binsoah* until the end of *Bamidbar, Devorim.*

פרשת שלח
PARASHAS SHELACH
▶◀

שלח לך אנשים ויתרו את ארץ כנען

"Send out men for you that they may scout out the land of Canaan." (13:2)

Rashi cites the *Midrash* which questions the juxtaposition of the chapter discussing the spies upon the chapter dealing with Miriam's speaking *lashon hora* against Moshe. It states that the *Torah* sought to emphasize the spies' iniquity. They saw the punishment meted out to Miriam for slandering Moshe, and they, nonetheless, spoke *lashon hora* against *Eretz Yisrael*. They should have heeded the lesson inherent in Miriam's punishment.

Horav Chaim Shmulevitz, z.l., derives from this *Chazal* that Hashem's punishment is presented as a corrective measure, rather than punitive. It is Hashem's way of communicating displeasure with an individual's deeds and a warning to the recipient to mend his ways. Thus, the spies were held accountable for having witnessed Miriam's punishment for a deed similar to theirs, yet not taking the lesson to heart. He states this is the reason that punishment is meted out *"middah k'neged middah,"* measure for measure. Its purpose is to avail one the opportunity to become cognizant of his sin and to improve himself in the relevant areas.

The purpose of punishment is not to afflict the recipient, but rather to demonstrate to the sinner the area in which he is remiss. Regrettably, man sees that which he desires to see. It is a human tendency to rationalize and justify even the greatest miscreancy. Indeed, even after punishment, the sinner will attribute his punishment to another "mistake" he has committed.

Horav Shmulevitz, z.l., tells the following story in conjunction with his thesis. The wife of a famous *Torah* personality of the previous generation happened to differ with her husband regarding the suitability of a prospective son-in-law for their daughter. Although this prospective groom was a great *Torah* scholar, he limped. The physical impediment was a point of consternation for this woman. One morning while she was bringing a glass of warm milk to her husband before *shacharis*, she slipped and broke her leg. She felt this was Hashem's punishment to her for serving her husband a drink before his prayers. She could not bring herself to admit the real reason for her punishment. Rather, she substituted an honorable deed.

From the chapter of the spies and the condemnation against them for failing to take personal note of Miriam's punishment, we derive that one must learn a lesson even from another's punishment. Miriam's illness should have served as an object lesson for the spies. Indeed, it is easier to accept a personal lesson by viewing it through the perspective of another's affliction, since one's own personal vested interests can veil the truth. May we merit to be among those who reflect upon the focus of rebuke and accept its intended lesson.

***

ויקרא משה להושע בן נון יהושע

"And Moshe called to Hoshea Ben Nun, Yehoshua." (13:16)

The *Midrash* explains that Hashem took the *"yud"* of שרי and added it to הושע to form a new name, יהושע. *Horav Nissan Alpert, z.l.,* states that this attachment to Sarah was by specific design. In order for our people to conquer and rule *Eretz Yisrael*, it was necessary for Yehoshua to be imbued with Sarah's *hashkafa*, philosophy. Sarah emphatically expressed her opinion regarding the proprietorship of *Eretz Yisrael*. It belongs to *Bnei Yisrael* and to no one else. With determination and resolve, she demanded of Avraham, *"Cast out this maidservant and her son, for the son of the maidservant shall not inherit with my son with Yitzchak" (Bereishis 21:10).* Yishmael and his descendants have no portion in *Eretz Yisrael*!

Hashem chose Yehoshua to assume the leadership of *Bnei Yisrael* in order to guide them through the entrance into *Eretz Yisrael*. He was admonished not to deviate from Sarah's demand. *Eretz Yisrael* is ours, and we are not permitted to give away any portion of it to Yishmael's descendants. This concept applies as much in our day as it did in those times.

We may suggest another thought. By her words as well as her actions, Sarah implied the need for maintaining a pristine environment, untainted by the harmful influence of Yishmael. She implored Avraham to raise their child in a protected surrounding, conducive to the sublime education he would receive. She understood that Yitzchak's *Torah hashkafos* must be developed in a pure environment, completely detached from any outside influences.

This was the message to Yehoshua. He needed to stand resolute and maintain indomitable faith and trust in Hashem in the face of dissenting views from the other factions of *Bnei Yisrael.* In order to do so, he was responsible for immersing himself totally in the *Torah.* The juxtaposition of outside influences would taint his perspective. Just as it was true then, it is all the more relevant in contemporary society in which the harmful influences of the outside environment can so easily undermine our sense of values.

***

ויקרא משה להושע בן נון יהושע

"And Moshe called Hoshea Ben Nun, Yehoshua." (13:16)

Rashi cites the *Midrash* which states that Moshe pronounced a prayer over Yehoshua, *"May Hashem deliver you from the counsel of the spies."* Why did Moshe pray only for Yehoshua and omit his loyal companion Calev? Perhaps Yehoshua's close relationship with Moshe singled him out, so that the spies suspected him of sympathizing with his *rebbe,* Moshe. Calev, on the other hand, was of the rank and file, whose true sympathies could be concealed until a propitious moment. Indeed, this afforded Calev the opportunity to boldly speak up against the multitude in support of Moshe. This later earned him the Divine appellation of "*ruach acheres,*" another spirit.

Chazal interpret *"ruach acheres"* to imply that Calev played a double role. He told the spies that he was one of them, while his intentions were clearly sympathetic to Moshe. *Horav M. Swift, z.l.,* explains that people sometimes feel that the only way to silence the opposition is by acceding to their point of view. This is an effective approach only when the individual is convinced that he will emerge triumphant. Calev ascribed to this theory and succeeded. In no way does this technique give one license to lie. It is merely a statement of

200

fact. Their lives were in danger; the future of *Bnei Yisrael* was in danger. Such extenuating circumstances demanded a "creative" orientation. Yehoshua, the future leader of *Bnei Yisrael,* could not even momentarily deviate from his exalted position. His word must never be doubted; his associations and his deeds must always remain laudable. Consequently, Moshe felt the necessity to pray to Hashem for increased protection for Yehoshua.

***

ויאמרו כל העדה לרגום אתם באבנים

"And the whole congregation said to stone them with stones."
(14:10)

The *Talmud* in *Sotah 35a* says that they never aimed the stones at the men, rather they threw them in the direction of Heaven. There seems to be a dispute about what occured - were the stones originally aimed at Heaven? Or, rather, did Hashem's Cloud of Glory descend and "catch" the stones? We may suggest a homiletic rendering of this *Chazal. Bnei Yisrael* chose to hurl stones at their leaders, because of their "dissenting" views. They did not realize, however, that hurling "stones" or other epithets at *Gedolei Yisrael* is tantamount to hurling stones at Heaven! Our *Torah* leaders are Hashem's emissaries, and we must accord them the reverence consonant with this lofty station. This is referred to as *Kavod Ha'Torah*, respect for the *Torah.* Echoing the events of that fateful day, Hashem will always protect His devoted emissaries in their time of need.

We may be so bold as to suggest that in many cases the intent of those hurling "stones" at religious authority is -- in reality-- to cast aspersion upon the Almighty. Their moral cowardice restrains them from blatantly exposing their animosity towards Judaism and its tenets. Once again, these loathsome remarks will receive their response from Hashem. The codes and doctrine of Judaism are Hashem's mandate. The defamation of the *Torah* or its disseminators is reflective of an intention to sever relations with Hashem.

***

במדבר הזה יפלו פגריכם

"In this desert shall fall your carcasses." (14:29)

Several commentators question the justification of the severe punishment of *Bnei Yisrael.* Indeed, the report the spies presented was a direct and accurate response to Moshe's inquiries. Their only mistake was their <u>own</u> judgmental assessment of what they had seen, suggesting that *Bnei Yisrael* would be unable to successfully invade the land. They simply expressed their opinion!

We may suggest the following idea. *Bnei Yisrael* were taken out of Egypt and until now Hashem had well provided for them. Moshe was their leader, specifically chosen for this position by Hashem. The assessment of the given situation should have been made by their leadership. They were merely to deliver the facts and wait for a response. This is the meaning of *"emunas chachamim,"* trust in *Torah* scholars. The *"Daas Torah,"* *Torah* decision, which they render is the only decision which should be the determining factor in resolving a problem. The negative assessment of the spies and the ensuing tragedy could have been prevented had they trusted in their *Torah* leadership.

QUESTIONS LEVEL- A

1. Why were the *meraglim* sent to *Eretz Yisrael?*
2. Did the *meraglim,* in any way, speak well of the land?
3. Did any of the *meraglim* feel that the land could be conquered?
4. What is given from the dough to the *kohen?*
5. Why was the *mekoshesh eitzim* placed under guard?

QUESTIONS LEVEL- B

1. Which part of *Eretz Yisrael* was considered the worst?
2. Who were the *Nephillim?*
3. Was the *mekoshesh* warned?

QUESTIONS LEVEL- C

1. What sign did Moshe give the *meraglim* for ascertaining the strength of the land's inhabitants?
2. How long should it have taken the *meraglim* to traverse the land from east to west?

3. Why are t*zitzis* worn only on a <u>four</u> cornered garment?

QUESTIONS LEVEL- D

1. A) On which day were the *meraglim* sent out? B) Which day did they return? C) On which day did they die?

ANSWERS LEVEL- A

1. To evaluate the strength of the people and land.

2. Yes, they said "it flows (with) milk and honey and its fruit was special."

3. Yes, Yehoshua and Calev.

4. *Challah.*

5. It was not clear <u>which type</u> of execution he warranted.

ANSWERS LEVEL- B

1. The southern part (*Negev*).

2. They fell from Heaven during the generation of Enosh.

3. Yes.

ANSWERS LEVEL- C

1. If they lived in open cities they were strong.

2. 40 days.

3. The four corners correspond with the four *leshonos* of *geulah* terms of redemption .

ANSWERS LEVEL- D

1. A) *Sivan* 29. B) *Av* 9. C) *Elul* 7 or *Elul* 17.

פרשת קרח
PARASHAS KORACH
▶◀

ויקח קרח
"And Korach took." (16:1)

The *Targum Onkelos* interprets Korach's "taking" as *"and Korach separated (himself)."* The *Sfas Emes* applies this concept in the following manner. In *Tana D'vei Eliyahu 25, Chazal* teach that one must always strive to attain the standard established by his ancestors. He must always ask himself, *"When will my actions reach those of my ancestors?"* One who is consistent in this self-expectation demonstrates the motivation which is so essential for continued spiritual development.

The *Sefas Emes* cites *R' Simcha Bunim of Paschischa* who states that the behavior of a Jew must be in consonance with that of the Jews throughout the ages. When one lives a traditional Jewish life, he thereby becomes a part of the continuum of Jewish life. He, in turn, becomes linked to the *Avos*, Patriarchs, and their remarkable way of life. Reciprocally, this relationship serves as an everlasting *zechus*, merit, in the individual's behalf.

Korach's tragedy emerged when he "separated himself" from the chain of tradition. His attempt to develop a lifestyle independent of *Torah* mandate represented his first break in the chain of *Mesorah*, tradition. By severing the chain of tradition, he severed his relationship with *Klal Yisrael* and, consequently, sealed his own tragic destiny.

***

ויקח קרח
"And Korach took." (16:1)

Korach's downfall at least partially originated in his own logistic approach to *Torah* law. His lack of respect for Moshe, which was a result of his overwhelming jealousy, caused him to judge right and wrong without consulting his teachers. This divergence from the *halachic* process contributed to Korach's total rejection of the *Torah* way.

Rashi cites an example of Korach's distorted approach to *Torah* law. He clad his followers in garments made entirely of *techeles*, blue wool. They came before Moshe, questioning if a garment made entirely of blue wool requires *tzitzis*. Moshe undoubtedly responded that *tzitzis* is a requirement even on such a garment. Korach immediately berated Moshe declaring, *"If one thread of blue can exempt a garment made of another material, surely a garment made completely of blue wool should be exempt from tzitzis."* Korach's absurd reasoning illustrates how far one can stray from the prescribed *Torah* path. We may, nonetheless, question Korach's choice of *halachic* law upon which to dispute.

Horav M. Feinstein, z.l., offers a meaningful homiletic insight into this matter. White, a pure color, connotes pure activity, untainted by personal prejudice. On the other hand, blue and other colors, being admixtures, symbolize biased activity. We should, therefore, wear a garment which is entirely white to reflect our proclivity to pure thought and action. We place one blue strand of wool in the *tzitzis* to alert us to the many obstacles which confront us in our quest for spiritual advancement. Korach made his mistake specifically concerning a garment which was entirely blue, since this indicates that even the most "crooked act" can somehow be justified. This was his error. There is never an acceptable rationale for evil.

***

ויקח קרח... ודתן ואבירם... בני ראובן

"And Korach took . . . and Dasan and Aviram . . . the sons of Reuven." (16:1)

Rashi notes that the *Torah* mentions Dasan and Aviram's lineage. He explains that, since the tribe of Reuven encamped on the south in close proximity to Korach, they developed an association with Korach. This relationship enabled their involvement in Korach's dispute. This seems puzzling. Throughout their sojourn in the wilderness, we find Dasan and Aviram described as Moshe's archenemies who instigated every incursion. Their incessant bickering and complaining resulted in many tragic consequences.

Horav Chaim Elazary, z.l., suggests the following difference between the insurgent attitude of Korach and Dasan and Aviram's orientation. Even though Dasan and Aviram undoubtedly exhibited flagrant disrespect towards Moshe, he was not the target of their disobedience. Their desire was simply to return to Egypt. They never disputed Moshe's legitimacy as leader of *Klal Yisrael.* In contrast, Korach's prime objective was to usurp Moshe as leader. His blatant defiance of him was his method of degrading Moshe's position as leader. This insurrection was the first of its kind in our history. Perhaps this is why Korach's punishment was so frightening. He was the first person to question *Klal Yisrael's* leadership, and, therefore, his punishment was symbolic, commensurate with the evil that he had wrought.

Our *Torah* leaders represent the stability and uniqueness of our nation; to question their legitimacy or to dispute their authority is to disdain one of the basic tenets of our faith.

***

ויקח קרח

"And Korach took." (16:1)

כי כל העדה כולם קדושים

"For all the congregation is holy." (16:3)

Referring to the controversy stimulated by Korach and his henchman, the *Mishnah* in *Avos (5:20)* remarks, *"Any controversy that is L'shem Shomayim" (for the sake of heaven) will have a constructive outcome. Which controversy is considered L'shem Shomayim? This is the controversy between Hillel and Shamai. And which is considered not L'shem Shomayim? This is the controversy of Korach and his entire company."*

The *Malbim* questions the use of "Korach and his company" as a paradigm of a *"machlokes she'lo l'shem shomayim."* Surely there were other infamous conflicts more appropriate to be mentioned. The disputes surrounding the lack of water and meat and the controversy in connection with the spies obviously fit into this category. Indeed, Korach's controversy even involved *halachic* discourse; i.e. Who is to

206

be sanctified for service in the *Mikdash*? Who shall offer the *korbanos*? Does a *tallis* made entirely of *techeles*, "blue wool," require *tzitzis*?

Horav Elchanan Sorotzkin, z.l., offers a profound solution to this question. It was precisely the *halachic* issues and the false facade which they engender that represents the core of this problem. These questions were no more than deceitful pretense, an attempt to veil the real miscreancy that was behind Korach's rhetoric. Korach did not have the dignity to come forward to directly debate the issues. His goal was social status and power. Every religious quotation was merely a method for concealing his true intentions.

The danger that subtly abounds in such a conflict is far greater than one which is overtly controversial. The Korach type of dispute is a rationalization of the evil within a person. Such a person presents actions motivated by self-aggrandizement as noble and altruistic. He veils the desire to obliterate religious tradition under the quest for modernity. When one is confronted face to face with evil, he can deal with the issues much more directly than when this evil is hidden behind righteous pretense.

***

ברית מלח עולם

"An eternal covenant of salt." (18:19)

How is Hashem's gift of the priestly blessings to Aharon and his sons to be compared to a covenant of salt? *Rashi* presents an analogy. Just as salt does not rot-- and even acts as a preserving agent for many things -- so, too, this covenant maintains its virility in order to preserve Aharon's dynasty forever.

Horav D. Feinstein, Shlita, derives a powerful implication from this *pasuk*. Even if some *Kohanim* deviate from the prescribed path of service to Hashem, some will always stalwartly uphold the covenant. Thus, just as salt never rots, maintaining its ability to preserve foods, so, too, the covenant will safeguard Aharon's priestly family. Thus, the covenant will ensure *Bnei Yisrael's* continued holiness throughout ensuing generations.

We may wonder why it is that some *Kohanim* and other individuals who hold positions of spiritual leadership tend to deviate from the path of *Torah* and "burn out." Perhaps the analogy to salt can resolve our question. As salt is a preservative, so, too, are our spiritual leaders. Their prime function is to promulgate the legacy of *Torah*, to conserve and perpetuate our heritage. They must view themselves as responsible for the continuity of *Klal Yisrael.* When this vision becomes distorted as a result of vested self-interests and personal prejudice, the leaders leave themselves vulnerable to the blandishments of the *yetzer hora.* Only by viewing themselves as a preserving agent will our leaders maintain the ability to safeguard the precious legacy of our heritage.

QUESTIONS LEVEL- A

1. Who was Korach's great grandfather?
2. When Moshe sent for Dasan and Aviram, did they come?
3. Did Moshe receive any personal gifts from *Bnei Yisrael?*
4. May *Kodshei Kodoshim* meat be eaten by a *Kohen's* daughter?
5. How does the *Torah* refer to *terumah* (in this *parsha*)?

QUESTIONS LEVEL- B

1. A) Where did *shevet* Reuven camp? B) Who were their neighbors?
2. Who was appointed as *Nasi* over *Beni Kehas?*
3. May a *Kohen's* wife eat *terumah*?

QUESTIONS LEVEL- C

1. What secret was taught to Moshe by the *Malach Ha'Ma'ves?*
2. The *bris* made with Aharon is referred to as *Bris Melach,* covenant of salt. What is salt's uniqueness?

QUESTIONS LEVEL- D

1. At the time of *Churban Bayis Rishon,* what happened to Aharon's *mateh*?

ANSWERS LEVEL- A

1. Levi.
2. No.
3. No.
4. No.
5. ראשיתם (18:12) (referring to the first part of the oil, wine, and grain.)

ANSWERS LEVEL- B

1. A) In the south. B) Kehas and his family.
2. Elitzaphan Ben Uziel.
3. Yes.

ANSWERS LEVEL- C

1. He was taught that offering *ketores* will stop a plague.
2. It is wholesome and lasting, and it preserves other foods.

ANSWERS LEVEL- D

1. King Yoshiyahu hid it together with the other testimonial objects and holy vessels.

פרשת חקת
PARASHAS CHUKAS
►◄

ויקהל משה ואהרן את הקהל אל פני הסלע ויאמר להם שמעו נא המורים
המן הסלע הזה נוציא לכם מים

**"And Moshe and Aharon gathered together the assembly before
the rock and said to them, 'Listen you rebels; are we to bring
forth to you water out of this rock?'"** (20:10)

The *Ramban* cites the *Rambam* who states in *Moreh Nevuchim* that
Moshe *Rabbeinu's* sin consisted of expressing himself in anger
towards *Bnei Yisrael*. His statement, *"Listen you rebels,"* signified a
weakness on his part. For an individual of Moshe's exalted stature to
express himself in such a manner was considered a *chillul Hashem*,
desecration of Hashem's name. People considered Moshe to be a role
model. They emulated his actions and words in the hope of achieving
such success. How could Moshe then appear to be angry,
demonstrating such an evil trait? *Horav E. Shach, Shlita,* suggests that
a fundamental and central principle may be gleaned from the words of
the *Rambam*. This concept focuses primarily upon those who hold
positions of spiritual leadership, either in a communal or educational
realm.

Undoubtedly, Moshe *Rabbeinu* did not become angry in accord
with our perception of anger. He did not possess even the slightest
vestige of anger. Nonetheless, since he was *Klal Yisrael's* virtuous
leader, who served as the paradigm for all men to emulate, he
appeared angry. This perception could not be tolerated, since it
created a *chillul Hashem*.

It is the nature of people to seek ways to discredit their
spiritual leadership, so that they have implied license to perform
every form of iniquity. One who accepts spiritual leadership is privy
to every form of critique. He must always be aware that he stands
beneath the microscopic eye of his community and students, who will

emulate his behavior.

Horav Shach reiterates the enormous responsibility which rests upon the shoulders of educators. Their function is to imbue and inculcate *Torah* into the hearts and minds of Jewish children. For the most part, the image of the next generation is placed in the hands of the educator to shape with the "tools" of *Torah* values and perspective. The *mechanech*, educator, should be caeful to reflect the model image of virtue and ethicality, refinement and dignity which befits a *Torah* personality.

***

ויסעו מקדש ויבאו בני ישראל כל העדה הר ההר

"And they journeyed from Kadesh, and the Bnei Yisrael came, the whole congregation, to the Har Ha'Har." (20:22)

Rashi cites a *Midrash* which is particularly relevant in contemporary times. The pillar of cloud which travelled before *Bnei Yisrael* leveled out the mountains and flattened the hills which stood in *Bnei Yisrael's* path. There remained, however, three mountains which resisted the shattering clouds: *Har Sinai* was spared, since the *Torah* would be given on it; *Har Nevo* was to be Moshe's burial place; and *Har Ha'Har* was singled out as Aharon's burial place.

Horav M. Swift, z.l., poignantly expounds on this *Midrash*. He draws an analogy between the significance represented by the stated purpose of these mountains and important aspects of Jewish life. Throughout our tenuous history, mountains of all kinds have crumbled to extinction. Mountains, fortunes, fame and glory, even life itself, all have been decimated. One mountain has endured, the mountain upon which Aharon transferred his vestments and charge to Elazar, his son. This mountain symbolizes the transmission of our heritage from father to son, generation to generation. On this mountain, Moshe comforted Aharon saying, *"Happy are you to see your crown rest upon your son's head."* A father could pass on in serenity, knowing that he had successfully conveyed the message of the past to the future generation. Such a mountain could never be eliminated.

Har Nevo, on which Moshe spent his last moments before taking leave of *Bnei Yisrael,* could not be destroyed. Until this day no one has been able to locate Moshe's grave. *Moshe Rabbeinu's* burial place defies discovery and alludes detection. His *neshamah*, soul, was bound up with Hashem, Who attended to his mortal remains. A significant message can be gleaned from this concept. While others have transformed the burial place of their leaders into shrines, our immortal leader's burial place remains unknown. Moshe began the overwhelming ascent upward. He continued to even greater heights of distinction, to walk in eternity.

There is yet a third mountain, *Har Sinai*. The mountain upon which the *Torah* was given represents the resoluteness of Jewish life to resist the challenging forces of the changing times. Whether the challengers appear in the form of reformers to distort our legacy or as apologetic moderates to sterilize our heritage, whether they came from within or without, not one letter of the *Torah* has been altered. The mountain of *Torah* resists change! We have seen in our own generation how a small group of dedicated Jews overcame adversity, prevailed against indifference, and surmounted ignorance in order to build a proud *Torah* community in this country. The mountain representing *Torah* devotion resists all adversity and will continue to grow stronger.

The lesson of these mountains is clear. We must be resolute in our commitment to preserve our *Torah* legacy. We must consistently grow by seeking more knowledge of its profundities, and we must be cognizant of our inherent obligation to see that this legacy is transmitted to future generations. With this tripartite commitment, the winds of change will never level the heights of our achievements.

***

ויפשט משה את אהרן את בגדיו וילבש אתם את אלעזר בנו

"And Moshe undressed Aharon of his garments, and put them upon Elazar, his son." (20:28)

Chazal describe the uniqueness of this undressing of Aharon. Normally, Aharon would first have to remove all of his garments, so that Elazar could don his undergarments first. As Aharon removed his outer garment, however, Elazar immediately put it on. This became Elazar's undergarment. As Aharon continued by removing this undergarment, it, in turn, became Elazar's outergarments. There is a

212

profound homiletic lesson to be derived herein. Aharon's inner "garments" or essence, the way he acted in the privacy of his own home, was reflected externally by his children. Children invariably reveal the actual values and outlook presented in their home.

How fortunate are the parents whose deep inner sense of Jewish values is revealed in the constructive activities of their children. One may be able to build an external facade of piety for the world. This sham, however, will eventually be exposed through the negative life activities of his children. We must forever be vigilant to keep the inner character of our lives in order, so that the next generation will be bequeathed a heritage which is pure and unimpeachable.

***

וישלח ישראל מלאכים אל סיחן... אעברה נא בארצך לא נטה בשדה
ובכרם לא נשתה מי באר בדרך המלך נלך עד אשר נעבור בגבלך.

"And Yisrael sent messengers to Sichon . . . let me pass through your land we will not turn aside into field or into vineyard, we will not drink of the water of the wells, by the kings highway we will go until we have passed your border." (21:21,22)

ולא נתן סיחן את ישראל עבר בגבול ויאסף סיחן את כל עמו
ויצא לקראת ישראל המדברה

"And Sichon would not permit Yisrael to pass through his border, and Sichon gathered together all his people and went against Yisrael into the wilderness." (21:23)

In this narrative, the *Torah* relates how Moshe requested Sichon's permission for *Am Yisrael* to pass through his land. He promised Sichon that nothing would be touched and no one would be harmed. Sichon's response was swift and emphatic. He not only prohibited their entry, but he subsequently waged war against them. This reaction is puzzling! What fear gripped Sichon that caused such terrifying concern, catalyzing his immediate attack on the Jews? They were not his enemies. It was not their desire to ravage his country. They were basically peace loving people who wanted access to their promised land.

Horav Chaim Zaitchik, z.l., suggests that Sichon's fear was of a sub-conscious nature. He feared the spiritual influence the Jewish

213

people would have upon his nation. In short, Sichon feared the truth. To expose his barbarian people to the refinement, nobility, and *middos tovos,* good character traits, which are paradigmatic to *Torah* Jews, was a "dangerous" gamble to take. Therefore, Sichon painted a gruesome picture of *Bnei Yisrael.* They were slaves who had rebelled against their masters, the Egyptians. This "ungrateful" people went on to destroy and pilfer their host nation, destroying anyone who crossed their path. Were he to allow *Bnei Yisrael* to enter his country, his people would come face to face with realty. Perhaps man's greatest apprehension is the fear of the truth.

Sichon was gripped by the fear that his people would be "trespassed" by *Bnei Yisrael.* The jealousy and consequent self-depreciation were more than he could handle. His people's self-esteem would suffer irreparable damage, confronting the truth that *Bnei Yisrael* were not as he had represented them. The false propaganda with which he attempted to indoctrinate his people was to be exposed by *Bnei Yisrael.* This was Sichon's greatest fear. He must stop *Bnei Yisrael's* entry into his land at all costs.

It is not at all surprising that a similar situation exists in our own times. There is an amazing rate of return to the *Torah* way of life. Many people are finally acknowledging the reality of their misguided perceptions. After years of alienation from *Torah*, they are embracing the true Jewish way of life with increased fervor and deepened commitment. Some people embrace the same misperceptions which have been responsible for so much of our suffering. They advocate these be used as the panacea to the Jews' problem in today's complex society. It must be our goal to adopt the truth of the *Torah* in every aspect of our lives, as individuals and as a society. Indeed, there is no substitute for the truth.

QUESTIONS LEVEL- A

1. The *Kohen* who performs the ritual of *Parah Adumah* is *tameh* until the _____.

2. A) One who comes in contact with a dead body is *tameh* for _____ days. B) Does this same *halachah* apply if one is beneath the same roof as a dead body?

214

3. How many times did Moshe strike the stone?

4. Who became *Kohen Gadol* after Aharon?

5. Which two kings, who were defeated by *Bnei Yisrael,* are mentioned in this *parsha?*

QUESTIONS LEVEL- B

1. A) What three things were taken with the *Parah Adumah?*

B) To what do these three things correspond?

2. Who is referred to as מחוקק?

QUESTIONS LEVEL- C

1. The ashes of the *Parah Adumah* are divided into _____ parts.

2. What is another Hebrew word used to describe a *Navi?*

QUESTIONS LEVEL- D

1. What is the significance of *Har Ha'Har* (double mountain) in regard to *Aharon?*

ANSWERS LEVEL- A

1. Evening.

2. A) Seven. B) Yes.

3. Twice.

4. His son, Elazar.

5. Sichon, Og.

ANSWERS LEVEL- B

1. A) Cedar wood, hyssop, and scarlet. B) The three thousand men who died as a result of sinning with the golden calf.

2. Moshe.

ANSWERS LEVEL- C

1. Three.

2. *Malach.*

ANSWERS LEVEL- D

1. Its name symbolizes the two crowns which Aharon had acquired during his lifetime: the crown of *Torah* and the crown of *Kehunah.* (*Tiferes Tzion*)

פרשת בלק
PARASHAS BALAK
▶◀

ותרא האתון את מלאך ד'... ותט האתון מן הדרך ותלך בשדה

"And the donkey saw the angel of Hashem... and the donkey turned aside out of the way and went into the field." (22:23)

ויעמוד מלאך ד' במשעול הכרמים גדר מזה וגדר מזה

"And the angel of Hashem stood in a hollow way between the vineyards, a fence (being) on this (side) and a fence (being) on this (side)." (22:24)

יוסף מלאך ד' עבור במקום צר אשר אין דרך לנטות ימין ושמאל

"And the angel of Hashem again passed, and stood in a narrow place, where there was no way to turn either to the right or to the left." (22:26)

Horav Chaim Ehrentrau, z.l., points out that the three places at which the angel stood opposite Bilaam, barring his path, symbolize man's three points of digression from freedom towards his ultimate loss of *bechirah*, free-will. In the beginning, the road towards sin appears to be a wide opening, from which it is easy to turn away to the right or left -- or even turn back. This was Bilaam's original situation. He could have returned to his home and redeemed himself.

The sinner who remains adamant, continuing along his path of evil, encounters a narrower path. Although return from this path is conceivable, it is difficult. He is now constricted on both sides, locked into a tight and awkward position. Just as Bilaam was fenced into the narrow path in the vineyards, man must work diligently to perform *teshuvah*, repentance. The path of return still remains accessible.

As the sinner reaches the third rung on the ladder of sin, the situation changes. At this stage one has nowhere to turn, neither to the right nor to the left. The *teshuvah* process is no longer imminent. The sinner has lost his opportunity to choose between right and wrong, since he has been completely overwhelmed by the power of

216

the *yetzer hora*. That Bilaam conceded his own arrogance serves as a lesson for us in our daily battle with the *yetzer hora*.

***

ויאמר בלעם אל מלאך ד' חטאתי כי לא ידעתי כי אתה נצב לקראתי בדרך

"And Bilaam said unto the angel of Hashem, 'I have sinned for I did not know that you stood against me in the way.'" (22:34)

Bilaam's statement seems enigmatic. How could it be considered sinful if, in fact, he was not aware of the angel's presence? The commentators explain that this ignorance is in itself a sin. There are situations in which one must be acutely cognizant of who he is and before whom he stands. For example, a child can never justify striking a parent. Similarly, the king's closest aide can not claim that he is not aware of the king's identity. Likewise, a prophet must always be cognizant of the presence of the Eternal. For Bilaam to assert that he was unaware of the angel's presence is in itself a sin. This is Bilaam's refrain to the angel, "I sinned by not knowing, because as a prophet I must at all times be aware of an angel's presence before me."

There is a story concerning *Rav Chaim Sanzer, z.l.,* which should be noted by all community leaders, spiritual as well as lay leaders. *Rav Chaim* once asked the rabbi of a nearby city why he did not respond to the dire need of one of his congregants. The rabbi replied, "I was unaware of his serious situation." *Rav Chaim* was taken aback and responded, "Regarding Bilaam, it is written that he said, 'I sinned because I did not know." This teaches us that lack of knowledge is in itself a sin. A community rabbi must consider it his personal mandate to know if one of his members is suffering. If he does not know, he has sinned."

This statement should have a profound effect on everyone. It is indisputably our moral obligation to sensitize ourselves to the needs of the community. We must seek out individuals who are in need. Biding time often results in tragedy for the one in distress. Coming forward to request assistance requires an amazing amount of courage. It behooves us to find a way to prevent one who is in need from undergoing this humiliating experience. Perhaps in the merit of helping others, we will not have reason to be concerned for ourselves.

217

את שבעת המזבחות ערכתי

"I have set up the seven altars." (23:4)

Bilaam emphasizes to Hashem that he had instructed Balak to erect seven altars. *Rashi* explains that Bilaam emphasized the number of altars for a specific reason. By virtue of erecting seven altars, Bilaam sought to negate the combined efforts of Avraham, Yitzchak and Yaakov, who had built seven altars through their combined efforts. Bilaam foolishly thought that he could equate his altars to the altars erected by the Avos, Patriarchs, by merely constructing the same number of alters.

Horav D. Feinstein, Shlita, suggests that perhaps Bilaam attributed a special significance to the number seven. Since *Bnei Yisrael* had seven altars to their credit, he erected the same number of altars in order to prevail over theirs. This is why Bilaam uses the word שבעת, which indicates a septet, rather than שבע, which is simply the number seven.

We may wonder why Bilaam's altars could not prevail over the merit of the Patriarch's altars. We may suggest the following thoughts. Although Bilaam possessed many supernatural powers, he was not capable of overwhelming the strength of the *Avos.* The power generated by a group, especially one representing three generations of devotion to Hashem, is awesome. May this be a lesson for us. When *Klal Yisrael* works together as a unified group, those who dare challenge the Jews will do so to no avail. This was Bilaam's error. It is not sufficient to erect altars. These altars must be imbued with the same devotion and *mesiras nefesh,* self-sacrifice, that is reflected by the altars of the *Avos.*

We may suggest another reason for Bilaam's lack of success. Bilaam built the altars solely for one reason, in order to destroy *Klal Yisrael.* One cannot build for the purpose of destruction and hope to succeed. While it may momentarily seem that things are working out in his favor, the negative orientation will not endure. This idea applies to so many instances in which individuals or organizations find excuses for creating new institutions. If one's objectives are noble and true to their stated purpose, they have a legitimate reason for existence. The efforts of those establishments whose goal is destruction and whose foundation is cemented with obsessive loathing, however, will be sabotaged by their own self-hatred. Bilaam's failure should serve as a lesson to us all in our approach to building community and institutions, so that *Klal Yisrael* will prosper and flourish.

***

לא הביט און ביעקב ולא ראה עמל בישראל

"None has beheld iniquity in Yaakov, and neither has one seen perseverance in Yisrael." (23:21)

Rashi explains that Hashem does not scrutinize the sins of *Bnei Yisrael*. He attempts to look away from their iniquities as much as possible. *Horav D. Kronglas, z.l.,* questions *Rashi's* statement based upon various instances in the *Talmud* in which it is clearly stated that Hashem does, in fact, scrutinize our sins. He cites specific cases in which it is clear that oversight is not one of Hashem's attributes; on the contrary, He is very exacting in His judgement.

Horav Kronglas explains this contradiction in the following manner. People tend to have two distinct standards for judgement: one for their friends and one for those who are not their friends. When one sees his friend engaged in an activity of a questionable nature or hears some form of slander concerning him, he will seek every opportunity to vindicate his friend. The true friend never delves into his friend's activities or relationships, so that he will not uncover any unpropitious evidence about him. In short, one is inclined to judge his friends favorably.

The opposite holds true when one is judging an enemy. Not only will he condemn an enemy's actions at every opportunity, but he will also attempt to uncover incriminating evidence with which to censure his enemy.

The *pasuk* states that Hashem does not behold their iniquity. The word used by the *Torah* is הביט, which implies deep scrutinizing. This relates to Yaakov, denoting a lesser degree of spiritual stature. Hashem does not wish to scrutinize the sins of those Jews who are spiritually and morally weak; rather He prefers to view their sins as simple errors. This is because they are only on the level of *"Yaakov,"* the level of the common masses. Regarding one who has attained the *"Yisrael"* level, the *pasuk* states that Hashem does not even "see," ראה

their slight deviations. As far as Hashem is concerned, these digressions from the path do not even exist.

This positive attitude only takes place when Hashem sees His people being considerate of one another and judging each other favorably. If, however, they judge their fellow Jew harshly, they will be treated similarly by Hashem. The way we act towards our fellow Jew is the standard by which Hashem will respond to us.

QUESTIONS LEVEL- A

1. What did Balak want Bilaam to do for him?

2. Who appeared to Bilaam in the middle of the night?

3. Which powerful person saddled his own donkey?

4. *Bnei Yisrael* rise up from their sleep as a _____ or _____ to serve Hashem?

5. Which *pasuk*, which is a part of our daily *tefillah*, did Bilaam say?

QUESTIONS LEVEL- B

1. How many altars did the *Avos* build?

2. Who advised Moav to incite *Bnei Yisrael* to sin through immorality?

QUESTIONS LEVEL- C

1. A) Which great *tzaddik's* action preceded an action performed by Bilaam? B) What was this action?

2. What inspired Bilaam to say *Ma tovu ohalecha Yaakov?*

QUESTIONS LEVEL- D

1. A) How many times was Bilaam tested by Hashem? B) How is this alluded to in the *parsha*? C) To what does this number correspond?

ANSWERS LEVEL- A

1. Curse *Bnei Yisrael*
2. Hashem.
3. Billam.
4. Lion or lioness
5. *Ma tovu Ohalecha Yaakov.*

ANSWERS LEVEL- B

1. Seven. Avraham built 4, Yitzchak 1 and Yaakov 2.
2. Bilaam.

ANSWERS LEVEL- C

1. A) Avraham. B) He saddled his own donkey in preparation for the *akeidah*, while Bilaam did the same in preparation to cursing *Bnei Yisrael*.
2. He noticed that the doors of the *Bnei Yisrael's* tents did not face each other.

ANSWERS LEVEL- D

1. A) 10. B) The word מלאך is mentioned ten times. C) Avraham was tested ten times and successfully demonstrated his devotion to Hashem.

פרשת פנחס
PARASHAS PINCHAS
▶◀

בקנאו את קנאתי בתוכם
"In that he was jealous for My sake." (25:11)

Through his zealous action, Pinchas was in fact carrying out the
halachah of הבועל ארמית קנאין פוגעין בו, *"One who is intimate with a
gentile is to be struck down by zealous people."* This injunction refers
to those who are so sensitive about the sanctity of Hashem's Name
that any incursion against it is intolerable. Why, then, is Pinchas
lauded and praised? Indeed, he was doing only what was expected of
him.

Horav M. Gifter, Shlita, explains that this *halachah* is unique
in that its fulfillment is to performed only by one who is a *"kana'ie,"* a
zealot. He explains that the concept of *kana'us*, is mistakenly
associated with extremism. A *"kana'ie"* is one who is קנא לאלקיו, so
zealous for Hashem that he is willing to give up everything he
possesses for Hashem, even his own life. The source of this
zealousness is the recognition that the fulfillment of Hashem's will is
ultimately the foundation of life. Every activity in life is a reflection
of this awareness.

Zealousness is the perfection of one's spiritual essence.
It is the culmination of an educational process which stimulates man
to progress from his natural inclination towards laziness to the
sublime height of spiritual peace. In this state, he is prepared to
dedicate his life to the service of Hashem. How distant is the *Torah's*
perspective of zealousness from extremism!

***

השיב את חמתי מעל בני ישראל בקנאו את קנאתי בתוכם
ולא כליתי את בני ישראל בקנאתי

"(Pinchas) has turned away My wrath from the Bnei Yisrael in that he was jealous for My sake among them (so) that I did not consume the Bnei Yisrael in My jealousy." (25:11)

In its purest form, zealousness is contingent upon three criteria. The zealot must perform his act totally *"le'shem shomayim,"* for the sake of Heaven. There should be no personal prejudice or vested interest which "motivates" his urgent reaction. Second, it is imperative that the zealot not remove himself from the community. He must challenge any incursion from within. Running away and hurling stones at the sinners does not reflect true *kana'us*, zealousness.

Horav Nissan Alpert, z.l., points out that a third contingency is regrettably often overlooked. Those individuals who exhibit unbounding devotion to Hashem's ideals may react zealously and swiftly to any incursion against the *Torah*. They ignore, however, one very important point: the welfare of those who erred and sinned. How often do we hear the term *"ye'mach she'mam"* (let their names be blotted out) regarding those who sin. One should take note of the *Torah's* text regarding Pinchas' act, *"And I did not consume Bnei Yisrael in My jealousy."* Pinchas' goal was to prevent Bnei Yisrael's death, not to destroy them. Our goal in *kana'us* is to save Judaism, not to see it destroyed. Undoubtedly, there are times when Hashem's Name is profaned and swift unrestrained reprisal is warranted. This response, however, should be executed with dignity, with an attitude reflecting the lofty necessity for this action.

***

ושם איש ישראל המכה... זמרי בן סלוא ושם האשה המכה
המדינית כזבי בת צור

"And the name of the man of Yisrael who was slain . . . (was) Zimri ben Salu . . . And the name of the woman who was slain, the midyanis (was) Casbi bas Tzur . . . (25:14,15)

The *Yalkut Reuveni* cites the *Ra'mah Mi'Panu*, who states that the famous *Tanna* Rabbi Akiva was the *gilgul nefesh,* reincarnation, of Zimri. The wife of Turnus Rufus, on the other hand, who later became Rabbi Akiva's wife, was in reality the *gilgul* of Casbi. Indeed, the

223

illicit advances which Casbi made to Zimri were "corrected" through her future *gilgul's* marriage to Rabbi Akiva. He explains that this is the reason that Rabbi Akiva died in such a torturous manner, by having his flesh raked off his body with metal combs. When Zimri came before Moshe with Casbi, he grabbed her by her hair and asked, *"This woman, is she forbidden or permissible? If you say she is forbidden, then who permitted you to marry the daughter of Yisro?"* Because Zimri grabbed Casbi by her hair, Rabbi Akiva, who was Zimri's *gilgul*, was destined to have his skin torn off with metal combs.

Horav M. Wolfson, Shlita, suggests that a profound insight may be noted. Zimri's act of immoral defiance caused a plague during which twenty four thousand Jews perished. Rabbi Akiva's students, who died during the period between *Pesach* and *Shavuos*, also numbered twenty four thousand! This amazing insight can be further advanced by reflecting upon the relationship between the stated "mistake" of Rabbi Akiva's students and the sin committed by *Bnei Yisrael*, which resulted in the devastating plague.

Chazal teach that Rabbi Akivah's students died because of their lack of respect for one another. Contrary to mistaken opinion, they were not sinners. Indeed, they were the greatest scholars. Despite their lofty level of *Torah* erudition, however, their character development seemed slightly lacking. Hashem assesses His devotees with a very precise measure, leading to severe punishment. Lack of respect for one another indicates selfishness. This seemingly innocuous form of self devotion can be a precursion to greater forms of self worship, such as immorality and, ultimately, idol worship. These sins, which represent the tragic flaw of *Bnei Yisrael,* were the cause of the terrible plague which decimated twenty four thousand of them.

A lesson can be gleaned from Rabbi Akiva's students and their failure. The greatest evil invariably has its roots in innocent behavior which, when allowed to germinate, can grow to terrible proportions. One should be constantly vigilant to take note of any behavioral deviation and make the proper adjustments, so that it does not grow into an irreversible condition.

ראובן בכור ישראל בני ראובן חנוך משפחת החנוכי
"Reuven, the first-born of Yisrael, the sons of Reuven (of) Chanoch the family of the Chanochi." (26:5)

Rashi explains the *Torah's* intent in emphasizing B*nei Yisrael's* genealogy. The gentile nations might think that they would be able to dominate the Jewish mothers, just as the Egyptians dominated the Jews' lives. Hashem, therefore, placed His Name upon them in everlasting testimony to their pure lineage. This statement seems puzzling. Do the gentiles study *Torah* so that they can become versed in our genealogy? Even if they were to study *Torah*, would they believe, as we do, in the *Torah's* immutability?

Horav Chaim Elazary, z.l., explains that the *Torah* was given to *Klal Yisrael* to study and believe. Hashem did not intend to teach its profundities or truths to the gentiles. Indeed, the *Torah* has frequently stimulated anti-semitism throughout history. *Chazal* state that *Har Sinai* was the place from which *"sin'ah,"* enmity toward *Yisrael* emanated. *Torah* will protect us only to the extent that it remains the source of our confidence and pride. Armed with this resource, we are enabled to confront the philosophical challenges that we face from external and even internal origins.

It is human nature to be affected by talk and innuendo. If the gentile nations slander our lineage, we may subconsciously begin to believe them. Such aspersions, can succeed in causing depression and disbelief among the uneducated and spiritually weak. Therefore, the *Torah* seeks to counteract this negative inference and to affirm our belief in Hashem by clearly stating our genealogy.

The notion that we are transformed by the beliefs of others is very real. If people say something often enough, we will slowly begin to accede to their chatter. Although we may express total disdain and vehemently deny their allegations, our subconscious minds will begin to raise questions. This fear of subconscious impression can only be counteracted by total immersion in *Torah*. As the source of our pride and the benchmark or our identity, the *Torah* will give us the tools to face the challenges we confront throughout life.

***

ויאמר ד' אל משה קח לך את יהושע בן נון איש אשר רוח בו

"And Hashem said to Moshe, take Yehoshua ben Nun, a man of spirit." (27:18)

The relationship between Yehoshua, the disciple, and Moshe, the *rebbe*, serves as the paradigm of a *rebbe-talmid* relationship. Yehoshua's constant attachment to his *Rebbe*, symbolized by the fact that he never allowed even one word of *Torah* to escape unheard, was a basic reason for his advancement to *Am Yisrael's* leadership. His faithfulness and devotion were exemplary; his commitment and diligence were unprecedented.

The *Talmud* in *Bava Basra 75a* relates that when Yehoshua succeeded Moshe, the elders of the generation remarked, "*The face of Moshe was like the sun, while the face of Yehoshua was like the moon.*" Most commentators interpret *Chazal's* statement to be derogatory towards Yehoshua. He was unable to supplant Moshe in leadership and glory. The *Chofetz Chaim*, however, suggests a different approach to understanding this *Chazal*. Although Yehoshua's luster paled in Moshe's shadow, the elders realized that Yehoshua reflected Moshe's brilliance on a lesser level. Just as the moon reflects the sun's brightness, so, too, Yehoshua simulated Moshe's luster. We may derive from here an important lesson. A student should aspire to captivate his *rebbe's* teachings and personality, so that the student reflects his *rebbe's* character with his very nature.

QUESTIONS LEVEL- A

1. Zimri was the *Nasi* of the tribe of _____.

2. After which event in this *parsha* does Hashem "count" *Bnei Yisrael*?

3. From which sons from his first wife did Yehudah have grandchildren?

4. Was Tzlafchad a member of Korach's assembly?

5. How does the *Torah* describe Yehoshua?

QUESTIONS LEVEL- B

1. What two letters did Hashem add to the names of the tribes?

2. Was all of Moshe's glory transferred to Yehoshua?

3. The ram offered on *Pesach* corresponds to the ram of _____?

QUESTIONS LEVEL- C

1. *Bnei Yisrael* trace their genealogy according to the tribe of their __.

2. The ___ Jews who died in the plague were from the tribe of _____.

3. Was Asher's daughter, _____, still alive during this last census?

QUESTIONS LEVEL- D

1. The __ bullocks offered on *Succos* represent the ____ of the world. What do the _____ lambs represent?

ANSWERS LEVEL- A

1. Shimon.

2. After the plague.

3. *Sheilah.* 4. No.

5. איש אשר רוח בו "*a man in whom there is spirit.*"

ANSWERS LEVEL- B

1. *Yud, Hay.*

2. No.

3. Yitzchak.

ANSWERS LEVEL- C

1. Father.

2. 24,000, Shimon.

3. Serach, Yes.

ANSWERS LEVEL- D

1. 70, 70 nations. 98, 98 curses in *Parashas Ki Savo.* This indicated that the *karbanos* shield us from these curses.

פרשת מטות
PARASHAS MATOS
►◄

אלף למטה אלף למטה לכל מטות ישראל תשלחו לצבא

"Of every tribe a thousand, of every tribe a thousand, throughout all the tribes of Yisrael you shall send to the war." (31:4)

Rashi explains that the phrase *"throughout all the tribes of Yisrael"* includes the tribe of *Levi* with the other tribes. The commentators find this statement difficult to understand. In the next *pasuk*, the *Torah* clearly states that only twelve thousand men, representing twelve tribes, went forth as soldiers. *"And there were delivered out of the thousands of Yisrael, a thousand of every tribe, twelve thousand armed for war."* If the tribe of *Levi* was included among the soldiers, there should have been thirteen thousand!

Rav Avrahom Mordechai M'Gur, z.l., suggests the following explanation. As stated in this *parsha*, Moshe's imminent departure from this world was contingent upon this war, as it is stated, *"Avenge the vengance of Bnei Yisrael; afterward you shall be gathered unto your people."* When *Bnei Yisrael* saw that their beloved leader would die soon after this war, they were undoubtedly reluctant to go forward to enlist in this endeavor. It is for this reason that the *Torah* states, *"They were delivered."* They were compelled to go, even against their will. The members of the tribe of *Levi*, however, had previously proven themselves to be unique. Their devotion to Hashem transcended even the closest family ties. When they were implored to kill those who had sinned with the Golden Calf, they went forward resolutely to perform this task. They did not distinguish family members. Their complete focus was upon faithfully carrying out their mission.

Hashem's will transcended the love the tribe of *Levi* had for their *rebbe*, Moshe. They were probably the only tribe which was willing to go forward and perform the deed of their own volition.

Consequently, thirteen thousand soldiers, including the tribe of *Levi*, entered the army. Twelve thousand of those soldiers, however, had to be "persuaded" to enter this service. One thousand of them went on their own.

We may derive from this *pasuk* that objectivity on the part of a *Ben Torah* is imperative. A true *Torah* devotee should be able to transcend his own sensitivities toward family and tendencies towards nepotism. Personal loyalties and considerations of kinship should not cloud one's total commitment to Hashem. Indeed, the *Sefer Ha'Chinuch* explains that the tribe of *Levi's* objectivity was the prime reason for their designation as the protectors of the unintentional murderers who fled to the *Arai Miklat,* Cities of Refuge. Their compassionate quality and their profound spiritual affinity especially suited them for this role.

The *Leviim* were trusted not to kill an unintentional murderer, even if he had slain a good friend or close relative of theirs. Following the episode of the Golden Calf, the *Leviim* demonstrated that their total commitment to Hashem and His *Torah* went beyond any personal attachments and allegiances. The *Leviim's* total adherence should serve as a powerful paradigm for us all.

***

ויגשו אליו ויאמרו גדרות צאן נקנה למקננו
פה וערים לטפנו

"They came close to him and said, 'we wish to build here sheep enclosures for our sheep and cities for our children.'" (32:16)

בנו לכם ערים לטפכם וגדרות לצנאכם

"Build for you cities for your children and sheep enclosures for your sheep." (32:24)

Chazal describe the dialogue between Moshe and the tribes of *Bnei Gad* and *Reuven* in the following manner. First they asked for sheep enclosures. Afterward, they requested cities for their children. Moshe corrected them by saying, *"Do not turn the unimportant into the essential and the essential into the secondary. First you must provide for your children, and then for your possessions."* *Chazal* explain that their obsession with their material needs caused these tribes to be the first to be exiled.

How true this has been throughout history. As soon as there is a modest improvement in our material sustenance, we tend to neglect our most sacred treasure, the *Torah*. We have shamelessly relegated the *Torah* to an inferior status as soon as opportunity for material advancement emerges. We should realize that all advancement becomes worthless if our awareness of *Torah* values becomes sullied. If *Torah* precepts do not dominate our life, then what value does it have?

Our noblest fulfillment should be the success of having reared children "*b'derech ha'Torah,*" in the *Torah* way. Our greatest symbol of Divine trust is the ability to dedicate ourselves and our family to *Torah* first and foremost. The desire to care for the "sheep" or our material security, while relegating *Torah* education to a distant second place catalyzes in the downfall of Jewish family values and *Torah nachas*. Indeed, financial worries are justified, but we are not permitted to sacrifice our most precious *Torah* treasures in order to pursue material pleasures. The *Tanna* in *Avos 3:21* states, "*If there is no flour (referring to material security), there is no Torah.*" This is indeed true, but we are not free to sacrifice *Torah* in the pursuit of "flour."

QUESTIONS LEVEL- A

1. What phrase is used by the *Torah* that means "*he should not break his word?*"

2. Were all the tribes represented in the war against Midyan?

3. A) How many Midyanite kings were killed in battle with *Bnei Yisrael*? B) Which gentile prophet was also killed?

QUESTIONS LEVEL- B

1. Which two righteous women were descendants of Amon and Moav?

2. Did *Shevet Levi* go to war against Midyan?

QUESTIONS LEVEL- C

1. Which *Kohen* was a משוח מלחמה?

2. Did Moshe demand that *Bnei Gad* and *Bnei Reuven* remain after the war for the division of the land?

QUESTIONS LEVEL- D

1. Which *Kohen* was the descendant of a Midyanite priest?

ANSWERS LEVEL- A

1. לא יחל דברו.
2. Yes.
3. A) 5. B) Bilaam.

ANSWERS LEVEL- B

1. רות המואביה, נעמה העמונית.
2. Yes.

ANSWERS LEVEL- C

1. Pinchas.
2. No.

ANSWERS LEVEL- D

1. Pinchas was the grandson of Yisro.

פרשת מסעי
PARASHAS MASEI
▶◀

את שש ערי מקלט
"The six cities of refuge." (35:6)

After Moshe endured the forty years of travel and travail with *Bnei Yisrael* in the wilderness, he was distressed at not being able to share in their forthcoming joy, entry into *Eretz Yisrael*. The *Abarbanel* explains that Hashem, in an attempt to console Moshe, gave him the task of teaching *Bnei Yisrael* the *mitzvos* relating to *Eretz Yisrael*, He also charged him with five specific missions which Moshe was to initiate, but which would not be completed until after his death. They were: to conquer and seize the land from its present inhabitants; to divide it fairly among the twelve tribes; to set its boundaries; to designate the forty-two cities for the *Leviim*; to set aside the six cities of refuge.

We may question this form of consolation. Would it not be even more difficult for Moshe to teach about *Eretz Yisrael*, knowing fully well that he was prohibited entry? Would it not take an amazing personal forbearance to be able to transcend his own feelings regarding his imminent death in order to teach *Klal Yisrael* about the promised land? The *Abarbanel* explains that, even though he knew he would not enter *Eretz Yisrael*, the realization that he was part of the process of entry consoled him.

We should take note of the above statement. Often we tend to avoid involvement in various activities because we will not receive due recognition for our efforts. This is misguided. The mere realization that we are part of a process which will enhance *Torah* activity should motivate our inclusion in any activity. One who seeks complete recognition for his efforts is guilty of a covert form of arrogance.

***

והיו לכם הערים למקלט...לנוס שמה כל מכה נפש בשגגה

"And they shall be for you cities of refuge . . . so that anyone who inadvertently kills a person shall be able to escape there."
(35:12,15)

One who killed *b'shogeg*, inadvertently, was to remain in the city of refuge until the death of the *Kohen Gadol*. Consequently, not all killers received the same punishment. While some had to remain a considerable length of time, some were liberated quickly. Not so with the deliberate killers. Each one received a similar punishment. Why is there such a discrepancy between the punishments of the deliberate and the inadvertent murderer? The *Korban Chagigah* offers an interesting response, which serves as a lesson in regard to appreciating the apportionment of punishment.

In the case of the intentional murderer, it is difficult to ascertain the extent of deliberateness. Therefore, all willful murderers receive the same punishment. In regard to the unintentional, we are faced with varied definitions of accident. Indeed, there are situations of inadvertent murder that could be viewed as negligent and those which can be viewed as voluntary. Hashem, Who knows the truth, discerns between these degrees and determines His punishment accordingly.

One whose act of violence borders on the deliberate will find himself remaining in the city of refuge for a longer period than one whose act was clearly accidental. Hashem's punishment is always *"middah k'neged middah,"* measure for measure. The retribution will always be commensurate with the transgression. While no person will receive more punishment than he deserves, neither will an individual receive less than his due.

QUESTIONS LEVEL- A

1. How many מסעות are mentioned?

2. A) Where did *Bnei Yisrael* camp after they left Kadesh? B) What happened there?

3. How many cities were designated for the *Leviim*?

QUESTIONS LEVEL- B

1. From where were the *Meraglim* sent forth?
2. What is an *Even Maskis*?

QUESTIONS LEVEL- C

1. In proportion where were there more *Arai Miklat* in *Eretz Yisrael* or *Ever Ha'Yarden*?
2. Who was the eldest of Tzlafchad's daughters?

QUESTIONS LEVEL- D

1. When was the letter *"yud"* added to סין to transform it to סיני?

ANSWERS LEVEL- A

1. 42.
2. A) *Har Ha'Har.* B) Aharon died.
3. 48.

ANSWERS LEVEL- B

1. Rismah.
2. A figured stone which the pagans would bow down upon with outstretched hands and feet.

ANSWERS LEVEL- C

1. *Ever Ha'Yarden.*
2. Machlah.

ANSWERS LEVEL- D

1. *Yud* corresponds with ten, the number of commandments given on *Har Sinai.* The extra letter was added at that time. *(Rokeach)*

ספר דברים
Sefer Devarim

Dedicated by

Mark and Peggy Yagour and Family

In loving memory of his mother
Miriam Yagour
מרים בת יעקב יוסף ע"ה
נפ' ג' תשרי תשנ"ו

*Through persecution, misery and illness,
her faith remained undaunted.*

*Her life personified love,
sensitivity and kindness.*

*Her love and devotion to her family
will always be a source of
inspiration to us.*

"תנו לה מפרי ידיה ויהללוה בשערים מעשיה"
*'Give her the fruits of her hand and let her be praised
in the gates by her very own deeds.'* (Mishlei 31.31)

פרשת דברים
PARASHAS DEVORIM
▶◀

יסף עליכם ככם אלף פעמים ויברך אתכם כאשר דבר לכם

"May He make you so many more like you a thousand times, and may He bless you as He has promised you." (1:11)

Just as *Moshe Rabbeinu* was on the verge of leaving *Am Yisrael,* he offered up a *tefillah*, prayer, that the nation be blessed with amazing future growth. He adds one word, however, which sheds light on the *Torah*'s perspective upon Jewish survival. Moshe says, *"May He make you so many more like you."* The true blessing is that the future generations are *"like you,"* following in the traditional path paved by their ancestors with blood, sweat, and tears.

In order to insure that the Jewish children of today and tomorrow serve as links in the chain of tradition, it is essential that they be imbued with the values of yesterday. Every incident which has occurred throughout our history, sad as well as joyous events, must become part of our children's personal "experience." They must be sensitized to our past, so that their future will reflect our heritage.

In contemporary times, we find many individuals who are searching for a common ground upon which to interface the lifestyle of the old traditional grandfather with that of his modern day grandchild. Alas, they have very little in common, unless the child was raised with ככם, *"like you,"* in mind. Many have been blessed with abundance, but Jewish survival is subject to another criteria, ככם, *"like you."* Today's blessing must coincide with the pattern of yesterday's values.

Horav M. Swift, z.l., homiletically applies this idea to a remarkable *Midrash*. The *Midrash* states that when Moshe was about to bid farewell to the people whose troubles he had shouldered for forty years, he began repeating the entire *Torah* to them. They looked at him and questioned his presence of mind. Perhaps he was old and had no rational understanding of the new country and the lifestyle that they were about to encounter. They immediately held up their children and asked Moshe, *"What have you provided for the future of these children? What pleasures can they enjoy out of life? What careers can they establish for themselves?"*

Moshe's response was to relate *Klal Yisrael's* history. He knew that the emotional approach would not stand the challenge of time. You can appeal to children not to neglect their old father and mother, but the response will be short- lived. Their retort is simple, "Times have changed, our parents are living in a different time frame. They are old fashioned. This is not the old country; it is a new world." Moshe did not appeal to their emotions. Instead, he presented them with an historical account of *Klal Yisrael's* existence as a nation. He gave them facts, figures, dates, and places. He recounted their iniquities and their strife. "Do you think that Hashem has allowed you to survive and has vanquished your enemies for naught? Hashem has cared for you for a reason, and He will continue to care for you throughout your future!" To paraphrase *Horav* Swift, *"No man is senile who cries 'look to history and take the lesson to heart.'"*

Both as a collective nation and as individuals, we have prevailed over the challenges of oppression and survived the most tragic catastrophes. The idea that we were liberated from tyranny and miraculously saved from terrifying death in order to enable our children to enjoy the pleasures of life (relegating *Torah* and tradition to the old fashioned grandparents) is not only absurd, but blasphemous! We must take the lesson of history. We were saved for a purpose. Our mandate is to live as our ancestors lived and build as they built, so that when our numbers increase, they will increase ככם, *"like you,"* in the tradition of our ancestors.

***

איכה אשא לבדי טרחכם ומשאכם וריבכם

"How can I myself alone bear your cumbrance and your burden and your strife?" (1:12)

The *Midrash* in *Eichah* distinguishes among three prophets who prefaced their prophecy with the word *"Eichah."*

The first was Moshe, who remonstrated about his obligation

238

to deal personally with all of *Klal Yisrael's* strife and complaints. Yeshayahu, the second, lamented *Bnei Yisrael's* infidelity with the words איכה היתה לזונה, *'How had the faithful city become like a harlot?"* Third, Yirmiyahu, who beheld *Klal Yisrael* in their disgrace, said, איכה ישבה בדד, *"Alas, she (Klal Yisrael) sits in solitude."*

These three statements apply to our people in the various stages of their development and ultimate disgrace. *Horav M. Rogov, z.l.,* explains that Moshe, who was with us during our period of glory, lamented the constant bickering and complaints to which he was subjected. During Yeshayahu's tenure, Moshe's burden would have been viewed as a source of "joy." The counsel and authority of *Torah* leaders was no longer in demand. The members of *Am Yisrael,* who were so faithful under Moshe's leadership, had transferred their loyalty to other authorities. They had strayed as a harlot.

This digression reached a greater proportion during Yirmiyahu's time. At least Yeshayahu saw the Jewish people before him. As long as the Jew exists, there is always hope for his return to the faith. In Yirmiyahu's time, regrettably, this was not the situation. The country had been ravaged and laid to ruin. The people were driven into exile. This was the greatest lament, for there was no longer anyone with whom to communicate.

Perhaps we can derive a simple lesson from this *Midrash.* We often bemoan our lot in life, not realizing that it is all relative. What we may view as hardship may be enviable to one who has less or suffers more. We should learn to view our fate in the proper perspective it reflects the decision of Hashem, who in His infinite wisdom recognizes what is best for us.

***

ותרגנו באהליכם ותאמרו בשנאת ד' אתנו הוציאנו מארץ
מצרים לתת אתנו ביד האמרי להשמידנו

"And you murmured in your tents and said 'because Hashem hated us, He has brought us forth out of the land of Egypt to deliver us into the hand of the Emori to destroy us." (1:27)

In *Parashas Shelach* the *Torah* extensively addresses the sin of the *meraglim,* spies. In this *parsha,* a new dimension to this sin is revealed as Moshe recounts *Klal Yisrael's* past iniquities. In their unfounded complaint against Hashem, *Klal Yisrael* added the above statement, *"Because Hashem hated us, He took us out of Egypt."* Such harsh criticism is not offered in any other context. In fact, this explains the eternal punishment effected by the sin of the *meraglim*. *Klal Yisrael* experienced the greatest miracles in Egypt. The Red Sea was wondrously split before their eyes. They were fed *manna* in the desert. Is there any reason to imagine that Hashem's beneficence was rooted in hatred toward them? Such a statement is not only the epitome of ingratitude, but it is also totally ludicrous!

Displacing responsibility in this manner is the result of a negative self-image. *Bnei Yisrael* were attempting to protect themselves from their anxiety by projecting their own shortcomings and unacceptable impulses upon Hashem. This defense mechanism was a reaction to their subconscious feelings of failure. Thus, they were blinded to Hashem's real love for them. They should have realized that Hashem, although He was aware of their imperfections, took them out of Egypt and cared for them out of unbounded love. This form of *Chillul Hashem,* desecration of Hashem's Name, is not to be tolerated.

Horav M. Wolfson, Shlita, suggests that *Parashas Devorim,* which is read on *Shabbos Chazon,* the *Shabbos* before *Tisha B'Av,* carries with it a special mandate. In this *parsha,* the *meraglim's* sin, which was the precursor of *Tisha B'Av,* is emphasized more intensely than a sin of ingratitude. It stresses our rejection and misrepresentation of Hashem's love. We took Hashem's acts of kindness and misconstrued them in the most reprehensible manner. It is, therefore, our obligation during this time to delve into the various events of life which we have encountered in order to attempt to appreciate their positive aspects. Through this endeavor, we will merit to see that wonderful day on which *Tisha' B'Av* will be transformed into a *Yom Tov.*

***

ונסב את הר שעיר ימים רבים. ויאמר ד' אלי לאמר. רב לכם סוב
את ההר הזה פנו לכם צפונה

"And we circled Mount Seir many days. And Hashem spoke to me saying 'you have long passed this mountain, turn you northward.'" (2:1,2,3)

The *Midrash* interprets the phrase פנו לכם צפונה *"turn you northward,"* as הצפינו לכם לתורה *"hide yourselves for Torah."* This *Midrash* suggests a profound idea. Throughout our history, we have attempted to solve all of our problems with one common panacea, assimilation. If only we would develop a greater, more open-minded relationship with the gentile world, we would be accepted as equals and all of our problems would dissipate.

Unfortunately, a perusal through Jewish history indicates the opposite. Every time we have attempted to break through the religious barriers by assimilating with our gentile neighbors, we have been driven back in the most cruel and bestial manner. On the contrary, we experienced our few "moments" of reprieve when we remained separate, not groveling as cowards willing to shed our identities in return for gentile recognition and acceptance.

Horav M. Rogov, z.l., points out that this is the meaning of the *pasuk.* Hashem says to *Bnei Yisrael, "You have long passed this mountain."* Stop encircling *Har Seir,* attempting to ingratiate yourselves in Eisav's eyes. The only hope and salvation for *Bnei Yisrael* is when you "hide" themselves in the *Torah.* Through our complete devotion to *Torah* and *mitzvos,* we will develop a unique sense of Jewish pride. This will be our source of courage and strength throughout the *galus,* exile, as we wait for the ultimate salvation, the advent of *Moshiach.*

QUESTIONS LEVEL- A

1. Which two kings did Moshe defeat prior to his death?

2. The judges were told to judge the people _____.

3. Hashem "carried" *Bnei Yisrael* in the wilderness like a ____ carries his _____.

4. Where did *Bnei Yisrael* camp for the longest time?

5. Whose descendants were promised the land of *Moav?*

QUESTIONS LEVEL- B

1. The _____ chased *Bnei Yisrael* as _____ chase a person. Why are they compared to this insect?

2. Which of Lot's daughters displayed greater *tznius*?

QUESTIONS LEVEL- C

1. What merit did Lot have to deserve to inherit two countries from Avraham?

2. At what point did Hashem stop addressing Moshe face to face with an expression of endearment?

QUESTIONS LEVEL- D

1. Hashem originally promised Avraham that his descendants would inherit the land of _____ nations. When they sinned, they lost this privilege. A) What was their sin? B) When will we possess Eisav's territory?

ANSWERS LEVEL- A

1. Shichon and Og.

2. Righteously.

3. Father, son.

4. Kadesh.

5. Lot.

ANSWERS LEVEL- B

1. Emori, Bees, just as a bee dies immediately upon stinging a person, they too died after touching *Bnei Yisrael.*

2. The younger one.

ANSWERS LEVEL- C

1. When Avraham said that Sarah was his sister, Lot kept quiet.

2. After the sin of the *meraglim.*

ANSWERS LEVEL- D

1. 10. A) Golden Calf. B) In the time of *Moshiach.*

פרשת ואתחנן
PARASHAS VAESCHANAN
►◄

ואתחנן אל ד' בעת ההיא לאמר
"And I beseeched Hashem at that time, saying." (3:23)

Chazal state that Moshe prayed 515 prayers, entreating Hashem to permit him to enter *Eretz Yisrael*. He was even willing to enter as an animal, sustaining himself on grass and water, as long as he could be in *Eretz Yisrael*. When Hashem denied him this request, he asked to be transformed into a bird which could fly throughout the land. Hashem also denied Moshe this plea. This *Chazal* demands an explanation. What could Moshe have accomplished in *Eretz Yisrael* as an animal or a bird? If he could not perform *mitzvos* in *Eretz Yisrael* what value would his merely dwelling there have?

Horav E.M. Shach, Shlita, explains that Moshe's request was profound. He cites the *Rambam* in *Hilchos Yesodei Hatorah 2:2*, who says that man can achieve a deeper understanding and appreciation of Hashem's eminence by reflecting upon His creations. When one realizes the infinite wisdom and boundless power of Hashem, he will, in turn, develop a greater sense of reverence and love for Him. One need only to open his eyes and reflect upon that which he perceives.

As *Horav* Shach explains, one need not delve on every aspect of Creation. Even if he were to contemplate only one minute facet of Hashem's creations, the effect would be profound. Moshe *Rabbeinu*, the most humble of men, viewed himself simply as a vehicle for sanctifying Hashem's Name in this world. His whole life and entire essence was dedicated to that goal. His desire to enter *Eretz Yisrael* was selfless. He adjured Hashem to avail him the opportunity to continue sanctifying His Name. When the opportunity for human endeavor was rejected, he requested to continue his service even as another creature. As long as he could enhance *"kavod Shomayim,"* honor of Heaven, Moshe was favorably inclined to accept. This is but

243

another example of the selfless devotion exhibited by the unique leader of *Klal Yisrael.*

***

וראה בעיניך

"And see with your eyes." (3:27)

Rashi explains that Hashem responded to Moshe's request that he be permitted to see the "good land" by showing him the entire land. *Horav Nissan Alpert, z.l.,* questions this response. Did Moshe merely want to "see" *Eretz Yisrael?* The *Talmud* in *Sotah 14A* states that Moshe's yearning for *Eretz Yisrael* originated from a deep longing to perform the specific *mitzvos* which are applicable only in *Eretz Yisrael.* Why, then, did Moshe want to "see" the land, and what was Hashem's response?

Horav Alpert explains that Moshe cherished *Eretz Yisrael* for its holiness. He sought the opportunity to imbue *Klal Yisrael* with his unique love for the land. He sought entry into *Eretz Yisrael* specifically for this reason. Moshe *Rabbeinu,* the quintessential leader, lived for his people. His primary goal was to impart this orientation to them. Moshe specifically requested of Hashem, אעברה נא ואראה which is translated as, *"Let me go over and see."* This phrase may be interpreted as, *"I will enable them to see. I will reveal the sublime sanctity which is the essence of Eretz Yisrael."* Hashem responded that when *Bnei Yisrael* would see Moshe standing on the mountain, full of yearning for the land, they would, in turn, be inspired with love for *Eretz Yisrael.* Moshe's love for *Eretz Yisrael* focused on the land as a vehicle by which to achieve heightened spiritual awareness.

***

ועתה ישראל שמע אל החקים ואל המשפטים... למען תחיו
ובאתם וירשתם את הארץ

"And now Yisrael, listen to the statutes and the laws . . . so that you may live and go and take possession of the land." (4:1)

Horav S.R. Hirsch, z.l., notes that this *pasuk* presents the *Torah's* prescription for life. Free-willed obedience and adherence to the laws mandated by Hashem allows us truly to "live." Only by devoting all of our energies to the observance of Hashem's laws do we attain life.

His laws must shape our thought processes and regulate our sensitivities. If *Torah* does not regiment our life, if its values are not our values, then we have not lived; we have merely existed. Free-willed obedience to the *Torah* serves as the criterion for our individual lives, transforming mere existence into true living. So, too, it is the sole condition for our national life to be granted credence and acceptability in our own land.

***

ואהבת את ד' אלקיך בכל לבבך ובכל נפשך ובכל מאדך

"Love Hashem, your G-d, with all your heart and with all your might." (6:5)

The *Talmud* in *Berachos* explains *"with all your heart," "levovcha,"* is the plural form of *"lev,"* which implies two hearts or two distinct natural drives, the good nature and evil nature of a person. This statement seems enigmatic. How does one serve Hashem with his evil inclination? Should not evil be uprooted? *Horav Moshe Rosenstein, z.l.,* posits that serving Hashem with one's evil impulse is actually easier and less complex than serving Hashem with one's good nature.

Horav Rosenstein explains that to love someone means to relinquish one's possession to the other person. The ability to surrender an object, to forego and sacrifice one's possession so that another individual can benefit, is an expression of love. To love Hashem with the evil inclination means to abolish all envy and desire for honor, to surrender one's proclivity for self-gratification in order to sacrifice everything for the sake of Hashem.

We now confront an apparent contradiction. If love is defined as sacrifice, then how does one abolish his good nature and "sacrifice" it in the service of Hashem? Such a submission seems puzzling!

Horav Rosenstein presents another understanding of loving Hashem with the *yetzer tov* and the *yetzer hora*. The concept of "good" has regrettably become a misnomer. Intended good, in reality, is sometimes blemished, thereby becoming bad. The definition of good is relative. At times certain developments which are the "result" of this initial good can actually cause more harm than benefit. In such a case, "good" is really "bad."

One's desire to perform that which is correct and good should emanate from an aspiration to serve Hashem. If this is the case, one will always be retrospective in his approach to "doing good," examining every facet of this endeavor, so that it conforms in all aspects to the dictates of Hashem. Unfortunately, our good deeds can be motivated by the wrong inclination or as the *Baalei Mussar* put it: the product of a *"frum yetzer hora."* In order to serve Hashem with one's good nature, one must be cognizant of the true nature of one's "good" intentions. He must also demonstrate the ability to abstain from these deeds when they conflict with the will of Hashem.

Love and sacrifice take on various forms. To sacrifice one's good nature because of possible conflict with the will of Hashem is a sign of true love for Hashem.

***

ושננתם לבניך

"And you shall teach them diligently to your children." (6:7)

Rashi explains that *"your children"* refers to one's students. Indeed as *Rashi* notes, *"talmidim,"* students, are often referred to as *"banim,"* children. It seems puzzling that the *Torah* would refer to students as children, thereby attributing to the *rebbe*, teacher, the status of a father. *Chazal* clearly state that a *rebbe* has greater *halachic* status than a father, since the *rebbe* "brings" the student into *"Olam Ha'bah,"* while the father brings him only into *Olam Ha'zeh.*

Horav M. Feinstein, z.l., explains that, just as a father bequeaths his child specific natural traits, so, too, a *rebbe* imbues his student with his own unique personality. A student should reflect his *rebbe's* character, just as a son reflects that of his father.

We may suggest a similar idea to be derived from here regarding the *rebbe-talmid* relationship. A *rebbe* should view his students as his own children. The love and concern which are synonymous with parenthood should be reflected by a teacher toward his student. Undoubtedly, when the student senses this special affection, he will reciprocate in kind.

***

QUESTIONS LEVEL- A

1. Whom was Moshe told to encourage?

2. Egypt is compared to an _____ _____?

3. Moshe separated _____ cities on *Ever Ha'Yarden* to serve as _____.

4. How many times are the *Aseres Ha'dibros* mentioned in the *Torah*?

5. Were *Bnei Yisrael* permitted to take pity on the gentile nations residing in *Eretz Yisrael*?

QUESTIONS LEVEL- B

1. To what does לבנון refer?

2. A) Where were *Bnei Yisrael* originally commanded regarding the laws of *Shabbos*? B) Which other one of the *Aseres Hadibros* were they commanded to observe (at this place)?

QUESTIONS LEVEL- C

1. What was unique about Moshe's preparation of the *Arai Miklat* on *Ever Ha'Yarden*?

2. Who referred to his *rebbe* with the appellation of אבי אבי?

QUESTIONS LEVEL- D

1. Moshe *Rabbeinu* was "buried" outside of *Eretz Yisrael*. A) Why does Hashem cause great *tzaddikim* to be buried outside *Eretz Yisrael*? B) Which great *Navi* was buried in *Bavel*?

ANSWERS LEVEL- A

1. Yehoshua.

2. Iron furnace.

3. Three. *Arai Miklat.*

4. Twice.

5. No.

ANSWERS LEVEL- B

1. *Bais Ha'mikdash.*
2. A) Marah. B) Honoring parents.

ANSWERS LEVEL- C

1. They did not offer asylum until the cities in *Eretz Yisrael* were established. Yet, he wished to perform this *mitzvah* prior to his demise.

2. Elisha referred this way to Eliyahu *Ha'Navi.*

ANSWERS LEVEL- D

1. A) So that their merits will protect their fellow Jews who are also buried outside *Eretz Yisrael.*

B) Yecheskel.

פרשת עקב
PARASHAS EIKEV
►◄

ואכלת ושבעת וברכת את ד' אלקיך על הארץ הטובה אשר נתן לך

"And you shall eat and be satisfied and bless Hashem your G-d for the good land which He has given you." (8:10)

This *pasuk* implies that *Bircas Ha'mazon* is not merely a formal offering of gratitude for the meal which we have eaten. Rather, it proclaims our acknowledgment that Hashem is the source of all things. Indeed, we even submit our thanks to Hashem for providing us with our land. This seems enigmatic. Imagine being invited to someone's home for dinner and, after the meal, thanking the host for the use of his furniture and home during the course of the meal. This expression of gratitude is undoubtedly excessive. Why, then, is it necessary to specifically mention the land during *Bircas Ha'Mazon*?

Horav B.Z. Baruk, z.l., offers the following analogy in response. A person who was hunger stricken and thirsty is walking in the desert, completely exposed to the elements. Suddenly, a plane lands as if from nowhere. A beautifully furnished home complete with a table laden with various delicacies ready for his consumption appears before him. Obviously, in such a situation, the individual's gratitude would extend beyond a simple acknowledgment of the delicious meal. He would indicate his appreciation for everything. Similarly, we should acknowledge that every meal we enjoy is a brand new creation, resulting from Hashem's beneficence. We have fallen victim to the sin of complacency by taking everything for granted. Regretfully, we reflect upon Hashem's favors only when we are denied them. Increasing our awareness would neutralize this apathetic attitude.

***

ואמרת בלבבך כחי ועצם ידי עשה לי את החיל הזה. וזכרת את
ד' אלקיך כי הוא הנותן לך כח לעשות חיל

**"And you say in your heart my power and the might of my hand
has gotten me this wealth. But you should remember Hashem
your G-d, for it is He who gives you the power to get wealth."**
(8:17,18)

Horav E. Dessler, z.l., explains that all which comprises an
individual's creative personality, including his capacity to earn a
livelihood, his intelligence, foresight, business acumen, and skill, are
the products of Hashem's beneficence. In fact, every facet of one's
existence is derived from Hashem. The miracle of physical and
mental health is not the direct result of the nutrition inherent in the
food we eat. Rather, Hashem employs the food as a vehicle by which
He imparts this seemingly natural blessing.

Horav Dessler cites *Targum Onkelos,* who explains that the
thought process which catalyzes every endeavor is actually the work
of the Almighty. Hashem gives us the "ability" to make our
livelihood. No part of our good fortune can be attributed to our own
merit. How disparate is *Torah hashkafah,* philosophy, from that of
contemporary society, which lauds and venerates the "self-made"
man! One should realize that the "self-made" man is really one who
has merited to be the recipient of a major gift from Hashem. Perhaps,
if we were to be more cognizant of the origins of success, our
appreciation of our gifts would be enhanced.

***

ובאהרן התאנף ד' מאד להשמידו ואתפלל גם בעד אהרן בעת ההיא

**"And Hashem was very angry with Aharon to destroy him. And I
prayed for Aharon also the same time."** (9:20)

Rashi explains that להשמידו, *"to destroy him,"* refers to the destruction
of children. During the sin of the Golden Calf, Hashem dictated that
Aharon was to be punished by the death of his children. Only through
Moshe's entreaty on his behalf were two of his sons spared, although
two did die. The *Mizrachi* derives from *Rashi's* statement that Nadav
and Avihu died as a result of Aharon's involvement in the Golden
Calf. This idea, however, is inconsistent with *Rashi* in *Shemos 24,*
where he states that they died as a result of beholding the glory of

250

Hashem while they were in an unsanctified state. Their deaths were delayed until the day of *Chanukas Ha'Mishkan*, dedication of the *Mishkan*, so as not to mar the sublime joy of the giving of the *Torah*.

Horav Y. Salant, z.l., clarifies these conflicting statements in the following manner. Hashem's form of retribution is unique in that it only affects the individual who deserves punishment. In fact, if anyone else is afflicted, it is because they are also culpable. Hashem weighs every situation, and He will refrain from punishing the guilty party if an innocent person will be needlessly affected. Nadav and Avihu sinned and merited immediate retribution. Aharon, however, would have needlessly suffered. Consequently, their fate was delayed. When Aharon became involved in the Golden Calf, the previously delayed punishment became effective. Only through Moshe's prayers were two of Aharon's sons spared. We should be ever retrospective in searching for the hidden message in every situation which confronts us. Every event which we experience has a purpose and a meaning behind it.

***

ובני ישראל נסעו מבארת בני יעקן מוסרה שם מת אהרן

"And Bnei Yisrael journeyed from the springs of Bnei Yaakon to Mosera, there Aharon died." (11:6)

The *Ramban* suggests that *Har Ha'Har*, upon which Aharon died, was actually a mountain ridge stretching from *Mosera* to *Kadesh*. Aharon climbed up to the ridge in *Kadesh* and died on top opposite *Mt. Mosera*. This explanation resolves the apparent contradiction concerning the place of Aharon's demise, *Mosera* or *Har Ha'Har*.

Horav Yekusiel Grunwald, z.l., offers a homiletic rendering of this *pasuk* which suggests a profound message. *Mosera* was the place where brother fought against brother with casualties falling on each side. After Aharon's death, the Clouds of Glory departed, causing much consternation among *Bnei Yisrael*. Afraid of war with the king of Arad, the people appointed a chief to take them back to Egypt. In *Mosera*, the tribe of *Levi* battled against them. In the ensuing battle, both sides suffered. The first blood to be shed between brothers was in *Mosera*. In reality, the spirit of Aharon, which is synonymous with peace, departed in *Mosera*. Even when a person physically dies, his spirit and legacy can live on in the heart and mind of his followers. His demise is final only when this spirit no longer serves as an inspiration to others.

***

כי אם שמר תשמרון את כל המצוה הזאת

"For if you will guard and continue guarding all this command "
(11:22)

It is not sufficient to study *Torah*. An individual must constantly review his *Torah* studies, so that they remain in his mind and becoame integrated into his personality. Indeed, the *Sifri* ascribes to this *pasuk* the admonition to repeat again and again that which we have learned. The *Torah* warns that, just as one has to be careful not to lose any penny that he has earned, he should likewise vigilantly guard against losing any *Torah* knowledge which he has acquired. In *Iyov 28:7, Torah* knowledge is compared to both gold and glass. Like gold, it is difficult to acquire, while like glass, it is easy to drop and lose.

We may suggest another reason for the analogy to glass. When glass falls and breaks, it splinters into sharp jagged pieces which are dangerous to anyone who touches them. Similarly, coming in contact with one who, due to a lack of dedication, has forgotten various aspects of his *Torah* wisdom is hazardous to one's spiritual health. *Torah* is not a secular subject which is studied merely to be remembered. Rather, it represents the lifeblood of our people and must be constantly reviewed, so that its students become thoroughly imbued in its value.

QUESTIONS LEVEL- A

1. If we observe the *mitzvos*, all the evil diseases which existed in _____ will be taken away from us.

2. Were the gentile nations of *Eretz Yisrael* deserving of remaining there?

3. The first *Luchos* were written with the _____ of Hashem.

4. Did Moshe throw down the first *Luchos*, or did they fall from his

hands?

5. When Moshe was instructed to prepare the second *Luchos*, what else was he told to build?

QUESTIONS LEVEL- B

1. Did *Bnei Yisrael* grow out of their clothes during their stay in the desert?

2. Moshe was on *Har Sinai* _____ times. During which time was he not in eminent good-will?

QUESTIONS LEVEL-C

1. Did Moshe's *tefillah* on Aharon's behalf have any effect?

2. What is the significance of the word היום (11:13) in regard to *mitzvah* observance?

QUESTIONS LEVEL- D

1. Hashem does not permanently entrust the keys to three vital matters to angels, but rather, he holds them for Himself. What are they?

ANSWERS LEVEL- A

1. Egypt.

2. No.

3. Finger.

4. He threw them down.

5. An *Aron* made of wood.

ANSWERS LEVEL- B

1. No, their clothes grew with them.

2. 1) Three, 2) The second time.

ANSWERS LEVEL- C

1. Yes, Hashem spared two of his sons.

2. *Mitzvos* should be as new and fresh to us as if they had been heard this very day.

ANSWERS LEVEL- D

1. Rain (livelihood), bearing children, and *techiyas ha'maisim*.

פרשת ראה
PARASHAS RE'EH
►◄

ראה אנכי נתן לפניכם היום ברכה וקללה

"Behold I set before you today a blessing and a curse." (11:26)

This phrase is usually interpreted as, *"I put before you two things, a blessing and a curse, of which you must choose one."* This translation emphasizes two distinct paths which are available to man: the path of good which leads to life and the path of evil which leads to the contrary.

Horav M. Swift, z.l., offers another interpretation for this *pasuk.* He renders *"blessing and curse"* literally as being one unit. Every blessing carries within it the potential that through misapplication will be transformed into a curse. People who have been endowed with wealth may shower this blessing upon their children in various ways, only to discover that this blessing has been the source of their child's failure in life. This same fortune spoiled them and led them astray. How many fortunes have destroyed marriages and families? An abused blessing thus contains the ingredients of a curse. The converse also holds true. Sometimes that which seems to be a curse can be transformed into a blessing.

Horav Swift explains that this idea is expressed during our *Rosh Chodesh bentchen* prayers. We ask for *"a life in which the wishes of our hearts will be fulfilled for (the) good."* What is the meaning of the added expression *"for (the) good"*? Does anyone desire something that is not for good? Unfortunately, some things, although they may seem fine in our eyes, are not "viewed" by Hashem in the same positive light. Hashem knows what is truly "good" for us. We, therefore, entreat Him to grant us the "good" which only He knows is truly beneficial for us.

We may advance this thought further. Due to a misguided sense of values, people often lose the ability to discern between blessing and curse. They perceive an individual who "appears" blessed, but in reality is cursed -- and vice versa. Some individuals view the apparent lack of material excess consistent with the lifestyle of many *Bnei Torah* as a bitter curse. On the other hand, other insecure individuals are secretly envious of the success attained by those who have deserted the *Torah* lifestyle. The *Torah* emphatically states that blessing is only *"if you shall listen"* and curse is *"if you shall not listen."* The prescribed guidelines for success, happiness, and blessing are clear. We have only to open up our eyes and see!

***

וסרתם מן הדרך

"And (you) will turn aside from the path which I have commanded you this day." (11:28)

Rashi derives from this *pasuk* that one who worships idols is in reality turning away from the entire *Torah*. *Rashi's* words seem superfluous. Obviously one who is an idol worshiper has no relationship with the *Torah*! *Horav Y.D. Soloveitchik, z.l.*, explains this *pasuk* in the following manner. Some individual Jews who, despite their commitment to *Torah* observance, still believe in various forms of idol worship. Indeed, the *Navi Sheker*, the false prophet, uses Hashem's Name in an effort to promulgate idolatry! This is a grave mistake. To believe in Hashem is to believe in nothing else. Hashem is the sole Supreme Being who created this world from nothing and guides every aspect of it at every moment. To deviate from this belief or to ascribe any form of collaboration to Him is pure blasphemy.

***

ונתת את הברכה על הר גריזים ואת הקללה על הר עיבל

"And you shall set the blessing upon Mount Gerizim and the curse upon Mount Eival." (11:29)

Why did Hashem designate two distinct mountains for curse and blessing? Would it not have been equally effective to have both blessing and curse upon the same mountain? Indeed, were not the *Leviim* the ones who stood between both mountains and recited both blessings and curses? The *Kehilas Yitzchak* explains that Hashem could have understandably issued blessing and curse from the same mountain. He wanted, however, to teach us a valuable lesson. The

255

place from which goodness and blessing emanates must be separate from the place which breeds evil and curse.

A Jew should seek to go to such a place which is *totally good.* Thus, he will be secure in his hope for success. Although it is conceivable for one to achieve spiritual success even in a place which is evil, the hazards preclude the likelihood for such achievement.

This was Hashem's message. The Jew must pursue every opportunity to detach himself from anything which is evil. The ability to distinguish between good and evil is truly a blessing.

***

אחרי ד' אלקיכם תלכו ואתו תיראו ואת מצותיו תשמרו ובקלו תשמעו ואתו תעבדו

"After Hashem your G-d you shall walk, and Him you shall fear, and His mitzvos you shall keep, and unto His voice you shall listen, and Him you shall serve." (13:5)

In *Parashas Eikav (10:20)* the *Torah* makes a similar statement, *"You shall fear Hashem, worship Him, and cling to Him."* One idea distinguishes these two seemingly redundant *pesukim.* The first *pasuk* is written is the singular, whereas the *pasuk* in our *parsha* is written in the plural form. This implies two different audiences.

Horav A.M. M'Gur, z.l., offers the following explanation for the apparent redundancy and change in focus. Under stable conditions, each individual can concentrate upon developing and enhancing his own spirituality, even in seclusion. During times of spiritual turbulence, however, the moral fiber of society deteriorates and blasphemers openly flaunt their diatribe. The power of the individual is rendered too weak to withstand the pressure upon him. The talents and powers of the entire *Torah* community must then be coalesced to provide the spiritual sustenance with which to defend our heritage against all incursions. Only with such support will we succeed in dispelling the harmful influence generated by these pressures.

In our *parsha,* the *Torah* addresses the danger to the Jewish community resulting from the false prophets. The previous exhortation regarding our relationship with Hashem is reiterated. This time, however, it is presented in the plural form. We are thereby instructed to combine our concerted efforts to repel this onslaught. We are required to work as a community to express proudly our spiritual heritage and our determination to observe *Torah* and *mitzvos*.

One postscript should be noted. While it is wonderful to have everyone working "together" for the sake of Heaven, they must function under one banner of *Torah* leadership. If everyone continues doing his "own thing" without the guidance and inspiration of *Gedolei Yisrael, Torah* leadership, our only achievement will be the defeat of our objectives.

***

פתח תפתח את ידך לאחיך לעניך ולאבינך בארצך

You shall open your hand to your brother, to the poor, to the needy, in your land." (15:11)

There are four levels of *tzedakah*. First is one who is *"your brother."* One's family takes precedence in charity. Second is *"your poor."* The poor citizens of one's city are to be cared for before one accepts responsibility for the poor of another city. The third degree is *"your needy."* He who is most needy is to be helped first. Last is *"in your land,"* the poor of *Eretz Yisrael*.

The laws regarding charitable donations are unambiguous. One does not contribute according to his heart's sentiments. *Torah* provides a prescribed manner and order for giving. The needy person or organization should meet the standards and criteria set forth by the *Torah*. All too often we make decisions regarding our charitable donations based solely upon our affinity with an organization or individual. If the *Torah's* standard for charity is met, we no longer have license to render a decision based upon religious affiliation or personal prejudice.

Rav Shalom M'Belz, z.l., suggests a novel interpretation of this *pasuk*. When one's hand is open, the fingers are not all the same size. Once one's hand is closed as in a fist, however, all of the fingers seem equal in size. The *Torah* demands *"Open up your hand."* Notice that there are various "sizes" or situations which call for different approaches to *tzedakah*. Not all of the poor are the same. One's decision should not be based upon a "closed" hand, in which all the fingers seems to be the same. We are adjured to proffer our contributions each according to its own unique degree of importance.

257

As Hashem bestows upon us the ability to contribute, so, too, does He issue us the framework for distribution of our *tzedakah*.

QUESTIONS LEVEL- A

1. What was the first thing *Bnei Yisrae*l were to do in *Eretz Yisrael*?

2. Which tribe did not have a portion in *Eretz Yisrael*?

3. What is the *Torah's* stated reason for the prohibition against eating blood?

4. What is an עיר הנדחת?

5. What special description is given to *Klal Yisrael* in this *parsha*?

QUESTIONS LEVEL- B

1. Who receives the firstborn of one's herd?

2. A) The *Bais Ha'Mikdash* was built in the portion of land belonging to _____. B) Why then does the *Torah* state מכל שבטיכם (12:5), implying all the tribes?

QUESTIONS LEVEL- C

1. Does the prohibition of בשר בחלב apply to an unclean animal?

2. Who is more needy, an עני or an אביון?

QUESTIONS LEVEL- D

1. Was there ever a case of an עיר הנדחת?

ANSWERS LEVEL- A

1. Destroy all the idols.

2. *Levi*.

3. The blood is the *"nefesh,"* the soul and life of the animal.

4. A city whose inhabitants turned to idol worship.

5. Children of Hashem.

ANSWERS LEVEL- B

1. *Kohen.*

2. A) Binyamin. B) They all gave money for the purchase of the land.

ANSWERS LEVEL- C

1. No.

2. אביין.

ANSWERS LEVEL- D

1. The *Talmud Sanhedrin 71* states that there never has been and never will be a case of an עיר הנדחת. The *Talmud Sandhedrin 113A,* however, states that Yehoshua treated Yericho as an עיר הנדחת.

פרשת שופטים
PARASHAS SHOFTIM
►◄

והיה כשבתו על כסא מלכותו וכתב לו את משנה התורה הזאת.
והיתה עמו וקרא בו כל ימי חייו למען ילמד ליראה את ד' אלקיו
ולבלתי רום לבבו מאחיו ולבלתי סור מן המצוה

And it shall be when he sits upon the throne of his kingdom and
he shall write him a copy of this law . . . and it shall be with him.
And he shall read therein all the days of his life that he may learn
to fear Hashem his G-d . . . that his heart not be lifted up (in
arrogance) above his brethren and that he not turn aside from the
mitzvah." (17:18,19,20)

The *Torah* implies that the king must seek *shleimus*, perfection, not
only as king, but also as an individual Jew. He is not permitted to
allow his exalted position to go to "his head." Arrogance is an
unbecoming character trait for anyone, especially a Jewish king. All
too often, one who is constantly involved with communal
responsibility forgets his obligation to himself. One's personal
spiritual perfection should not defer to his communal endeavors.

One who devotes himself to *Klal Yisrael* undoubtedly has
enormous *zechusim*, merits. These merits will support him in his
time of need. Nonetheless, as *Horav D. Bliacher, z.l.,* observes, the
Torah implores the king not to depend upon these merits, but to
personally endeavor to perfect himself. The quest for perfection is
effected through the writing and constant use of his own *Sefer Torah.*
This concept is illustrated by *David Ha'melech,* who often spent the
night engrossed in *Torah* study and praise to the Almighty. The
following morning he was available to the Jewish leaders in order to
involve himself in communal problems.

Every *Torah* leader should be aware of this obligation. All too
frequently, one defers his own spiritual advancement for the sake of
others. This is a grave mistake. If one's personal spiritual dimension

260

is not perfected, he has no right to act in a leadership role. Indeed, rather than help others, he may ultimately cause irreparable damage.

***

תכין לך הדרך ... והיה לנוס שמה כל רצח

"You should prepare the way . . . (so) that every murderer shall flee there." (19:3)

The *Torah* implores *Bnei Yisrae*l to *"prepare the way"* for the unintentional murderer, availing him the opportunity to reach the safe haven of the *Arai Miklat.* Indeed, they prepared road signs which pointed the way to the nearest city of refuge. The *Talmud* in *Makkos 10b* states that just as Hashem shows the way for the unintentional sinner, He certainly does the same for the righteous. *Horav A.H. Lebowitz, Shlita,* notes that Hashem places "road signs" for all of us, directing us to the correct path to follow for a successful life.

The unintentional murderer found his way referring to the signs. When he came to a fork in the road, the sign pointed him in the correct way. We, too, have signs to follow when we reach a fork in the road of life. We are mandated to analyze the *Torah* and determine the meaning of its message to us. Our course in life is charted by Hashem's *halachos*, laws, which illuminate every step of our journey through life.

Our devotion to *halachah* will determine how simple or difficult it will be for us to recognize the message of our personal road signs. The greater our affinity to *Torah* law, the easier it is for us to find our way through the maze of confusion to which we are subjected in life.

Horav Lebowitz sums up his thesis with a profound observation. The reason that the murderer found it difficult to course his way was his lack of familiarity with the area of the city of refuge. Had he been near home, he would have had no problem reaching his destination. Likewise, the more we discover ourselves to be at home in *Torah*, the easier it will be for us to discern its message and to chart our path through life.

***

ונשל הברזל מן העץ ומצא את רעהו ומת הוא ינוס אל אחת הערים האלה וחי

"And the iron flies from the wood and finds his fellow man and he dies, he shall flee to one of these cities and live." (19:5)

The unintentional murderer was required to flee for the safety of his life to one of the designated cities of refuge. In *Parashas Masei,* the *Torah* states that the murderer was to remain within the confines of the city until the death of the *Kohen Gadol.* If the murderer were to leave the city prior to the *Kohen Gadol's* death, he may have been killed by his victim's closest kinsman.

The *Mishnah in Makkos 2:7* states that the *Kohen Gadol's* mother would provide food and drink for the exiled murderer, so that he would not pray for her son's death. Indeed, the *Talmud* explains that the *Kohen Gadol* was held partially accountable for the inadvertent death of the victim and the murderer's subsequent exile. The responsibility of a *Torah* leader is all encompassing. Had the *Kohen Gadol* prayed with increased fervor for *Klal Yisrael's* welfare, this incident might not have occurred.

Horav Y.Z. Segal, z.l., notes the importance of a *Torah* leader's communal responsibility. The potential effectiveness of the exiled murderer's prayers is indicated by the fact that the *Kohen Gadol's* mother sought the opportunity to prevent their being offered. This observation is magnified with the awareness of the type of person the sinner is. What kind of self-indulgent individual would pray for the *Kohen Gadol's* death, so that he could leave the city of refuge? Nonetheless, the sinner's sordid prayers could have had an influence upon the *Kohen Gadol's* life. Heightened responsibility accompanies his exalted position.

Indeed, as *Horav Segal* notes, it is difficult to understand how preventing the sinner's prayers would have saved the *Kohen Gadol.* Was his life hanging in the balance of the sinner's prayers?

He explains that by nature the sinner sought the *Kohen Gadol's* demise. He controlled his prayers only in deference to the *Kohen Gadol's* mother. Consequently, it was the *Kohen Gadol's* mother's effort which helped him to overcome his predisposed evil inclination. This accomplishment served as a great source of merit for the *Kohen Gadol.* Such is the power of כבישת הרצון, control of one's natural desires.

We glean two important lessons from this. It is our personal and collective obligation to care for those who are in need. Those who are suffering, regardless of the source of the affliction, must be sustained and comforted. We should also seek to improve our interpersonal relationships by restraining ourselves whenever our actions might be harmful to others. Perhaps through this reciprocal awareness, we will merit to see an end to all our suffering with the advent of *Moshiach*.

***

מי האיש הירא ורך הלבב ילך וישב לביתו

"What man (is there) who is fearful and fainthearted let him go and return to his house." (20:8)

After the *Torah* lists those who were free to return home from battle, it mentions the one who is faint-hearted. One who lacks the courage to represent his people in battle should return home lest he instill this fear into others. In *Sotah 44a* the *Talmud* adds that this fear is more than an apprehension concerning battle and brush with death. This fear applies to one who is ירא מעבירות שבידו, *"fearful of the sins in his hand"* One who is afraid of the transgressions he has committed will affect the success of his brethren. He must depart from the field of battle.

Horav M. Swift, z.l., explains that these are no ordinary sins. After all, no man is perfect. We refer here to one who is fearful of the sins committed *"by his own hands."* There are times when circumstances drive man to lose control and sin. The way one has been raised, his family background and social environment, leave an indelible imprint upon his personality. Such a sinner is not to be condemned. He must be shown the correct path, through study, encouragement, and sympathy. The unforgivable sin that is contagious is the one of בידו, one who has the ability to help others but has not. One who has the power in "his hands" to help, but does not, commits an unpardonable sin. One who has the means, בידו, but refuses to lend assistance, truly has reason to be afraid.

We may suggest another interpretation of the term בידו. We often find excuses to rationalize our wrongdoings. For every *aveirah*, sin, we find a *teretz,* excuse. A time comes, however, when all of our excuses simply no longer work. We can no longer blame our parents, teachers, and rabbis for our failure to adhere to Hashem's *Torah* and *mitzvos.* These are עבירות שבידו, sins that were in our hands. We have been afforded the opportunity to do the right thing. No one has distracted us from following Hashem's mandate. No one has compelled us to transgress. It has all been within "our hands" to do well, but we have failed. This is unforgiveable! When one sees that he has no one to blame but himself, he is gripped by an overpowering fear. This apprehension can be overcome through *teshuvah,* repentance, and reaffirming one's obligation to Hashem and His people.

QUESTIONS LEVEL- A

1. What were *Bnei Yisrael* commanded not to build, even as a place of worship?

2. What is the punishment for one who deliberately worships idols?

3. To which country are we commanded not to return?

4. In this *parsha,* how does the *Torah* refer to *terumah?* 5. If one moves over his neighbors boundary line, which *aveirah* does he transgress?

QUESTIONS LEVEL- B

1. Is the tongue of a cow included in the לחיים?

2. What is the punishment for a prophet who withholds his prophecy?

QUESTIONS LEVEL- C

1. Does a *Kohen* who has a blemish receive a portion in *Eretz Yisrael?*

2. A) How many *aveiros* does one who removes the boundary of his neighbor transgress? B) Does this apply outside of *Eretz Yisrael?*

QUESTIONS LEVEL- D

1. After settling *Eretz Yisrael* the Jews are commanded to perform _____ *mitzvos.* What are they?

ANSWERS LEVEL- A

1. A מצבה, a pillar of a single stone.

2. Death by stoning.

3. Egypt.

4. ראשית דגנך (18:4).

5. לא תסיג גבול רעך.

ANSWERS LEVEL- B

1. Yes.

2. מיתה בידי שמים.

ANSWERS LEVEL- C

1. No.

2. A) Two, לא תגזול, לא תסיג .

B) Outside of *Eretz Yisrael* he only transgresses לא תגזול.

ANSWERS LEVEL- D

1. Three. 1) To appoint a Jewish king based upon the guidance of a *Navi* and the *Sanhedrin*. 2) To destroy Amalek. 3) To build the *Bais Ha'Mikdash (Rambam Hilchos Melachim)*.

פרשת כי תצא
PARASHAS KI-SEITZE
▶◀

כי יהיה לאיש בן סורר ומורה... ורגמוהו כל אנשי עירו באבנים ומת

"If a man has a stubborn and rebellious son .. and all the men of his city shall stone him with stones that he die. (21:18,21)

Rashi offers the reason for this extreme punishment. The *ben sorer u'moreh*, rebellious son, is punished because of what he may become in the end. The *Torah* delves into his final intentions. In order to satisfy his insatiable desires, after first consuming his father's wealth, he will stand at the crossroads and rob people. In order to satisfy his "needs," he may even murder. Consequently, the *Torah* said, let him die innocent rather than guilty.

This approach to retribution is, however, not consistent with *Rashi's* thesis in *Bereishis 21:17*. When Yishmael was condemned to die as a child, the *pasuk* states באשר הוא שם, as he is there. *Rashi* interprets this to mean that Hashem punishes an individual commensurate with his present state. Yishmael was currently an innocent child who was not deserving of death. If such is the case, why is the rebellious son judged according to "future actions"?

Horav C.M. Katz, z.l., responds in the following manner. Life on *Olam Ha'zeh,* this temporary world, has meaning and value only as long as it serves as a corridor to *Olam Ha'bah.* We spend our lifetime in this world as an opportunity for passage to the real world. When the *Torah* sees that the rebellious son has determined the course of his life to be antithetical to *Torah* standards, his life no longer has value. A life which will never lead to eternal life has no meaning.

This profound statement obviously does not preclude the opportunity for *teshuvah*, repentance. By all indication the rebellious son has charted for himself a course of evil and self-destruction from which there is no return. How diligent must we be that every endeavor of our life focuses upon the reality of true life, rather than the folly of mere existence!

266

כי יהיה לאיש בן סורר ומורה...איננו שמע בקול אביו ובקול אמו...

ואמרו בננו זה סרר ומורה איננו שמע בקלנו

**"If a man has a stubborn and rebellious
son that will not listen to the voice of his father or the voice of his
mother . . . and they shall say . . . 'this our son is stubborn and
rebellious he will not listen to our voice.'"** (21:18,20)

The *halachos* that abound regarding the *ben sorer u'moreh*, rebellious
son, preclude its practical application. Indeed, in *Sanhedrin 71A* the
Talmud states that there has never been an incident of *ben sorer
u'moreh* which culminated in the boy's execution. According to the
Talmud, the *parsha* of *ben sorer u'moreh* was included in the *Torah*
for the sole purpose of study and reward. This indicates the
importance of the *parsha's* message regarding the proper method for
the education of children. Nonetheless, the approach to teaching the
specific message presented seems questionable. Why did the *Torah*
not simply state the positive factors concerning effective parenting?
Evidently, proper fulfillment of this lifelong responsibility is so
crucial that it cannot simply be read, it must be studied and
contemplated over and over until one has become totally imbued with
its message.

Chazal derive many lessons from the specific wording of the
text which focus upon the uniqueness of the parent-child relationship.
Hashem, our Father in Heaven, directs us in the correct manner of
raising our children. We are responsible to follow His mandate as
interpreted by our *Torah* scholars, so that we merit to see *Torah
nachas* from our children.

The *Torah* characterizes the *ben sorer u'moreh* in these words,
*"he does not listen to the voice of his father and the voice of his
mother."* Horav M. Gifter, Shlita, explains the distinction between
"kol," voice, and *"divrei,"* speech. He posits that *"divrei"* applies to an
intelligible voice, whereas *"kol"* is used even for a sound which is not
comprehensible. The source of the *ben sorer u'moreh's* insurrection is
his tendency to listen to his parents only when their guidance "make
sense" to him. If he fails to understand, or if he is not in total
agreement with their thinking, he refuses to accede to their wishes.

A child must learn the value of respect for parents. This can be effected only when the child realizes that the source of parental authority is, in reality, Hashem. One must subordinate to his parents' wishes because Hashem has commanded him to do so. True, parents should attempt to explain the reasoning behind their directives, commensurate with a child's level of maturity and comprehension. Nevertheless, obedience to parents is Hashem's mandate and not subject to human approval.

When the parents bring their son to the *Bais Din,* court, they say, *"This son of ours." Chazal* explain that both parents must come and together point to their son. They should be in complete harmony regarding his insubordination. If they are not in agreement, their child receives mixed messages. A child who receives mixed messages from his parents will, in turn, manipulate one against the other in order to fulfill his own desires.

It is also important for parents to "see" their child. They must perceive who he is. Being mindful of a child's personality and natural tendencies is an integral part of parenting. A child who is not understood by his parents is not to be blamed for his rebelliousness. Situations occur in which, due to their own shortcomings, parents emotionally destroy their children. Such a child cannot be deemed a *ben sorer u'moreh.* A child is not born evil. Rather, he may be either improperly educated or not educated at all. As parents, we have an enormous responsibility to provide for the physical and spiritual future of our children. Fulfilling our obligation towards our children takes priority over all other responsibilities

***

כי יקרא קן צפור ...והאם רבצת על האפרחים או על הבצים ...
לא תקח האם על הבנים

"If a birds nest by chance be (found) before you . . . and the mother sitting upon the young or upon the eggs, do not take the mother with the young." (22:6)

The *halachah of Shiluach Ha'Kain,* sending away the mother while keeping the eggs for oneself, is especially striking in that it applies only to birds and not to wild beasts. Throughout *halachah,* these two are considered the same, i.e. the law of covering blood after *shechitah* applies likewise to a wild beast and a fowl. Why should one be permitted to take a young deer away from its mother? *Horav Zalmen Sorotzkin, z.l.,* suggests an explanation from which we may derive a profound insight into a parent's relationship with his children.

Animals, as well as humans, give birth to offspring which have naturally common physical features and traits. Fowl, on the other hand, lay eggs which do not hatch for a while. During this maturation time, the affinity which is natural in the human and animal world should not logically develop. Nonetheless, an almost unnatural boundless love develops between the mother bird and its "egg." Although birds are not able to distinguish their features and characteristics, they transcend uncertainty to shower maternal love upon their young. This is manifest by the act of resting on top of the eggs until the baby birds are prepared to fend for themselves. Consequently, the mother bird's pain and anguish at losing her young is far greater than that of her animal counterpart.

What a wonderful lesson for us. How often do we base our relationship with our children solely upon our personal proclivity towards them? Our love is all too often expressed in consonance with how much of "ourselves" we see in "them." There are even those who, if they do not "see" a promising potential in their children, tend to ignore them. A parent's love and relationship with his child should not be contingent upon specific charachteristics. It should be boundless and unconditional. Perhaps the mother bird's unrestrained devotion to her young could well serve as a lesson for us all.

***

ארבעים יכנו לא יוסיף

"Forty (stripes) he may give him, he shall not exceed." (25:3)

Rashi explains that the number forty is not accurate, since he only receives thirty-nine lashes. Various explanations are offered by the commentators to explain why the *Torah* chose to write the number forty when -- in reality -- it should read only thirty-nine. The *Divrei Yecheskel* offers an explanation which carries within it a profound message.

Man must realize that, regardless of one's level of achievement, it is inconceivable to attain the degree of sublime purity necessary to stand before Hashem. Likewise, whatever our lot in life, it is still not sufficient compensation for that which we "owe" Hashem. Nonetheless, we are implored to do our utmost to serve Hashem. Upon repenting, we must seek contrition by doing our maximum and hoping that it will effect penance for our sins. Above all, man must be aware that he has not completed his mandate.

This is the *Torah's* message. You have received thirty-nine lashes, but be aware that you should have had a greater punishment. Whatever our lot in life, we must thank Hashem for His beneficence in sustaining us despite our deficiencies and iniquities.

QUESTIONS LEVEL- A

1. The parents of the *ben sorer u'moreh* refer to their son as a _____ and a _____.
2. May the burial of one who is executed by *Bais Din* be delayed?
3. What must one make for the roof of his house?
4. Is one permitted to accept interest from a Jew?
5. How many *malkos* does one receive from *Bais Din*?

QUESTIONS LEVEL- B

1. Do the *halachos* concerning a *yefas toaar* apply to a Canaanite woman?
2. Is the *mitzvah* of *chalitzah* performed in any language?

QUESTIONS LEVEL- C

1. What is the punishment for the husband who slanders his wife?
2. How long is the prescribed time for *bal t'aacher?*

QUESTIONS LEVEL- D

1. What is the rationale behind the removal of the shoe during *chalitzah?*

ANSWERS LEVEL- A

1. זולל וסובא, glutton and drunkard.

2. No.

3. A מעקה, a fence around the roof.

4. No.

5. 39.

ANSWERS LEVEL- B

1. Yes.

2. No, only in *Lashon Ha'kodesh*.

ANSWERS LEVEL- C

1. *Malkos* and payment of 100 silver coins.

2. שלש רגלים.

ANSWERS LEVEL- D

1. True mourning for the deceased begins at this point. Now he is truly "dead," since he has no successor through *yibum* (*Rabbeinu Bachya*).

פרשת כי תבוא
PARASHAS KI-SAVO
►◄

ועתה הנה הבאתי את ראשית פרי האדמה אשר נתת לי

"And now, behold I have brought the first of the fruit of the land which you have given me, Hashem." (26:10)

Chazal interpret the word ועתה, *and now,"* as meaning "immediately". Behold, with obvious joy I immediately come to share <u>my</u> fruits with Hashem. Is there any doubt that he is offering <u>his</u> fruits to Hashem? What *chiddush*, new idea, is he stating by emphasizing his prior ownership of the fruit? *Horav Yosef N. Kornitzer, z.l.,* explains that clearly everything belongs to Hashem. Indeed, nothing which we give Hashem is <u>ours;</u> it really belongs to Him. Consequently, what portion of <u>our</u> <u>own</u> belongings do we personally possess in *mitzvah* performance?

He offers the following response. We do not have possession of the actual *mitzvah.* There is, however, a specific essential component of each *mitzvah* which is inherently ours. This is our sensitive involvement in its performance. The alacrity, joy and enthusiasm one applies to his *mitzvah* performance is <u>his</u> part of the *mitzvah.* The *tefillin, tzedakah* money, and *matzos* belong to Hashem, but the emotion, fervor, and excitement belong to man.

This is man's confession to Hashem. And now I come to You, Hashem, with <u>Your</u> fruit which <u>I</u> am bringing. The joy inherent in my offering gives <u>me</u> license for its possession.

***

לא אכלתי באני ממנו ולא בערתי ממנו בטמא ולא נתתי ממנו למת

"I have not eaten of it in (during my period of) mourning, neither have I put away while (I was) unclean, nor have I given of it to the dead." (26:14)

This seems to be a three part statement. *Horav M. Swift, z.l.,* applies this *pasuk* to three types of Jews whose distorted sense of (Jewish) values preclude their proper observance of *Torah* and *mitzvos*. The first type is the Jew whose religious life centers around his period of mourning. His observance of Judaism is manifest through his expression of grief. In modern times, *shiva* has been diminished by the "enlightened Jew" from seven days to one night. Next, we find the Jew whose mixed sense of values distorts his perspective. He can no longer discern between *"kodesh,"* holy, and *"tamei,"* unclean. His total devotion to charitable causes knows no bound. Unfortunately, he substitutes his enthusiasm for rational deliberation. He gives indiscriminately to all, whether or not they are *halachically* worthy of receiving *tzedakah*. There is yet a third type of Jew whose entire *Yidishkeit* is concentrated upon the dead. The funeral, monument, and hiring of a *kaddish* reciter are the cornerstones of his Jewish theology.

These three Jews do not represent the average sinner. They are committing sins due to their lack of prudence and good sense. They want to be religious, and they even think of themselves as religious, but they do not know how and when to be religious. They give *tzedakah*, but they do not know to whom to give.

The individual who comes to the *Bais Ha'mikdash* responds to these three particular weaknesses; "*I have not eaten from it during mourning.*" My period of mourning was not my prime focus of religious observance. '*I have not put it away while unclean.*" I never gave of myself and my fortune indiscriminately to all causes alike. *"And I did not give of it to the dead."* My sentiments towards Judaism have not focused upon death. As *Horav Swift* says, a Jew must be discriminate in spiritual endeavor. The cognitive ability and objective knowledge required for this discernment is truly a blessing. Not everything which appears to be good is truly good. Likewise, bad may not be so bad after all. The guidance and direction received from our *gedolim*, *Torah* leaders, is an invaluable source of illumination for our spiritual quest.

***

אלה יעמדו לברך את העם... ואלה יעמדו על הקללה... וענו הלווים ואמרו

"These shall stand to bless the people . . . and these shall stand for the curse . . . and the Leviim shall speak and say . . . "
(27:12,13,14)

Rashi cites the *Talmud* in *Sotah 32a* that describes the procedure for giving the blessings and curses. Six tribes ascended to the summit of *Har Gerizim,* and six tribes ascended to the summit of *Har Eival.* The *Kohanim* and *Leviim* stood below in the middle. The *Leviim* turned toward *Har Gerizim* and recited the blessing, while both groups responded with *Amen.* Afterwards, this same procedure was followed reciting the curses, but this time they faced *Har Eival.*

Horav M. Shternbuch, Shlita, suggests a profound lesson to be derived from this *pasuk.* The tribe of *Levi* received no portion in *Eretz Yisrael.* Indeed, this tribe has been synonymous with a lack of material sustenance. Their whole earthly "possession" consists of the *Torah.* Looking for support from their brethren, their lot in life has appeared bleak. The other tribes have represented prosperity and good fortune. They are viewed by the "world" as fortunate. Nonetheless, the success or failure of *Bnei Yisrael* hinges upon the tribe of *Levi. Klal Yisrael's* future is dependent upon the tribe of *Levi's* devotion to successful *Torah* study. They stand in the "middle," effecting blessing or curse.

Bnei Torah may stand at the bottom of the ladder of material accomplishment. Their spiritual achievement, however, is the determining factor for everyone else's success. As always, appearances may be deceiving. The individual who, according to man's limited vision, is "suffering" on the bottom of the pole may be at the summit of success in the eyes of the Eternal. *Bnei Torah,* the spiritual heirs of the tribe of *Levi,* should be nourished and sustained, so that *Klal Yisrael* may continue to endure.

***

ארור אשר לא יקים את דברי התורה הזאת לעשות אותם

"Cursed (be he) that confirms not the words of this Torah to do them." (27:26)

As translated above, this *pasuk* is ambiguous. How does one "confirm" the words of the *Torah?* The *Ramban* offers various interpretations of the word יקים from which we may derive important lessons. First, the *Ramban* states that the word *"yakim"* means to "uphold and accept" the validity of the *Torah* in all generations. Consequently, the curse applies to anyone who denies the relevance of any part of the *Torah*. Accordingly, it is our obligation to impress upon all Jews the *Torah's* relevance as a living source of guidance for modern society.

Second, the *Ramban* cites the *Yerushalmi* in *Sotah 7:4*, which interprets this curse as referring to one who has the power to uplift the *Torah*, yet refrains from doing so. It is imperative that we see to it that everyone is availed of the opportunity to study *Torah*. No child should be turned away from *Torah* study, due to financial concerns, family problems, or just not fitting into the image of its student body that the school would like to project. Conversely, those who support Jewish education are worthy of the prosperity, joy and happiness which preceded the curse.

The *Ramban* cites another interpretation which focuses upon the literal translation of יקים: Hold it up and do not let it fall down. The *Torah* must be placed in the *Aron Ha'kodesh* in such a manner that it is settled with dignity and not likely to fall down. In truth, everything in a *shul* must be respected, including the physical structure and its holy appurtenances. This same level of decorum should likewise be reflected by the congregants, who should show the proper reverence for a *makom kodesh*, holy place.

Last, the *Ramban* says that the *pasuk* refers to "holding up" the *Torah* high for all to see. The one who is honored with *Hagbahah*, lifting up the *Torah*, should unfurl it so that it can be viewed by all of the men, women and children present. In a deeper sense, this idea alludes to our responsibility to provide *Torah* to all members of the community, regardless of their age or background. As the *Torah* scroll is raised up high for all to see, so, too, should its message be transmitted to everyone, so that it can sustain us all.

***

תחת אשר לא עבדת את ד' אלקיך בשמחה ובטוב לבב

"Because you did not serve Hashem your G-d with joy and gladness of heart." (28:47)

This *pasuk* implies that the source of all the punishment is serving Hashem with a lack of joy. The *Arizal* states that precisely because *Klal Yisrael* served Hashem in a lackluster manner, without vitality and joy, they would ultimately serve their enemies. Joy is an essential

275

component of *avodas* Hashem, serving Hashem. Indeed, if we would not have failed to serve Hashem with joy, we would not have been exiled.

The *Yalkut Me'am Loez* explains this idea with a simple, but profound analogy. The king of a certain country had a son that was not controllable, His unrestrained acts of self-indulgence often were a source of embarrassment to his father. Whenever his father was about to punish him, the son would put on a sweet angelic smile. When the father observed the happiness and sweet innocence in his son's eyes, it became difficult for him to execute his planned punishment.

This, explains the *Yalkut*, is a powerful deterrent from punishment. When Hashem sees the apparent joy and happiness emanating from an individual's *avodas* Hashem, He defers punishment. Joy in performing *mitzvos* is essential. Even if a person is intellectually aware of the significance of *Torah* and appreciates the value of *Torah* life, he must experience this through joy. Unless one recognizes the inherent joy with which Judaism imbues us, he may turn elsewhere to pursue happiness.

QUESTIONS LEVEL- A

1. The *parsha* begins with the *mitzvah* of _____.

2. *Bnei Yisrael* were commanded to place the ____ stones on *Har* ____.

3. The stones for the *mizbe'ach* can not be cut with _____.

4. In the curses, the Jews will run from the enemy in _____ paths.

5. We are told in the curses that a nation described as a _____ _____ will attack us.

QUESTIONS LEVEL- B

1. There were _____ curses before *Har Eival*. This number corresponds with _____. Who was excluded?

2. What is a צְלָצַל?

QUESTIONS LEVEL- C

1. What is the meaning of כִּלְיוֹן עֵינַיִם?

2. A person thoroughly understands neither the knowledge of his teacher nor the wisdom of his studies before ___ years?

QUESTIONS LEVEL- D

1. On *Rosh Hashanah* we recite various *"yehi ratzons"* (*simanim*). One of them is contained in this *parsha*. What is it?

ANSWERS LEVEL- A

1. *Bikurim.*
2. 12, Eival.
3. Metal.
4. Seven.
5. עז פנים.

ANSWERS LEVEL- B

1. 11, 11 Tribes, Shimon.
2. A type of locust.

ANSWERS LEVEL- C

1. This refers to any hope which is not realized.
2. 40.

ANSWERS LEVEL- D

1. ונתנך ד' לראש ולא לזנב (28:13).

פרשת נצבים
PARASHAS NITZAVIM
►◄

אתם נצבים היום כלכם לפני ד' אלקיכם...לעברך בברית ד' אלקיך ובאלתו

"You are standing this day, all of you before Hashem your G-d . .
. that you should enter into the covenant of Hashem your G-d and
into His oath." (29:9,11)

פן יש בכם איש או אשה ... אשר לבבו פנה היום
מעם ד' אלקיך ללכת לעבד את אלהי הגוים ההם

"Lest there be among you a <u>man or woman</u> whose heart turns
away this day from Hashem our G-d, to go to serve the gods of
those nations." (29:17)

וילכו ויעבדו אלהים אחרים

"And <u>they</u> went and served other gods." (29:25)

The *Chofetz Chaim, z.l.,* explains that the moment when Moshe stood
before *Bnei Yisrael,* prepared to bring them into Hashem's covenant,
was filled with trepidation and uncertainty. On the one hand, Moshe
had shared with *Bnei Yisrael* Hashem's recognition of their lofty
accomplishments. His statement of unconditional love for them
reassured them of their future.

Immediately thereafter, however, Moshe admonished them
regarding the individual Jew who might have been leaning towards
idol worship. This individual's deviation from Hashem could fester,
bringing ruin to a whole nation! This seems unreal! How could an
entire community fall victim to the folly of one individual?

The *Chofetz Chaim* explains that this is reality. That which
seems foolish in the beginning evolves into a tolerated lifestyle. This
accepted standard of living becomes normative. If the individuals are
communal leaders or scholars -- role models -- this process of
acceptability progresses even more rapidly. Consequently, Moshe saw
fit to caution *Bnei Yisrael.* After living in Egypt and witnessing the

278

most decadent behavior, it was conceivable that a complacent attitude could develop among members of *Bnei Yisrael.*

Thus, Moshe reprehended, "*Lest there be among you a man or woman... whose heart turns away from Hashem.*" We are all gathered here because of that single Jew. Never forget the value of a single Jew! If the community does not concern itself with the single Jew, then <u>everyone</u> will be held accountable. We derive this from the end of Moshe's speech, in which he said, "*And <u>they</u> went and served other gods.*" Moshe now spoke in the plural, rather than in the singular. If the community does not look out for the individual, it is considered as if <u>they</u> <u>all</u> were <u>also</u> involved in the transgression.

Horav Y. Abramsky, z.l., notes that the importance of an individual has far reaching implications, especially in spiritual matters. He explains that at times one can deliver a profound lecture or *mussar* discourse before a large gathering, but only <u>one</u> person will grasp the message of the lecture. Imagine that one can teach a class for a period of time. Even if only one student has been affected, it becomes been well worth every minute of effort expended with the entire group!

As we search for *zechusim,* merits, during these days of awe, it would serve us well to concern ourselves with the individual Jew who falls between the cracks while we attempt to save the community!

***

פן יש בכם איש או אשה... אשר לבבו פנה היום... פן יש בכם
שרש פרה ראש ולענה

"Lest there should be among you a man or woman . . . whose heart turns away this day . . . lest there be among you a root that is fruitful (in) gall and wormwood." (29:17)

The *Ramban* explains that the individual whose slight deviation will eventually grow into blatant evil is at present a pious Jew. He stands in seeming direct contradistinction to the full-fledged believer in paganism. Nonetheless, the *Torah* combines the two into one group. Indeed, their only point of divergence is intellectual belief. To the unknowing onlooker, they may appear to be two very different people. One is an obvious heretic, while the other acts like he should be

279

grouped with the devout. The *Torah* says, however, that appearances are deceiving. The two individuals act distinctly, but their heresy is essentially similar.

Horav A.H. Lebowitz, Shlita, makes a profound observation from this concept. Two students can be sitting together studying in the same classroom. They may come from similar backgrounds, but if their paths diverge even slightly, they can be worlds apart ten years later. The slightest noticeable deviation must be immediately ameliorated, or it can end in spiritual tragedy. Even if the disparity is not immediately noticed, it can become evident in later years when this sinister behavior manifests itself in the way one raises his children.

Horav Lebowitz tells a story about *Horav E.M. Bloch, z.l.*, who was once waiting in the Chicago train station, preparing to board a train to New York. A few feet away stood a train about to leave in the opposite direction to California. He questioned his students concerning the distance between the two trains. When they responded that it was only a few feet, he disagreed, *"Theses two trains are 3000 miles apart, since one is going to California and the other to New York."* The message is clear. Two students can be standing next to each other, but if they face "different directions," they are worlds apart. We should never ignore the slight deviations in actions, thoughts, and even attitudes, either in others or in ourselves. That which seems to be innocuous today may manifest itself as evil tomorrow.

QUESTIONS LEVEL- A

1. Which two professions are emphasized as standing before Moshe that day?

2. What will happen to one who thinks he can do as he pleases and not listen to Hashem?

3. Why will all the land be destroyed?

4. What will Hashem do when the dispersed Jews repent?

QUESTIONS LEVEL- B

1. Why are זקנים mentioned before שטרים?

2. Which two other leaders made *Bnei Yisrael* stand in ranks (מצבה)?

QUESTIONS LEVEL- C

1. A) Which idols were left out in the open? B) Which idols were hidden?

2. To which type of sin does רוה refer? To which type of sin does צמאה refer?

QUESTIONS LEVEL- D

1. Which Jewish king erected a four-faced idol in the *Bais Ha'Mikdash*?

ANSWERS LEVEL- A

1. Wood choppers and water drawers.

2. Hashem will punish him with all of the curses.

3. Because *Bnei Yisrael* turned away from Hashem.

4. He will gather them together and bring them to *Eretz Yisrael*.

ANSWERS LEVEL- B

1. The more distinguished are mentioned first.

2. Yehoshua and Shmuel.

ANSWERS LEVEL- C

1. A) Those of stone and wood. B) Those of silver and gold.

2. A) Inadvertent. B) Willingly with desire.

ANSWERS LEVEL- D

1. Menashe.

פרשת וילך
PARASHAS VAYELECH
►◄

וילך משה וידבר את הדברים האלה... בן מאה ועשרים שנה אנכי היום
לא אוכל עוד לצאת ולבוא וד' אמר אלי לא תעבר...
ד' אלקיך הוא עבר לפניך

"And Moshe went and spoke these words ... a hundred and twenty years I am this day, I can no more go out and come in, and Hashem said to me you shall not go over. Hashem, your G-d, He will go over before you ..." (31:2,3)

Moshe's farewell address to *Bnei Yisrael* seems enigmatic. Why does Moshe mention his advanced age and "frailty" in his closing words? *Horav Chaim Sheinberg, Shlita,* cites the *Sforno* who adds insight to Moshe's words, "*I am a hundred and twenty years old this day.*" Do not grieve over my death, for according to nature I should not be alive until today. *"I can no longer go out and come in."* And even if I were to live, I would not be able to go out and come in on your behalf because of my advanced age. "*And Hashem has told me, 'You shall not go over'.*" Even if I were to live, I could not take you into *Eretz Yisrael.* Therefore, it is to your advantage that I die, so that you may enter into *Eretz Yisrael.* "*Hashem, your G-d, He will go over before you.*" You have no reason to grieve over the loss of my leadership, because, indeed, Hashem is your leader, and He will continue to provide for you.

Moshe *Rabbeinu* felt it was necessary to comfort *Bnei Yisrael,* who were obviously devastated by the knowledge of his impending death. The thought of losing their beloved leader forever cast them into a state of despair at a time when heightened joy was appropriate. *Bnei Yisrael* had just entered into the covenant with Hashem. In order to reinforce that contractual relationship it was critical that their resolve be strengthened and their spirits elevated. Moshe, the quintessential leader, roused himself during his last moments to reassure *Bnei Yisrael* that they would not be forsaken.

This, notes *Horav Sheinberg*, is the true hallmark of a *Torah* leader. He must be sensitive to the emotional concerns of his people. Moshe felt that his death would devastate *Bnei Yisrael* at a time when they should be overjoyed. Therefore, he minimized the effect of his demise to whatever extent possible. He allayed their concerns regarding his death and their consequent loss of leadership. Moshe neglected his personal emotions in deference to the need to nurture his flock.

Horav Sheinberg cites the *Siddur Ishei Yisrael*, who points out that this is the essence of our *tefillos*, prayers, on *Rosh Hashanah*. We do not ask favors for ourselves; we entreat Hashem that His Name and kingdom be universally exalted, that every human recognize that He is the source of all creation. When we defer our own personal requests and yield to *kavod Shomayim*, honor of Heaven, we will merit that our iniquities will be erased. We must be sensitive to the pain and anguish "suffered" by the *Shechinah*. On the *Yom Ha'din*, Day of Judgement, our *zechusim*, merits, are commensurate to the degree to which we are able to overlook our own personal needs and submit to the requirements of *kavod Shomayim* and our fellow Jew.

***

הקהל את העם האנשים והנשים והטף

"Assemble the people, the men, and the women, and the little ones." (31:12)

Rashi explains that, although the little children were clearly not capable of comprehending the experience, they accompanied the adults. Thus, those who brought them would be rewarded. In truth, the children that came along probably disrupted the adults to the point that they could not listen as intently as they would have desired. We may, therefore, wonder at the *Torah's* insistence that the children be present. Would it not have been preferable for the children to remain at home, in order to enable the adults to properly concentrate on their *avodas Hashem*, service to Hashem?

Horav N. Adler, z.l., suggests that herein lies the actual reward. The adults were implored to "sacrifice" some of their personal spiritual experiences, so that the children would be availed the opportunity to see, hear, and experience the sublimity of the moment.

283

As *Horav Adler* emphasizes, *Torah chinuch*, education, takes precedence over parents' personal needs. In regard to educating Jewish children in accordance with the true *Torah* spirit, our concern should focus on what is ultimately most beneficial for the children, not our personal preferences or affiliations.

QUESTIONS LEVEL- A

1. To whom did Moshe give the *Torah* when it was completely written?

2. During which year does *Hak'heil* take place?

3. Where did Moshe and Yehoshua stand as Yehoshua received his command from Hashem?

4. Did Moshe know that *Bnei Yisrael* would eventually sin after his death?

QUESTIONS LEVEL- B

1. Who reads from the *Torah* during *Hak'heil*?

2. What is the last *mitzvah* in the *Torah*?

QUESTIONS LEVEL- C

1. *Bnei Yisrael* were given a special assurance regarding the *Torah*. What was it?

2. Did *Bnei Yisrael* sin during Yehoshua's tenure as leader?

QUESTIONS LEVEL- D

1. Which king was praised for standing during the *Torah* reading of *Hak'heil*?

ANSWERS LEVEL- A

1. To the *Kohanim* and elders.

2. The eight year (the first year after *Shmittah*).

3. *Ohel Mo'ed.*
4. Yes.

ANSWERS LEVEL- B

1. The *Melech Yisrael.*
2. To write a *sefer Torah.*

ANSWERS LEVEL- C

1. It will never be forgotten.
2. No.

ANSWERS LEVEL- D

1. Agripas.

פרשת האזינו
PARASHAS HAAZINU
▶◀

קל אמונה ואין עול צדיק וישר הוא

"A G-d of faithfulness and without iniquity, just and right is He."
(32:4)

One does not need to possess an astute mind in order to comprehend that Hashem is the Creator. As *Horav Y. Neiman, z.l.,* notes, simple prudent logic dictates that one believe in Hashem. The ultimate test of *emunah,* faith, however, is when one notices occurrences which contradict human logic and thought patterns. The challenge to accept Heavenly decrees which seem harsh and perplexing is the ultimate test of human faith. At such a time, the individual must trust in Hashem with a profound belief that man cannot possibly begin to understand his Creator. The *pasuk* alludes to this. Man should strive to attain the level of עול אין, accepting that Hashem has no iniquity.

This unique form of *emunah* was exhibited by many Jews just fifty years ago during the Holocaust. Rarely have men and women demonstrated so much bravery, while hopelessly facing such cruelty and bestiality. We speak here of overwhelming spiritual bravery and invincible dedication to Hashem, His *Torah,* and *mitzvos.* The faith of the Jew confronted the destructive efforts of a diabolical enemy whose one goal was the annihilation of the Jewish people. They sought guidance in *halachah* and solace in *Torah* study. This was *emunah* at its most sublime and majestic moment.

Horav Neiman states that he once heard the *Chazon Ish, z.l.,* analogize perplexing events to a master tailor who takes shears and cuts up a beautiful piece of material. One can be assured that this is part of the process of creating a beautiful garment. Only a fool begins to question the tailor's motives in cutting up the raw material. The same principle applies to the conduct of the Almighty. The truth is that we do not begin to understand His actions. We do not grasp why

He makes these "incisions" in the best and most lovely part of His people. We must realize, however, that we are merely flesh and blood with a limited level of understanding. The fact that we do not comprehend Hashem's actions should in no way diminish our belief in Him.

The aged *Rebbe of Yarislav* once said that he merited living to a ripe old age because he never questioned the *Ribono Shel Olam.* Rather, he accepted everything lovingly. He remarked that he feared that if he would seek an answer, Hashem would say to him, "If you don't understand, just come up to Heaven and I will explain everything to you." Since he was not quite ready to entertain such an idea, he never asked questions. May we merit to achieve the devotion inherent in this profound degree of faith in the Almighty.

***

וישמן ישרן ויבעט שמנת עבית כשית ויטש אלקה עשהו

"And (then) Yeshurun waxed fat, (as often as you waxed fat, you became obese and overcome with fat) and (then) it forsook the G-d who made it." (32:15)

Horav S.R. Hirsch, z.l., notes that this is the first time that the name ישרן, straight and morally upright, is mentioned. This word designates and defines *Bnei Yisrae*l according to the ideal of its moral mandate. This implies that *Bnei Yisrael* should be *"yashar,"* straight, never deviating from the correct path of service to the Almighty.

Hashem desires that we ascend to the summit of achievement in the dual heights of human aims; the highest of material good fortune and spiritual/moral perfection. We are to serve as an illuminating example to the secular world that a life devoted entirely to spiritual and moral perfection by no means demands a renunciation of earthly happiness. On the contrary, a life devoted to *Torah* and *mitzvos* is in harmony with material wealth and enjoyment. Materialism can be sanctified by its dedication to moral deeds and spiritual developments.

*Bnei Yisrae*l, however, have a problem relating to abundance. The *pasuk* says, *"As often as you waxed fat, you became obese, and (you) became overcome by fat."* *Horav* Hirsch views this verse as being parenthetical to the beginning of the *pasuk*. It contains the essence of the historical perspective of *Klal Yisrael.* In suffering we thrive. In times of good fortune, we fall prey to the *yetzer hora,* evil inclination.

The history of *Klal Yisrael* has reflected that when we receive more "fat" to be transformed into energy and good works, we employ it instead to become slaves to this corpulence. We have not used the abundance for the common good. We have not been able to master our riches and good fortune for *Torah* and *mitzvos.* We should learn that whatever good fortune we receive, is granted for a purpose. It serves as an opportunity for greater moral and spiritual achievement. With this idea in mind, we pray to Hashem for abundance, so that we can use it to attain greater spiritual accomplishments.

***

כי לא דבר רק הוא מכם כי הוא חייכם

"For it is no (vain) (empty) thing for you; because it is your life."
(32:47)

As Moshe bids farewell, he implores *Bnei Yisrael* to charge their children with *Torah* observance and *mitzvah* performance, *"for it is no vain thing for you, it is your life."* The Hebrew word רק, which is usually translated as "vain," literally means "empty." *Horav M. Swift, z.l.,* suggests that viewed in this perspective, this phrase lends itself to an alternative meaning. A container is considered empty when its contents have been removed. On the other hand, this container is still viewed as a container, retaining its potential use for a similar purpose.

A gentile without *Torah* is a human being who has the potential to achieve his intended purpose in life. The gentile only remains "empty" of *Torah.* It is not part of his life. Without it, he is still a person. The converse is true by a Jew. A Jew who is "empty" of *Torah* is not merely "empty"; he no longer functions in the same potential capacity as he had previously. He no longer has the same meaning or value as a Jew, for the *Torah* is our only way of life. Indeed, it is our very source of living! If one denies the Jew his *Torah,* devoids his life of his *mitzvos,* his *tallis, tefillin, Shabbos,* and *kashrus,* then there is no longer anything uniquely Jewish about him. He is emptied of his real significance. To be a כלי רק, an "emptied vessel," is the antithesis of *Torah* Judaism.

As we stand before Hashem during these days of sublime judgement, let us not come before the Almighty "empty" handed. Let *Torah* penetrate into our inner being, so that the *"pintele Yid,"* the essential Jew within each of us, emerges. The goal is that our entire essence will be suffused with Jewish living.

***

ומת בהר ... כאשר מת אהרן אחיך

"And die on the mountain . . . as your brother Aharon died."
(32:50)

It seems that Hashem is promising Moshe that he will die in the same manner that his brother Aharon died. What did Moshe envy that was so unique about Aharon's death? *Rashi* explains that just before Aharon died, Moshe dressed Elazar, Aharon's son, in the priestly vestments, so that Aharon would have the *nachas* of seeing his son fill his position as *Kohen Gadol.*

Indeed, we find in *Parashas Pinchas (Bamidbar 27:16)* that Moshe entreated Hashem to bequeath his position of leadership to his sons. This seems puzzling. This *parsha* indicates that Hashem promises to honor Moshe's request. It would be inconceivable to think that Hashem would promise Moshe to give his sons leadership and instead appoint Yehoshua to this position. How, then, did Hashem grant Moshe's request? How did Moshe see his sons attain his greatness?

Horav D. Feinstein, Shlita, offers the following answer to this question. Moshe's distinction did not lie in his role as king or leader, but rather as the *Rebbe* of *Klal Yisrael.* He was the pre-eminent teacher who first introduced the *Torah* to us. Just as the biological father brings his child into this world, so does the *rebbe* bring the Jewish child into the eternal world of *Olam Ha'bah.* Indeed, in the eternal world, the *rebbe* is viewed as a father to his students.

*Moshe Rabbein*u, the quintessential teacher of *Klal Yisrael,* was promised that he would see his most devoted student, Yehoshua, accede to his position as *manhig,* leader, of *Klal Yisrael.* All of his spiritual children, the entire *Klal Yisrael,* have inherited his legacy of *Torah.* What greater joy and *nachas* can a *rebbe* have than to see his *talmidim* follow in the path which he has charted for them?

Moshe truly merited a death similar to Aharon's, for until this very day we, his spiritual heirs, study the *Torah* which he taught to that initial generation.

We may advance this thought further. There are some parents who structure their child's whole future in their mind. They have decided which career their child should embark upon. There are also those individuals who, themselves erudite *Torah* scholars, expect the same orientation for their sons. Alas, there is always the one child who doesn't fit the mold, whose aspirations and strivings are not in harmony with those of his parents. To some people, not having their son follow in their footsteps or predetermined future plans can be a crushing blow. This reality can destroy a relationship between parent and child and place a heavy strain on the whole family.

This foolish response is not *Torah* oriented. Parents must inspire and encourage their children, while guiding them towards their own individualized future. Negative responses to a child's choice can only destroy the child's self-image and will be self-defeat. Moshe *Rabbeinu's* sons did not assume his mantle of leadership. Moshe accepted Hashem's decision and instead joyfully transferred it to his student, Yehoshua. Moshe was not only *Klal Yisrael's* illustrious leader, he was also a parent whose love and respect for his offspring transcended his personal aspirations for them.

QUESTIONS LEVEL- A

1. Name the four different terms for rain or moisture mentioned in *Shiras Ha'azinu.*

2. How is the concept of history referred to?

3. Hashem protects us as the _____ of His _____.

4. How is the Torah referred to in this *parsha*?

5. On which mountain did Moshe die?

QUESTIONS LEVEL- B

1. Does a wicked person who does good receive reward? Where?

2. In reference to *Klal Yisrael*, what is the difference between נבל and לא חכם?

QUESTIONS LEVEL- C

1. When Hashem gave the *Torah*, from how many directions did He appear?

2. Why is Yehoshua referred to as Hoshea in this *parsha*?

QUESTIONS LEVEL- D

1. A) What is the hidden comfort in the words וחצי אכלה בם (32:23)?
B) What "arrows" will Hashem shoot?

ANSWERS LEVEL- A

1. רביבים, שעירים, טל, מטר.

2. ימות עולם.

3. Pupil, eye.

4. Our life.

5. *Har* Ne'vo.

ANSWERS LEVEL- B

1. Yes, in *Olam Ha'zeh*.

2. נבל is one who doesn't think about what Hashem has done for them in the past. לא חכם is one who doesn't have the foresight to understand what evil or good can appear in the future.

ANSWERS LEVEL- C

1. Four.

2. Although Yehoshua received the mantle of leadership at this time, he nonetheless acted humbly as he had previously.

ANSWERS LEVEL- D

1. A) "*All My arrows shall be spent, but the nation will not be destroyed*" (Rashi). B) The 98 curses stated in *Parashas Ki Savo*. The *Rokeach* also points out that the numerical equivalent of אכלה בם is 98.

291

פרשת וזאת הברכה
PARASHAS V'ZOS HABRACHA
▶◀

ד' מסיני בא וזרח משעיר למו הופיע מהר פארן

"Hashem came from Sinai, and rose from Se'ir unto them; He shined forth from Har Paran." (33:2)

Chazal derive from this *pasuk* that Hashem offered every nation on earth the opportunity to receive the *Torah*, only to receive a rejection from all of them. Why, then, does the *Torah* mention only two nations, *Se'ir* and *Paran*, the descendants of Eisav and Yishmael, respectively?

Horav Z. Sorotzkin, z.l., suggests the following explanation. Yishmael and Eisav had the opportunity to learn *Torah* and *mitzvos* from their parents. Yishmael spent his youth in Avraham's home, while Eisav was able to study from both his father, Yitzchak, and his grandfather, Avraham. Because the background of Eisav's children was more firmly infused in *Torah*, Hashem originally approached them. Even though they had a secure foundation for receiving the *Torah*, they nevertheless spurned it. The other gentile nations did not demonstrate such blatant impudence in their rejection of the *Torah*. People who have never been initiated into the profundity of *Torah* and the majestic beauty of a *Torah* lifestyle are not considered to be equally contemptuous in their rejection as those who have had that privilege.

***

האמר לאביו ולאמו לא ראיתיו ואת אחיו לא הכיר

"Who said of his father and of his mother 'I have not seen him' neither did he acknowledge his brothers." (33:9)

Rashi explains that the terms "father" and "brother" used in the *pasuk* does not refer to the *Levi's* real father or brother, since no member of the tribe of Levi had sinned. He, therefore, suggests that these terms refer to their mother's father or a brother from the same mother who,

292

in either case, was a *Yisrael*. If this is the case, why does the *Torah* emphasize the words father and brother?

Horav Nissan Alpert, z.l., suggests the following thought. The *Leviim* killed the sinners because of their zealousness for the sake of Hashem's Name. One might hypothesize that they had done this only because they had no relationship to the sinners and, therefore, no special sensitivity towards them. The *Torah* responds by viewing these sinners as family. The love of the *Leviim* for each and every Jew was tantamount to a family relationship. They considered every Jew to be their brother; every elder was considered their father! Nonetheless, when Moshe issued the command for avenging Hashem's Name, they responded immediately. Their love for Hashem transcended even their sensitivity towards their brethren.

***

ולזבולן אמר שמח זבולן בצאתך ויששכר באהליך

"And to Zevulun he said: Rejoice Zevulun in your going out, and, Yissachar, rejoice in your tents." (33:18)

The Yissachar-Zevulun relationship was truly unique. Indeed, Moshe blessed these two brothers concurrently, since Zevulun, who engaged in commerce, split his earnings with Yissachar, who devoted his time to *Torah* study. The *Zohar Ha'kadosh* explains that Yissachar and Zevulun shared equally. Zevulun shared his material abundance with Yissachar, while Yissachar enabled Zevulun to receive a portion in the World to Come. This "equality," however, seems puzzling. Is there any way to compare the eternal bliss of *Olam Ha'bah* to the limited material benefits of *Olam Ha'zeh*? Why, then, is this viewed as a parallel partnership?

Horav Ch. Elazary, z.l., explains that actually Zevulun was also the beneficiary of material advantage. As a result of Zevulun's support of Yissachar's *Torah* study, he attained the spiritual level of Yissachar. Thus, he benefitted from the sublime peace and joy accorded to one who devotes himself to *Torah* study.

Horav Elazary cites the *Rabbeinu Bachya,* who explains the reason that Yissachar's blessing was expressed in only two words. Moshe tells Yissachar *"And Yissachar (rejoice) in your tents."* He states that, in fact, these two words encompass every possible blessing. Moshe was telling the tribe of Yissachar to rejoice in *Torah* study, for there is no greater source of true happiness. As it says in *Tehillim 19:9*, *"The statutes of Hashem are upright; they make the heart rejoice."* This idea is especially relevant when we read this *parsha* on *Simchas Torah*, the festival on which we rejoice with the *Torah*. May the inherent joy stimulated by *Torah* study be the catalyst of inspiration for a life of contentment and bliss.

***

וימת שם משה

"And Moshe died there." (34:5)

The *Zohar Ha'kadosh* states that Moshe *Rabbeinu* died on *Shabbos* at *Minchah* time. Similarly, according to the *Zohar*, Yosef *Ha'tzaddik* and David *Ha'melech* also died on *Shabbos* during *Minchah* time. It is specifically for this reason that we recite three *pesukim* which begin with the word צדקתך, *Your righteousness*, as a form of צדוק הדין, which constitutes acceptance of Hashem's judgement at this time.

Horav Nissan Alpert, z.l., questions the reference to the time of Moshe's death. The *Torah* states that Moshe told *Bnei Yisrael*, *"I am one hundred and twenty years old today."* This implies that Moshe reached this age on the very day of his demise. If, as it was stated in the *Zohar*, this day was *Shabbos*, how was Moshe permitted to write thirteen *sifrei Torah?* It would be *chillul Shabbos*, a desecration of the sanctity of *Shabbos!*

Horav Alpert suggests the following novel response. Moshe *Rabbeinu*, in fact, died two deaths, a spiritual demise followed by physical cessation of life. On the sixth day of *Adar*, which was *Erev Shabbos*, Moshe *Rabbeinu* ceased to be *Rabbon Shel Kol Yisrael*, the *Rebbe* of all *Klal Yisrael*. His vast storehouse of *Torah* knowledge was transferred to Yehoshua on that day. On the next day, which was *Shabbos*, Moshe stood before *Bnei Yisrael* as an ordinary Jew in preparation for physical death. Someone of Moshe's sublime spiritual stature, a unique leader whose soul has been intrinsically bound up with the future of *Bnei Yisrael*, did not experience mortality in the common sense. His physical being was as pure as his spiritual essence. On the seventh day of *Adar*, Moshe "disappeared" from this earth.

וימת שם משה עבד ד'... ולא ידע איש את קבורתו עד היום הזה

"And there died Moshe, servant of Hashem . . . and no man knows his grave unto this day." (34:5,6)

It seems strange that the life of the pre-eminent leader of *Klal Yisrael* came to an end with so little attention directed to it. Indeed, the appellation used to describe the essence of the man who achieved the apotheosis of spiritual leadership is simply עבד ד', the servant of Hashem. *Horav S.R. Hirsch, z.l.*, explains that, in fact, this characterization of Moshe represents the ultimate tribute to him. Moshe's entire life was devoted to Hashem and His people. He was an "*eved Hashem*," servant of Hashem, in the truest sense of the word. He achieved total self-abnegation, so that his whole being was dedicated to serving as an instrument with which to convey Hashem's message.

Horav Hirsch notes that no physical lasting commemorative of Moshe remains. Our leader has departed from this world, yet no monument or stone exists in testimony to him. We do not even know the location of his gravesite. Moshe's whole earthly persona disappeared with his physical demise. All that survived of Moshe in this world is Hashem's Word. This was transmitted in the most precise manner, so that if a later descendant arises to assume his mantle of leadership, he will carry with him an echo of the words of Moshe *Rabbeinu*.

QUESTIONS LEVEL- A

1. Which tribe did not receive a specific *brachah*?

2. Which tribe was praised for not being involved in the sin of the Golden Calf?

3. Which tribe is compared to an ox?

4. Which words describe Moshe's relationship to Hashem?

5. For how long did the Jews mourn Moshe?

QUESTIONS LEVEL- B

1. A) Who is referred to as נזיר אחיו? B) Why?

2. Who is referred to as the מחקק?

QUESTIONS LEVEL- C

1. With which "hand" did Hashem "write" the *Luchos*?

2. Why was *bircas Binyamin* mentioned immediately after *bircas Levi*?

QUESTIONS LEVEL- D

1. A) Moshe composed _____ psalms of *Tehillim*. B) What are they? C) To what does this number correspond?

ANSWERS LEVEL- A

1. Shimon.

2. Levi.

3. Yosef.

4. עבד ד'.

5. Thirty days.

ANSWERS LEVEL- B

1. A) Yosef. B) He was separated from them when he was sold.

2. Moshe.

ANSWERS LEVEL- C

1. Right.

2. Bircas Binyamim concerns the *Bais Ha'mikdash* to be built in Binyamin's portion, while *bircas* Levi deals with *avodas ha'korbanos.*

ANSWERS LEVEL- D

1. A) 11. B) 90-101. C) This corresponds to his last blessings to the eleven tribes. (Shimon did not receive a blessing.)